PAUSE

By Lance Lang

A YEAR OF HOPE IN FIVE MINUTES A DAY

Published by:
The Treehouse Group, LLC

Pause: A Year of Hope in 5 Minutes a Day

ISBN: 978-0-9903118-5-0
Printed in the United States of America
Library of Congress Cataloging-in-Publication Data

First Edition

Cover Design: Zach Divilbiss
Interior Design: Curtis Stephens / The Treehouse Group, LLC
Editor: Adam Palmer
Proofreader: Ann Sandager

For information regarding author interviews or speaking engagements, please contact the public relations department – Lance@LanceLang.com.

Adam Palmer

Thank you for giving your heart and soul to this project
Your words will lay the foundation for millions of people
to find JOY, PRAYER, PEACE & GRATITUDE for decades to
come! You are so supportive, humble and special.

Ally Lang

God's had us on quite the journey in the months leading
up to this project. Thank you for never leaving my side
through all the ups and downs. And for always being there
to pick me up when the lights go down and the people
walk away. It's me and you til the end boo. Ride or die!

INTRO   PLEASE READ THIS!

Hey, thanks for picking up this devotional! I'm so pumped for you to take this 365-day journey with God. What you are about to experience has helped to transform my heart, reshape my soul, and give me practical tools to *fight depression, loneliness, comparison, greed, addiction, people-pleasing, ruminating thoughts, and so much more—* the struggles the enemy has used to try and slow me down, steal my calling, and rob my joy.

I'll be honest: there've been some days when the devil has won and beat me up, but as I have sought the Lord, He heard me, comforted me, and pointed me to different people, experiences, scriptures, and practices that have helped me rebuild my hope.

I desperately wanted to share this journey with you, because I know so many other people are fighting the same kinds of battles.

This devo is hopefully something different from what you may have experienced in the past. It's a combination of the ways I learn, the best ways I experience God, and a spiritual discipline (scripture memory) that I've always found challenging.

Depression, loneliness, comparison, greed, addiction, people-pleasing, and ruminating thoughts are, for the most part, under-the-skin types of problems. Here's what I mean: sometimes you can see symptoms, but a lot of times these struggles are held in secret. They aren't obvious to the outsider. Instead, the devil uses these challenges to slowly eat away at our God-given confidence, tear down our faith, and ultimately distract us from the mission we've been created to fulfill.

This devotional is a tool to help you fight back! It's not confusing or hard to accomplish: it's simple, practical, quick, and proven to help! Like I said, what you'll find here are all the tools that have helped me rebuild my hope and hold on to it!

That's what I want for you: for each day to be filled with hope as you step out to live the abundant, purposeful, FREE life God desires for you!

Flip through these pages and you'll see I've focused this entire devotional book around the scripture found in Philippians 4:4-9. Why? Because long ago, God showed me this passage and told me to memorize it, hide it deep in my heart, and share with everyone I could.

This passage has changed my life, and I know it will change yours.

I've broken up the year into four quarters to really focus on the four different aspects of our Phillipians passage: Joy, Prayer, Peace, and Gratitude.

January 1 through March 31: Joy

"Rejoice in the Lord always. I will say it again: Rejoice! Let your gentleness be evident to all. The Lord is near." (Philippians 4:4-5)

April 1 through June 30: Prayer

"Do not be anxious about anything, but in every situation, by prayer and petition, with thanksgiving, present your requests to God." (Philippians 4:6)

July 1 through September 30: Peace

"And the peace of God, which transcends all understanding, will guard your hearts and your minds in Christ Jesus." (Philippians 4:7)

October 1 through December 31: Gratitude

"Finally, brothers and sisters, whatever is true, whatever is noble, whatever is right, whatever is pure, whatever is lovely, whatever is admirable—if anything is excellent or praiseworthy—think about such things. Whatever you have learned or received or heard from me, or seen in me—put it into practice. And the God of peace will be with you." (Philippians 4:8-9)

As you will see, within these four quarters, each day has the same template to help you find a rhythm and cadence as you journey through the year: Proclaim, Prompt, Prod, Praise, and Pray.

Proclaim

Each day you will start by reading a selection of verses from our theme passage in Philippians. Read this at least once and read it OUT LOUD. I hope by the second or third week of the quarter, you will have it memorized and you can begin reciting it throughout your day as you need to. This passage is meant to become your foundation, which is why you will read it every single day for three months!

Prompt

This is the devotional for the day. It's usually only about 150 words, give or take, just enough to give you the concept, encouragement, teaching, or guidance you might need for the day. Use it as a launching pad, not a destination. My goal was to plant some ideas, share some insights, and let the Holy Spirit activate in you how this applies to what you are currently experiencing in your life.

Prod

This is an activation question that I am gonna ask you to respond to. I would encourage you to write your response, thoughts, prayers, ideas, confessions, or whatever IN THIS BOOK. If I didn't give you enough room, write on the side of the page, on the top of the page, whatever—just make it your own and take action! Fill up the pages with what God reveals to you! That's where change begins and hope is activated!

Praise

This is a song I want you to listen to. As you will see, there's a QR code that will take you to that specific song of the day, held in a custom Spotify playlist.

You can listen to it while you read, you can listen on the way to work, you can listen any way you want. But my suggestion would be to listen to the song, with headphones on or really loud in your car WHILE you pray to close each day's devo (more on that in the next section). This will help you to hear the words of the song, engage with the Holy Spirit, and truly have a moment with God. I am so convinced that God wants to spend alone time with you every day. Even if it's just these five minutes, He longs to give you the hope you need not just to survive the day, but to conquer it!

Pray

Every day closes with a prayer to get you going. Obviously make this prayer your own! Don't just recite it—make it personal. I've tried to provide a prayer path for those who might be new to praying, but even so, remember God wants a relationship with you, so talk with Him and make it personal. God does not desire for you to pray perfect, eloquent, religious prayers. He just wants to hear your heart, hear your requests, hear your gratitude and fill you with the POWER to live in freedom! God loves you!

FINAL PREPARATION

As you participate in this practice every day, you will definitely pick up a rhythm and that's good. That's the goal! Developing strong spiritual rhythms is an essential part of building a relationship with God. Remember that's what God desires: a real, authentic, transparent relationship with Him.

In preparation to dive in, I would also encourage you to try and complete the devos each day...

- · In the Same Place
- · At the Same Time of Day (In the Morning)
- · With the Same Spirit

Find a nice place that works for you. I have a chair in my closet where I can be alone and escape for a minute, and it's in that chair where I do my morning and evening quiet times with God. Think about where you can be each morning (or most mornings) and try to put this book there. It could be in your car, somewhere quiet at work, your kitchen table, the nightstand, wherever... just try and stay consistent. This will help you build your momentum!

The same goes for the time of day. Work hard to complete each day at the same time, especially try to build your mornings around it. It's just five minutes, so it's not hard, but it will take intentionality. I know if you have young kids, mornings can be a challenge, so you might have to wait until you've dropped them off at school or day care. Or you just might have to get up five minutes earlier than usual, get to your spot, and dive in! But please try to read this in the morning, many of the devos are set up to help you get started the right way, each day!

No matter where you read these devos or what time it is, if your attitude is not right, you won't get the most out of it. I want to strongly encourage you to focus on picking up the book with a smile on your face every morning. Yes, I am talking LITERALLY, not figuratively. Each day, as you get to your place, pick up your book with a smile and as you do, ask God to reveal Himself to you as you jump in!

Last Thing...

Obviously this devo has 365 days laid out that correspond with our calendar (well, 366 days, in case you're reading this during a leap year). If you are able to start the brand new year with this book in your hand, that's awesome! With that said, no matter when you pick this book up, just start reading on that day and keep going for a whole year. I know God will speak to you, whatever season you may be in or day of the year you choose to start. He is God, after all. He sees you, He loves you, and He longs to spend time with you.

Fight Depression,

Defeat Loneliness,

Eliminate Comparison,

Overcome Greed,

Destroy Addiction,

Ignore People-Pleasing,

Change Ruminating Thoughts,

And So Much More!

Proclaim

"Rejoice in the Lord always. I will say it again: Rejoice! Let your gentleness be evident to all. The Lord is near." (Phil. 4:4-5)

Prompt

It's a new year! Hooray! I love fresh starts and new beginnings. Not much gets me this jacked up. Today is THE day of new beginnings, a day when seemingly everyone in the world is taking advantage of the rolling of the clock and the last digit of the date ticking forward by one.

Today is also a day of revival and renewal, a day to rejoice over where God has brought you, a day to reflect with gratitude on all he's done in and through your life up to this point.

Joy is a gift we choose to open every day. But especially on the FIRST day of a new year.

As we enter this new year together, make a plan and a goal to receive joy into your life each day of the year. Let joy be the lens through which you view this new year, and watch what happens!

Prod

It's time for joy! How will you incorporate the choice of joy into your life today? Write it down.

Praise

 Listen to "Happy Day" by Tim Hughes

Pray

Jesus, thank you for your unbounded joy in my life. Help me to experience it today. I invite you into my heart and into my life. Lead me this year like never before. I know I need you, but more than that, I want you. I want you to fill my mind, my heart and my soul with JOY! A joy that can only come from you. I dedicate this year to you, thank you for another year to spend with you! Amen.

Proclaim

"Rejoice in the Lord always. I will say it again: Rejoice! Let your gentleness be evident to all. The Lord is near." (Phil. 4:4-5)

Prompt

SMILE MORE.

I wrote those words on my mirror when I lived in Hope is Alive's first sober mentoring home.

This was during a season when I was overworked and just found myself constantly mad at things and people. That's not a good combo for a recovering addict by the way...

During a Sunday Night Meeting, one of the speakers said, "We should be the happiest people on the planet, God has given us a second chance that none of us deserve." That encouragement stuck with me, so later that evening, I wrote that reminder on my bathroom mirror. ***SMILE MORE!***

It's easy to pick out the bad things and dwell on them. Just like it's easier to frown rather than smile. But when we use those 43 muscles it takes to smile, each time we are reminding our brain that we are JOY-filled people who have a lot to be thankful for and happy about.

Prod

Are you experiencing Jesus-joy today?

If so, how?

If not, what's ONE thing you can do (hint, try listening to this song with headphones on! It will make you smile!)

Praise

 Listen to

"10,000 Reasons"

by Matt Redman

Pray

Jesus, thank you for the radiant smile of joy. Let me share your joy with the world I encounter today. I ask that you would give me the willingness to SMILE today and the courage to share the smile you created with at least one other person who might need it! Amen.

Proclaim

"Rejoice in the Lord always. I will say it again: Rejoice! Let your gentleness be evident to all. The Lord is near." (Phil. 4:4-5)

Prompt

Read the scripture again, this time out loud. There's a whole world of encouragement in that exclamation mark, isn't there?

It's not just about rejoicing. That's why Paul first tells us to rejoice in the Lord always, and then explicitly says, like a modern-day preacher, "I'm going to say that again to make sure you get it: *REJOICE!*"

Sometimes we have to be reminded to rejoice, and we have to be reminded *emphatically*.

Don't take that negative first feeling for the truth—sometimes it takes a few times for joy to break through the gloom of our guilt and shame, the fire of our anger and fear. Don't stop trying. In fact, do more than just try, JUMP! Yes, you read that right, JUMP FOR JOY!

I dare you to try and jump in public and NOT smile. There's something almost biologically connecting when our feet leave the ground our face starts to smile. And joy begins to invade our hearts.

So, when you are weary, read this verse out and choose joy!

When you're worried. When we're woozy. Rejoice. *I will say it again: Rejoice!*

Prod

How can you remind yourself to choose joy today? JUMP every time you start to feel overwhelmed, defeated or down. I know it seems weird, but that's the point. God will find you in the weirdness and bring joy to your heart.

Praise

 Listen to

"Living Hope"

by Phil Wickham

Pray

Jesus, thank you for your joy. I'll say it again: thanks for your joy! Thank you for filling my heart with joy when I smile, when I think of all your blessings and even when I JUMP in the air. I love to experience all the ways you love me! Even when I feel kinda silly. Today, may your joy radiate throughout my body and may it feel amazing! Amen!

LANCE LANG

Proclaim

"Rejoice in the Lord always. I will say it again: Rejoice! Let your gentleness be evident to all. The Lord is near." (Phil. 4:4-5)

Prompt

I love The Message translation of Psalm 51:15, which reads, *"Unbutton my lips, dear God; I'll let loose with your praise."*

Joy is all around us when we choose not just to see it, but to say it. There's a reason why singing songs out loud moves us emotionally: this action connects our heart and emotions with the vision made plain in the words.

When we unbutton our lips and praise God for what He has done and declare out loud the things, people, and situations in our lives that bring us *joy*, then off fall the shackles of fear, anger, disappointment, depression, sadness, and any other crappy stuff you can think of!

Let your praise loose today and tell God or someone else you know about your joy, and trust all the great things happening in your life. Let the joy of your life be known to those around you.

Prod

Who will you let loose to about your joy today?

Make a plan to tell them something great that is happening in your life today, no matter how small. Remember, when you share JOY, you share JESUS!

Praise

 Listen to

"Great Are You Lord"

by All Sons & Daughters

Pray

Jesus, unbutton my lips so I can let loose with your praise today. You have made me new, giving me a fresh start and forgiving me for my sins. I want to share my joy with others; please help me to clearly know who you want me to share it with today, when I should share it and the best way to share it. I'm pumped to see what you do in my life today! Amen!

Proclaim

"Rejoice in the Lord always. I will say it again: Rejoice! Let your gentleness be evident to all. The Lord is near." (Phil. 4:4-5)

Prompt

I learned a lesson about joy from a friend of mine as she went through some really hard challenges with her immediate family. I watched as her family hurt her over and over, and I watched as she stood her ground.

No matter what was thrown her way, my friend bounced back every day and chose joy.

When her parents or siblings ignored her, spited her, or purposefully hurt her, my friend chose joy.

I couldn't really comprehend the way she was able to pull it off and still seem grounded in reality. So I asked her about it and she told me she'd developed her **"joy muscle."** Choosing joy over and over again in all the little things in her life had developed her joy muscles for the times that required heavy lifting.

Start developing your joy muscles and you'll also develop a muscle memory that will make joy a reflex. What a way to live!

Prod

How can you choose joy in a small thing today? Maybe at work? Home? A mundane task? A tough conversation?

Write down a moment today that you anticipate will be TOUGH to find JOY-FULL.

Make a commitment NOW to choose joy in this moment and any others like it.

Praise

 Listen to

"Who You Say I Am"

by Hillsong Worship

Pray

Jesus, thank you for this [NAME A SMALL THING] in my life. This moment, this person, this task, this experience... God, you know I struggle with this, but when I choose to give it to you FIRST, then I can find joy in it! So God, please prepare me now to do the heavy lifting of choosing JOY in the tough moment I know I am going to experience today. I am working to change my thinking, change my reactions, change my heart. But I need your help to do so. Thank you for having my back! Amen.

LANCE LANG

Proclaim

"Rejoice in the Lord always. I will say it again: Rejoice! Let your gentleness be evident to all. The Lord is near." (Phil. 4:4-5)

Prompt

"Rejoice in the Lord always." **Always?!** How is that even possible?

Those rare people who seem to embody this level of joy, just walking around life always seeming joyful and positive, sure can seem strange. But the truth is, I really want to be that person! So much so that I'm working overtime to try and find all their life hacks for staying positive.

While on this journey, God has shown me one that has really helped: every time someone tries to steal my joy, I quickly try to think about what might lead them to act that way and just say, "Bless 'em, God" in my spirit or even quietly aloud.

As I do that, I acknowledge that, **99 times out of 100**, they have something going on within that I don't know about. So whatever I feel from them, hear from them, or put up with from them is from a tender area of their life that is spilling out on me.

"Bless 'em, God" then becomes a trigger in my head and heart to smile, protect my joy, and move on with life. Always.

Prod

Are you willing to try this "Bless 'em, God" life hack today? Who are the people you are thinking about right now!? I know you got some...

Praise

 Listen to

"This Is Amazing Grace"

by Phil Wickham

Pray

Jesus, thank you for knowing our hearts even when we don't. I know you know how hurtful people can be. I'm really trying to overcome the pains that people can bring. As I come across those kinds of people today, please help me to bless them, just like you did. Amen.

Proclaim

"Rejoice in the Lord always. I will say it again: Rejoice! Let your gentleness be evident to all. The Lord is near." (Phil. 4:4-5)

Prompt

Joy is a habit. It can't be a random occurrence you hope happens to you—it has to be something reflexive, something you carry with you all the time. Fortunately, as you well know, habits are something you can develop.

Here's an example: when I first got sober, I started breaking my bad habits and making a new habit of praying on my knees **every night**, a habit I still (mostly) maintain. Even all these years later, I still pray on my knees nearly every night.

Habits and routines are really important as a rule, but especially as we step into a new year. It's been proven that the best way to establish a new habit and keep it is to create a "habit trigger," a simple pre-action that quickly and easily catapults you into your habit without you even knowing it.

I started incorporating these habit triggers into my nighttime routine, and in the past decade-plus, I've rarely missed out on closing the day with prayer.

Put a habit trigger into place for joy and watch how much easier it gets for you!

Prod

Brainstorm time! What habit triggers can you put in place to help you turn joy into a habit? Write them down!

Praise

 Listen to

"One Thing Remains"

by Bethel Music

Pray

Jesus, thank you for giving me wisdom as I create these habit triggers for joy. I know that all joy comes from you, so when I experience joy, I'm really experiencing you! Help me to experience your joy more today, and more regularly as it gets easier and easier for me. Amen.

Proclaim

"Rejoice in the Lord always. I will say it again: Rejoice! Let your gentleness be evident to all. The Lord is near." (Phil. 4:4-5)

Prompt

I love the song "Waymaker." I love to sing it loud and proud, because it helps remind me of who God really is.

Someone who lives with hope is someone who knows the characteristics of the God they serve, and that can lead us to sing loudly and joyfully about the way-making God we serve!

When you believe all these things about God, you can confidently step out in faith to accomplish what he has called you to. You can make the tough decision. You can have the challenging conversation. You start the new venture, admit the mistake, forgive the sinner.

No matter what it is you are facing today, rejoice! He will make a way!

Prod

Where in your life do you need God to make a way? Can you trust Him with that today?

Praise

 Listen to "Waymaker" by Leeland

Pray

Jesus, you're the Waymaker! Make a way for me today, and help me walk in that way. I can't make my own way—I've tried and failed, stumbled, got lost and just messed it all up. Over and over and over again. Please make the way for me today. I'm following you all the way! Amen.

Proclaim

"Rejoice in the Lord always. I will say it again: Rejoice! Let your gentleness be evident to all. The Lord is near." (Phil. 4:4-5)

Prompt

We're made to play.

If you want to see how hope can change you, then you have to get out and enjoy life. Quit whining, turn off the TV, and go play.

One of the most important aspects of keeping my dreams alive today is a laser focus on enjoying life to the fullest. Don't get me wrong—I can overwork myself with the best of them, but I try to play just as hard as I work. It's a huge part of my recovery and my hope-filled life.

I try to keep a wide variety of friends and when they want to do something fun (and sober), I make an attempt to practice what I preach and say YES! We have only a limited amount of time in this world and I don't want to waste *any* of it.

Trust me: when you come alive after being dead for so long, life feels way too good to sit around. You have to sink your teeth into it! To hold onto your joy this year, you have to practice PLAY!

Prod

When's the last time you experienced the joy of play?

- · What were you doing?
- · How can you weave this into your weekly or even daily rhythms?

Praise

 Listen to

"Dynamite"

by Tom Smith

Pray

Jesus, thanks for making me to play! I treasure that about myself. Every time I connect with the little child inside my heart, I can feel your joy overtake me. God, please help me find a moment through today to have some fun! Help me come alive in JOY! Amen.

Proclaim

"Rejoice in the Lord always. I will say it again: Rejoice! Let your gentleness be evident to all. The Lord is near." (Phil. 4:4-5)

Prompt

How's your routine? I find a ton of joy in my routine, for a lot of reasons. I know that might sound counterintuitive—how do you find joy in doing the same things over and over? Well, structure brings safety and simplicity, which brings my soul joy. The older I get, the higher on my priority list my soul gets.

In fact, here's an example: most every morning I drive to my local coffee shop, listening to worship music. I pick up a cold brew and my fave ooey-gooey blueberry scone. As I dine on this delicious treat on the way to the office, the joy in my soul sure seems to rise!

Now, is it the most healthy routine? ***Probably not.*** But it sure feeds my soul, and that's really important!

Ps. When I need my soul to feel loved, this is always my go-to song! For a long time, I would listen to it every time I was in the sauna at the gym.

Prod

How's your soul today?

Reflect on your routine, take stock, and make sure it's providing your soul the small things that bring it joy.

What can you do RIGHT NOW, to start a healthy routine that feeds your soul?

Praise

 Listen to

"Goodness of God"

by Bethel Music

Pray

Jesus, please help show me the small things I can do each day to encounter you, feed my soul, and grow as a follower. I know that, when my soul is healthy, I am more generous, more kind, and more loving. I am more like you, and that's what I really want. Thank you for loving me enough to give me so many little things that bring me joy—some of which only me and you know about. Thank you for loving me! Amen.

Proclaim

"Rejoice in the Lord always. I will say it again: Rejoice! Let your gentleness be evident to all. The Lord is near." (Phil. 4:4-5)

Prompt

You know a great way to maintain your joy? Growing your self-confidence.

You know a great way to grow your self-confidence? Maintaining your routine.

As we check off our list every day, our confidence grows. Routines help us accomplish tasks we never could have completed while drunk or high. As this self-assurance grows, our fear of the unknown begins to slowly diminish, and true, long-lasting change seems a little more possible.

Courage and self-esteem build within us as we successfully take on new responsibilities and start to say YES!

And the more we build that self-esteem, the more joy we can take in a job well done. With each new accomplishment, we lay another brick into our wall of joy.

Prod

· How's your routine today?
· What do you need to add to it to round it out?
· What's left to accomplish?

Praise

 Listen to

"We Say Yes"

by Elim Sound

Pray

Jesus, thank you for the joy of my routine! Give me new insight into my self-confidence today. My answer is yes, whatever it is you have for me and whatever it is that lies ahead! I say YES to you today, Lord. Amen.

Proclaim

"Rejoice in the Lord always. I will say it again: Rejoice! Let your gentleness be evident to all. The Lord is near." (Phil. 4:4-5)

Prompt

When you're on the road to discipleship, you're on a road that leads to a joy-filled future. And a way you can prepare for that future is through practicing your routine.

Your routine helps you to innately begin to develop skills that will serve you greatly in the days to come. I know I benefited immensely from things like waking up on time (or early!), making my bed, finding time to read my Bible or a life-affirming, faith-building book, and saying prayers daily.

These kinds of routine builders mimic the type of professional schedule that a lot of us addicts have failed to maintain in the past. Routines keep us focused and looking ahead, building up strategic planning and time-management skills.

Routines set us up for the future, building joy both now and in the time ahead.

Prod

What's a way you can build for your future in your routine? Ask God for guidance and make a plan to make it happen.

Praise

 Listen to

"Behold (Then Sings My Soul)"

by Hillsong Worship

Pray

Jesus, you're amazing. Thank you for helping me find you in the little things so that I can find you all along the road to my amazing future. Amen.

Proclaim

"Rejoice in the Lord always. I will say it again: Rejoice! Let your gentleness be evident to all. The Lord is near." (Phil. 4:4-5)

Prompt

As you journey through discipleship, it's imperative to maintain your spiritual connection. Everything relies on Jesus *because Jesus is the Author of our Joy.*

That's why a daily devotional like this is so important. Making a concerted effort to seek God each day will naturally grow your understanding of Him while also driving your faith levels up and up and up.

As you carve out daily time like this, time to consciously connect with God through prayer, meditation, and daily devotionals, He will reveal His truths to you. And then you'll gain momentum as you see how God's sovereign hand has guided and protected you, even in the depths of your addiction.

Jesus has ALWAYS been there, even when you couldn't feel or see Him. He's been running after you since the day you were born.

Prod

How is your daily routine spiritually? Is there anywhere you need to step up your game?

Praise

 Listen to

"Reckless Love"

by Passion

Pray

Jesus, I know you've always been with me, even when I didn't realize it. Let me feel your presence with me today. I know you're here, and I love you. Amen.

Proclaim

"Rejoice in the Lord always. I will say it again: Rejoice! Let your gentleness be evident to all. The Lord is near." (Phil. 4:4-5)

Prompt

God made us to be creative beings. It's one of the many aspects of our lives that brings us true joy! Just the simple act of creation, of turning nothing into something, can spark a happiness that lasts and lasts.

When you achieve a balanced and relaxed life—which you can do when you keep up your routine—you then have easier access to your intuition and creativity.

You know what else helps? Getting out and **DOING** something active, whether that's exercise in a home gym, a brisk run through the neighborhood, or just a walk in the park. Getting yourself moving can refresh your mind and help you get back to your true, creative self.

Within all of us lies a creative being; by maintaining a routine and tapping into what Jesus offers, we allow that person the freedom to thrive.

Prod

When's the last time you did something creative? Make a plan to be creative today: write a poem, draw a sketch, or do something else you enjoy, just for the sake of being creative.

Praise

 Listen to "Glorious Day" by Passion

Pray

Jesus, you have the biggest imagination in the history of the universe—thank you for making me imaginative, too. Help me to honor you with my creativity today. Amen.

Proclaim

"Rejoice in the Lord always. I will say it again: Rejoice! Let your gentleness be evident to all. The Lord is near." (Phil. 4:4-5)

Prompt

Part of being a human being in this world is that our joy eventually bumps into non-joy in others. It's just the nature of life. We don't all get along at all times, even those who really love us.

When someone you love does something to steal your joy and rob you of your passion, when someone tries to hold you down and keep you in a box: recognize those for the lies they are and then *pick up your hope.*

Write down a list of affirmations and remind yourself that who the Son set free is FREE indeed. Remember who you really are: you are victorious, you are a beloved child of the King of Kings, you were made for something great.

What you've been through doesn't define you, it's only refined you into the person you are today. Take joy!

Prod

Okay, you just read it, so now do it: write down a list of affirmations about yourself. What does the Bible say about you? Put it in a place where you'll be reminded who you really are.

Praise

 Listen to

"Christ is Enough"

by Hillsong Worship

Pray

Jesus, thank you for calling me your beloved! I am new because you make me new! Through everything I went through, you've been there to pick me up. You are enough for me. You are everything to me. Because of your love, I can love myself today. Thank you for being everything I need! Wow! Amen.

Proclaim

"Rejoice in the Lord always. I will say it again: Rejoice! Let your gentleness be evident to all. The Lord is near." (Phil. 4:4-5)

Prompt

Living the life of a world-changer is wrought with ups and downs, but the key to weathering that roller coaster ride is simple: live in joy.

It's really the only way to deal with setbacks and tough seasons. After all, that's what scripture tells us in James 1:2-4:

"Consider it pure joy, my brothers and sisters, whenever you face trials of many kinds, because you know that the testing of your faith produces perseverance. Let perseverance finish its work so that you may be mature and complete, not lacking anything."

Smile. Love. Give. Share.

Make a commitment right now to choose JOY in all circumstances today. I know people might say things, treat you poorly, the stock market could go down, you could get dumped, you could find your car with a flat, all kinds of stuff could happen. No matter what, choose joy!

Prod

When you encounter a trial today, say it out loud: *I CHOOSE JOY!*

Practice with me right now, repeat after me, *I CHOOSE JOY!* (Your turn!)

Praise

 Listen to

"How He Loves"

by Jesus Culture

Pray

Jesus, you're my joy. No matter what, no matter when, I find my joy completely in you. Thank you for loving me like you do. Thank you for caring about everything I care about. Thank you. Period. Amen.

Proclaim

"Rejoice in the Lord always. I will say it again: Rejoice! Let your gentleness be evident to all. The Lord is near." (Phil. 4:4-5)

Prompt

"There will be glory after this. No need to worry."

So go the lyrics to the song "Joy of the Lord" by Maverick City, which borrows its chorus from Nehemiah 8:10, which says, "the joy of the Lord is my strength."

Do you believe that's true? Because if you do, then you don't need to worry! Even in the midst of the greatest trials of your life, you can trust that God's given you the strength to last through them—and he's done that through the strength-giving gift that is His joy.

No matter what you're encountering, there's glory after it. As we discussed yesterday, no matter what comes your way, you can choose to say, *I CHOOSE JOY!*

How can we say that with confidence? Because the giver of JOY never gets tired. His strength is always well rested and ready to go. He never sleeps, gets tired, or takes a day off. When you need joy, ask for a dose from the God who is always ready to give.

Prod

Make yourself a joy reminder—a Post-it note on your bathroom mirror, a rubber band around your wrist, whatever you have handy—and use it to remember that the joy of the Lord is your strength. Each time you see the note or feel the rubber band snap, remember, it's not your strength, it's GOD's that brings joy.

Praise

 Listen to

"Joy of the Lord"

by Maverick City

Pray

Jesus, thank you for your joy! Help me to rely on it and remember that there's glory on the other side of what I'm dealing with today. Thank you for being an everlasting source of strength and joy in my life. Make yourself known in my life today! I want to live life with a smile that shows the joy in my heart! Amen.

Proclaim

"Rejoice in the Lord always. I will say it again: Rejoice! Let your gentleness be evident to all. The Lord is near." (Phil. 4:4-5)

Prompt

Hope is so real.

During my journey of sobriety, almost everything I've hoped for has come true. Even in the midst of my disappointments, God has brought me hope and often showed me that I wasn't dreaming big enough yet.

Despite that, **God has watered the dreams** and visions He planted inside of me and brought them to life. What was once only a small "hope" has now become a thriving organization helping hundreds of people every day.

Hope, when birthed inside the will of God, is the most powerful thing on this planet. It's these hopes that God uses to pull us to more fulfilled and free lives. It's these hopes that God uses to provide for the joys of our hearts.

I know God has planted hopes inside of you. Today is a great day to dream a little. To get alone with God, talk about the hopes in your heart and ask Him to guide you to the next step. Rarely is a big dream or big hope instantly accomplished or provided for; instead it's a series of small answers to prayers that God provides consistently over time that lead to the big hopes in your life coming true. So today, trust that God wants to hear all the seemingly small hopes in your heart so He can begin to lead you to something bigger than you could ever imagine.

Prod

What hopes has God planted inside you? Write them down—even the big ones. Go spend some quiet time alone with God today and talk to Him about what's on your heart. He can't wait to be with you!

Praise

 Listen to

"Holy Water"

by We The Kingdom

Pray

Jesus, you're my hope. You have given me this new life, this new heart and all these new hopes in my soul. Thank you for all the hopes and dreams you've planted inside me. Show me what I need to do—and what I need to leave for YOU to do today. Amen.

Proclaim

"Rejoice in the Lord always. I will say it again: Rejoice! Let your gentleness be evident to all. The Lord is near." (Phil. 4:4-5)

Prompt

If you look at it right—with God's perspective—life itself is a joy.

Think about it: we've been given the gift of new life! And that's not all: we've also been called by the Creator of Life Himself to the wonderful task of co-laboring with God to build His kingdom.

Even when this life brings us deep, exquisite pain like a career setback, a torn relationship, financial disaster, or the loss of a loved one, how can we do anything but revel in Christ's joy?

When we take God's eternal perspective on life, suddenly things can make a lot more sense. I get it, it's easier said than done. But you are doing the work right now to establish a fresh new JOY-FILLED perspective. Choosing to spend time with God, memorize His word, and build a healthy rhythm of joy is a huge step in the right direction.

Prod

Is there anything holding you back from looking at life from God's perspective? Name it.

Ask God to help you remove anything that is blocking you right now!

Praise

 Listen to

"YOUR NAME IS POWER"

by Rend Collective

Pray

Jesus, thank you for your vision. Guide me to see the world with your joy today. I need your help letting go of [NAME A BURDEN]. I need your help forgiving [NAME A PERSON]. I need your help keeping my eyes focused on your JOY! Please help me today see this world through a lens of Joy! Amen.

Proclaim

"Rejoice in the Lord always. I will say it again: Rejoice! Let your gentleness be evident to all. The Lord is near." (Phil. 4:4-5)

Prompt

There's an interesting thing about joy in the way it changes our perception.

Here's what I mean: think about the last time you were in a really terrible situation. This may have been back when you were still neck-deep in your addiction, struggling with how to parent your children or facing financial challenges. It can even be as recent as just feeling down this morning.

If you were to bring a negative perception to that situation, what would happen? Would it change anything?

What if you brought a positive, joyful perception? Would it change the situation itself?

The answer to both questions is probably "no." Your perception doesn't change the situation—it changes *YOU*. Choosing to **see with joy** makes situations more bearable and invites the Lord into them.

Choose to SEE TODAY WITH JOY! No matter what, commit to it right now.

Prod

Grab a sharpie, some Post-it notes and fill out ten of them with one word: JOY! Put the notes in different places you frequent. Each time you SEE them, let them be a reminder that you are choosing to see through the eyes of JOY!

Praise

 Listen to

"I Am Free"

by New Life Worship

Pray

Jesus, thank you for making me able to choose joy. Today, fill me with your Holy Spirit, ignite my heart with a joy that is unquenchable. I want to make JOY the number one option for me today! I need your help to shift my perspective as I face today. You are a joy giver, you are THE hope dealer, you are my sustainer and the creator of all good things. Thank you for giving me JOY today. Amen.

Proclaim

"Rejoice in the Lord always. I will say it again: Rejoice! Let your gentleness be evident to all. The Lord is near." (Phil. 4:4-5)

Prompt

Joy is a gift.

The thing about a gift is that it's something you have to be given. I mean, I guess you can give yourself a gift, which is, of course, something I've done on occasion (like when I treat myself to that extra breakfast scone).

But real gifts come from someone as a thoughtful expression that aims to bring joy to someone's life. But a gift **MUST BE RECEIVED.** Otherwise it just sits and collects dust, never reaching its full intended purpose.

Joy is a gift and it's something we must choose. Remember, it's on the menu because God put it there. He wants you to choose this gift and get the benefits of all its intentions. So don't put it off, don't ignore it, don't let it collect dust.

Unwrap this gift of joy that God wants to give you today!

Prod

Treat yourself to a little gift today, and when you do, reflect on the gift of joy God has given you.

Praise

 Listen to

"For All You've Done"

by HIllsong Worship

Pray

Jesus, thank you for the gift of joy. Help me to treasure it always. Amen.

Proclaim

"Rejoice in the Lord always. I will say it again: Rejoice! Let your gentleness be evident to all. The Lord is near." (Phil. 4:4-5)

Prompt

When's the last time you took joy in something God gave you? It could be something as small as your next breath or something as big as a relationship you treasure. When's the last time you have **LOOKED at a situation and seen the victory God** was giving you as a gift of JOY?

These are the kinds of things that, miraculous though they are, can become commonplace in our lives just through the sheer fact that they are part of our lives for so long.

But when we stop, and we reflect on them, and we take joy in them—then they come alive once more and become in our minds and hearts the gifts that they always were.

Take joy!

Prod

Find five things throughout the day that you would ordinarily overlook and determine to take joy in them.

Praise

 Listen to

"See The Victory"

by Elevation Worship

Pray

Jesus, let me look at this world through your joy-filled eyes and see you wherever you are. Help me to see the victory you have placed in my hands. Amen.

Proclaim

"Rejoice in the Lord always. I will say it again: Rejoice! Let your gentleness be evident to all. The Lord is near." (Phil. 4:4-5)

Prompt

I'm not a coffee guy. I'm an energy drink guy.

You know when you open a can, how you get that oh-so-refreshing sound of carbonation escaping? (Or maybe you remember that sound from your beer-drinking days?)

To me, that's the sound of joy.

Joy is effervescence. Joy bubbles up from within us. Joy can seem like an almost inexhaustible resource that never runs out.

At least, that's how God's joy is. We can't get there on our own—if we try, we'll just go flat. We have to rely on the joy of the Lord to refresh us daily, hourly.

Crack open your heart and let the joy come out!

Prod

Get a non-alcoholic carbonated beverage—energy drink, sparkling water, Diet Coke—and reflect on God's joy as you open it and listen to the sound.

Praise

 Listen to

"I Thank God"

by Maverick City Music

Pray

Jesus, thank you for your effervescent joy, bubbling up within me. Keep me from going flat today. I want to have a joy that overflows into the life of others today. Please fill me with a POP that others are drawn to, and as you do, give me the courage to speak JOY into their hearts! Amen.

Proclaim

"Rejoice in the Lord always. I will say it again: Rejoice! Let your gentleness be evident to all. The Lord is near." (Phil. 4:4-5)

Prompt

Do you let yourself get excited? Do you look forward with anticipation to what lies ahead?

While we do need to take things one day at a time, that shouldn't stop us from having not just a big vision for our future but an exciting one!

Because there's joy in excitement!

It's exciting when we put together those first thirty days of sobriety! It's exciting when we pay off that debt we owe! It's exciting when we get far enough along to celebrate others when they start achieving milestones we've already attained!

By the same token, it's exciting to look down the road with the vision of the Holy Spirit and see what God might have in store for us. Each day I get up expecting something BIG to happen. Why? Because in Jeremiah 29:11, God told me that He has plans for me that include hope and a future! That sounds like something big to me, and THAT gets me excited! Filled with joy!

Prod

What's ahead for you to get excited about? Share 3 things:

Give yourself permission today to believe that God wants to do the extraordinary in your life. Get excited and get joy-FULL!

Praise

 Listen to

"God's Not Done With You"

by Tauren Wells

Pray

Jesus, thank you for the gift of excitement. I believe that you have my life in your hands. Today, I commit to trusting you in every area of my life. I speak the name of Jesus and proclaim that my best days are ahead, that you are working all things together to bring about good in my life, and that something BIG is coming. God help me to see it today, and when I do, give me the confidence to chase after it with faith! Amen.

Proclaim

"Rejoice in the Lord always. I will say it again: Rejoice! Let your gentleness be evident to all. The Lord is near." (Phil. 4:4-5)

Prompt

Okay, here's a thought you've maybe had, probably when you were a kid. You were somewhere in public, like a mall or museum or something, and you saw a fountain. And as you watched it—assuming you watched it after you got entranced by all the money in the bottom of it—you started to notice how it never stopped.

That's the point of fountains, right? That they just flow and flow and flow, nonstop.

And that's what the joy of the Lord is like. It just comes up and flows out and out and out. As long as we don't allow that flow to get blocked by the cares of this life, we can draw on that neverending fountain of joy.

And don't you want to live a life that's overflowing with JOY? I know I do! I don't want to barely be operational or only occasionally feel joy—I want to be overflowing with God's love, joy, and passion! May God help us to be filled to OVERFLOW today!

Prod

Do you have anything blocking your joy fountain? Name it right now in the space provided! Spend time today listening to this amazing song and ask God to remove anything that's keeping you from living in a joy overflow today!

Praise

 Listen to

"Fountains"

by Josh Baldwin

Pray

Jesus, thank you for your fountain of joy in my life! You produced the water, you produce the flow, and Jesus, you can help me to remove anything that's blocking me. So today that's what I am asking for. I need your help! Please help me to remove bitterness, unforgiveness, lust, jealousy, comparisons, negative thoughts about other people, laziness, [LIST ANYTHING ELSE THAT MIGHT BE BLOCKING YOUR FOUNTAIN]. God, I ask you to remove these things that are blocking me from experiencing you fully today. In the name of your son Jesus, I pray these things. Amen!

Proclaim

"Rejoice in the Lord always. I will say it again: Rejoice! Let your gentleness be evident to all. The Lord is near." (Phil. 4:4-5)

Prompt

Sometimes joy needs a reboot. Routine is great and necessary, but it can sometimes lead to a dullness that gets in the way of our joy.

When you find yourself in that place, ask yourself how you can change things up *just enough* to find your joy again. It can be something as dramatic as taking a vacation or something as subtle as spending your morning prayer time walking instead of kneeling by your bed.

If you're in that spot where your joy needs to be refreshed, don't wait! Hit that RESET button today. Do something—still within the guidelines of your routine—to jostle your joy.

Prod

Make a slight—but healthy!—difference in your routine today to make room for God to show you unexpected joy. Here are some things I love to do to deepen my relationship with God. When I do these things, my joy is reset and refilled. He is the author and caretaker of joy after all!

- Go on a long walk
- Exercise 'til you can't anymore (full exhaustion)
- Call someone and tell them how grateful you are for them
- Spend time with an employee or co-worker who needs you
- Fill your spouse's or significant other's love tank by speaking their love language!

Praise

 Listen to

"I'll Follow"

by Cody Carnes

Pray

Jesus, thank you for joy in the routine—and for joy outside of it. Today I want to stop and seek you in a new and different way. As I do, please meet me there and fill me with the joy that only comes from you. Amen.

Proclaim

"Rejoice in the Lord always. I will say it again: Rejoice! Let your gentleness be evident to all. The Lord is near." (Phil. 4:4-5)

Prompt

Joy often looks like gladness. It's fun to be glad, isn't it?! I love being glad—when my joy radiates out like a big smile on my face.

But joy doesn't always take the form of gladness. Sure, it's awesome to feel glad, but sometimes joy shows up and it just looks like contentment.

All that to say: don't worry if you don't feel glad today! Gladness is not the end result—joy is. You can have a whirlwind of chaos going on in your life, but if you're content with what God is doing within you and through you, then you have joy!

Today, you might be a *"content type of joy"* day. That's okay. Thank God that you have everything you need because He gave everything He had for YOU!

Prod

When's the last time you felt content? Ask the Lord for the contentment of His joy today. This could be tough for you to just be okay with what you have. If so, share why contentment is tough for you.

Praise

 Listen to

"Kind"

by Cory Asbury

Pray

Jesus, I need your help to feel content. Sometimes I find myself just comparing everything I have and everything I do with others. My eyes wander to someone else's life and I just struggle with where mine is. But God, you call me your own. You tell me I am saved and sanctified, a light in the world. You call me your friend and a co-heir with Jesus. You tell me I am chosen, adopted, and made alive in Christ. Let me walk in these truths and fill my life with a contented joy today. Amen.

Proclaim

"Rejoice in the Lord always. I will say it again: Rejoice! Let your gentleness be evident to all. The Lord is near." (Phil. 4:4-5)

Prompt

Not that long ago, tidiness expert Marie Kondo took the world by storm with her radical new approach to hoarding. She encouraged people to go through their closets, garages, or wherever, pick up each item they owned, and ask themselves whether it "sparked joy" in them. If it did, they could keep it. If not: out it went.

I think this is a good practice not just for our physical stuff but also for our emotional and spiritual stuff. Is there a feeling you're hanging on to that doesn't spark joy? What about a relationship? A social media app? A rhythm in your routine? A habit?

If something in your life doesn't spark joy, ask yourself if it's really necessary to hang on to it. If not, trash it!

Prod

Think of your life and list the first five things that come to mind that do NOT spark joy.

What can you do to let these go this week? Or even today?!

Praise

 Listen to

"Monkeys at the Zoo"

by Charlie Peacock

Pray

Jesus, thank you for the things, people, and feelings around me that spark joy. I revel in them! I want joy to fill my life in all moments and seasons. Some of the things I listed today seem to steal my joy. I want to get rid of them. Please help me to find the courage and confidence to let go of anything that is robbing my joy! Amen.

Proclaim

"Rejoice in the Lord always. I will say it again: Rejoice! Let your gentleness be evident to all. The Lord is near." (Phil. 4:4-5)

Prompt

We have to take all the joy we can find these days, wherever we can find it.

So where are you looking? Are you looking to the simple things like finishing yet another day clean and sober? Or enjoying a nourishing meal with a friend or loved one? Or just having enough gas in your car to get you to work?

I know for me, when I take the time to recognize the small joy-fillers and joy-givers in my life, my joy meter goes up! Stuff like an inside joke with my wife, watching a good football game in the middle of the week, a song that just gets me fired up, or a new documentary. It's a small step to keep my soul where it needs to be and my spirit filled with the right things.

Joy can sometimes feel in short supply. That's why we have to seize it where we find it, and we can only find it if we're on the lookout for it. Keep your eyes open. Today's prompt will help.

Prod

Have you found joy today? Look for it in the small things. Start right now by sharing five JOY-GIVERS that others might not know about you.

Praise

 Listen to
"God is For Us"
by CityAlight

Pray

Jesus, thank you for helping me find joy today. You love me so much that you gave me all these small things that put a smile on my face. Thank you for your love. Thank you for caring about ME! Thank you for being FOR ME! Thank you for being my source of all GOOD things in my life. Fill me with joy today. Amen.

Proclaim

"Rejoice in the Lord always. I will say it again: Rejoice! Let your gentleness be evident to all. The Lord is near." (Phil. 4:4-5)

Prompt

Gentleness. It's underrated in our modern society for sure. We love to laud the brash, the powerful, the people who "tell it like it is." Social media celebrates the selfie pose, the self-promoter, the influencer.

Where is the place for the gentle?

According to our scripture passage, it's with us. WE'RE the ones in this world whose gentleness should be evident to all. WE'RE the ones who should be spreading gentleness throughout the world, because that gentleness is an indicator of joy.

Prod

Is it hard for you to be gentle as you go about your day? What does that mean to you?

Think of the gentlest way you can go through your day today. Choose right now to put this gentleness into play TODAY! See how it might spark JOY in those around you.

Praise

 Listen to

"Promise To The End"

by LO Worship

Pray

Jesus, thank you for filling me with your gentleness. I'm so glad I get to be like you to others. Help me to stay humble, kind, and gentle with your children today. I just want others to see YOU in me today. I love you, Jesus, and thank you for being my Savior and King. Thank you for your faithfulness to me. Amen.

Proclaim

"Rejoice in the Lord always. I will say it again: Rejoice! Let your gentleness be evident to all. The Lord is near." (Phil. 4:4-5)

Prompt

Here we are at the end of the first month of the new year. At midnight tonight, the clock will tick over to the next day, and that day will be February, and we'll be fully into the new year.

January ends. February begins. **THE CYCLE CONTINUES ON.**

But you know what doesn't end? The joy of the Lord. God's joy is the same today as it was yesterday and will be the same tomorrow. Days on a calendar, minutes on a clock—these mean nothing to our God! His mercies—and joys—are ever new, on today, the last day of the month, and tomorrow, the first.

Prod

Whether January was great or terrible, celebrate another month of life as it closes out.

Treat yourself to something nice today.

Praise

 Listen to

"You Will Be Found"

by Natalie Grant & Cory Asbury

Pray

Jesus, thank you for your ever-giving, neverending joy. Thank you for seeing me through this first month. I love how this song reminds me that no matter where I am, no matter what I do, you find me. I'm so grateful for your love for me and how it gives me joy in my heart. Thank you for a great first month of the new year! Amen.

Proclaim

"Rejoice in the Lord always. I will say it again: Rejoice! Let your gentleness be evident to all. The Lord is near." (Phil. 4:4-5)

Prompt

Does your every heartbeat feel like a blessing?

Because they are. Every single heartbeat, every single blink, every single blessing in your life should remind you that YOU ARE ALIVE!

Today's song, "I'm Alive" by Paul Zach and Page CXVI gets at this very notion. That it's a joy just to be alive today, because God gave you this day and the life you get to lead, no matter what the day holds for you.

My Dad loves to quote Psalm 118:24: "This IS the day the Lord has made; we will rejoice and be glad in it."

He's right! We should rejoice that we are alive another day.

As today's song says: "I'm alive, and I'm blessing every heartbeat." This can be your rallying cry today! Let's goooo!

Prod

Before you turn on today's song, take a few moments to sit quietly and reflect on your heartbeat. Pay attention to your pulse and ponder how every single one of those is a blessing from your heavenly Father. Once you are done, turn on today's song and try not to DANCE! I dare you!

Praise

 Listen to

"I'm Alive"

by Paul Zach and Page CXVI

Pray

Jesus, thank you for this heartbeat, and the next one, and one after that. I'm blessing every single one of these. This IS the day YOU have made, and I will rejoice and be glad that I am ALIVE. Amen.

Proclaim

"Rejoice in the Lord always. I will say it again: Rejoice! Let your gentleness be evident to all. The Lord is near." (Phil. 4:4-5)

Prompt

Today is a good day.

Oh, it might be a terrible day. It might be the worst possible day you've ever faced (probably not, though). Or maybe it's setting up to be a boring day of boring routines at a boring job doing boring things.

Doesn't matter. Today is a good day. **Say it! Out loud. Right now!**

If you say it and believe it, it won't matter if dynamite, disaster, or drudgery hit you the moment you get to work—however your day goes, it's a good one. So take joy in it.

Why? Because God made it. And as our verse reminds us, God is near. His love for us is greater than anything we will face.

We should have no worries today because, as today's song reminds us... God takes good care of us!

Prod

Say this three times out loud. Get louder each time. I know it feels weird—do it anyway!

Today is going to be a great day.

Today is going to be a great day.

Today is going to be a great day.

Praise

 Listen to "Sparrow" by Cory Asbury

Pray

Jesus, thanks for making this day. Thank you for being near to me—always. Thank you for giving me joy in this day! I choose to believe, with faith, that you will help me to make this day great! Help me to smile, be kind, and radiate joy to everyone I see. Amen.

LANCE LANG

Proclaim

"Rejoice in the Lord always. I will say it again: Rejoice! Let your gentleness be evident to all. The Lord is near." (Phil. 4:4-5)

Prompt

One of the immutable facts about joy is this: it is not a thing.

Joy cannot be bought or manufactured, and it cannot be licensed or packaged for sale. Joy arises from the presence of the Living God. We can turn to outside influences to help us recall joy or remember joy, but those are not the cause—*it's Jesus within us that makes our joy.*

Jesus gives us peace. Jesus gives us grace. Jesus embodies forgiveness. Jesus loves us no matter what. Jesus is our compass. Jesus is our rock. Jesus is our provider. Jesus lights the way. And because of all this and so much more, we have JOY!

So turn always to Him. Keep your eyes on Him. *Jesus gives us JOY!*

Prod

Where do you look for your joy? Spend three minutes meditating on your own source of joy.

Praise

 Listen to

"Your Love Never Fails"

by Jesus Culture

Pray

Jesus, you're amazing. I can't get enough of you! Thank you for dying so that I might have a life. I want to be the kind of person who radiates joy. As I spend more time with you, I can see how you were kind to others, accepting of all people, and serving anyone. You healed so many people and loved all. You embody joy—please fill my heart with that same joy right now! Amen.

Proclaim

"Rejoice in the Lord always. I will say it again: Rejoice! Let your gentleness be evident to all. The Lord is near." (Phil. 4:4-5)

Prompt

The joy of the Lord isn't just a great motivator or external force—it's also a great *internal* force.

In other words, joy makes us feel great about ourselves. And this is great news for us! Why? Because many of us (me included) get stuck in **cycles of comparison** all the time!

We compare our money, our moments, our misery, our marriages.

We compare our titles, our trips, our transportation, our trophies.

We compare everything and it rips joy from our hearts.

BUT... when we operate in the joy of the Lord, we don't need to worry about the opinions of others, or the things, or the stuff—because we know God is on our side and is taking care of us. We can just walk in the humble confidence of the Lord, spreading His goodness and gentleness wherever we go.

So walk on! Know God loves you and that that's really **ALL YOU NEED** to have joy in your heart!

Prod

Where do you struggle to compare? Use today's prayer time to ask God to step into those places in your heart and help you heal them.

Praise

 Listen to

"The Goodness of Jesus"

by CityAlight

Pray

Jesus, thank you for being on my side. Thank you for taking care of me. Thank you that you are all that I need. Thank you for reminding me today that comparison is a thief of joy. Today I am asking you to step into every place of comparison in my heart and heal me. Help me walk in your humble confidence today. Amen.

Proclaim

"Rejoice in the Lord always. I will say it again: Rejoice! Let your gentleness be evident to all. The Lord is near." (Phil. 4:4-5)

Prompt

Yesterday we talked about how we don't need to worry about the opinions of others when we walk in the joy of the Lord.

But here's another benefit and another set of opinions we don't have to worry about: our own!

Our minds can often be our biggest champions when we allow them, but more often than not, our minds can be our biggest obstacles. After all, how many times have we avoided a compliment or a promotion—or even love—because we were convinced we weren't worthy of it?

Stop! **THAT'S NOT JOY, AND IT'S NOT OF GOD!** You can set your opinion about yourself straight—you are a joy-filled creation of the Most High God! Walk in it!

Prod

In what ways is your own mind blocking you from experiencing God's joy? What are the negative tapes you played this week in your head?

Now, speak the truth of Jesus over each one of these and trust that HIS love is true and greater than any negative thought you can have.

Praise

 Listen to
"Jesus Have It All"
by Jeremy Riddle

Pray

Jesus, I give you all of my mind today. Fill it with your thoughts about me. Help me to truly believe what you say about me. I believe that you are for me, you love me no matter what, and that you want to be the guide to the thoughts in my mind. Amen.

Proclaim

"Rejoice in the Lord always. I will say it again: Rejoice! Let your gentleness be evident to all. The Lord is near." (Phil. 4:4-5)

Prompt

When was the last time you played? I mean, like, went out and just played for no real reason. Pick-up hoops with some friends, or an impromptu board game night, something like that.

There's a reason we find play pleasurable—it's because we're wired that way! God made us to love play because that's a way we learn about the world when we're kids... and well into adulthood.

That's because God is the author of joy, and play feels pretty darn joyful, doesn't it? When we play, we're bringing God's joy to the surface. What can you do to practice play today? I know it might sound weird, but this is how you keep JOY alive in your life.

Sometimes we have to intentionally stop the WORLD around us that just pushes us to perform all day, every day, and instead treat yourself to some play.

You need it, your family needs it, your soul needs it. So do it!

Prod

Organize a time of play with a small group of people TODAY, and have fun! Don't make any excuses. Trust that God will reveal Himself in this time and put a smile on your face.

Praise

 Listen to

"Wake"

by Hillsong Young & Free

Pray

Jesus, thank you for giving me the spirit of play. Let me enjoy you today! As I do, please make yourself known to me. Help me to see you for who you are, reveal your nature, your love, and your joy for me SO THAT I can feel joy for myself. Amen.

Proclaim

"Rejoice in the Lord always. I will say it again: Rejoice! Let your gentleness be evident to all. The Lord is near." (Phil. 4:4-5)

Prompt

Sometimes you just need a break.

That's okay! It's good to take breaks when you need them (as long as you do it in a healthy way and not try to take a break from your sobriety or something really critical!). We live in a busy world that seems to get busier by the day—a little self-care is often a recipe for health.

I am a huge evangelist for time off. Not because I'm lazy, but because I have learned the value of time set apart with God. I've felt just how full my soul can be with God's love when I choose to step away from my normal life, get alone with God, and just seek Him. I'm telling you: ***I come back to my world CHANGED!***

So if you're having trouble hearing the Lord and finding the joy he's always bringing you, maybe you need to interrupt what's going on and take a little break.

Make space for you and God to be together. Cut out all the other noise (as best as you can) just to seek Him and watch as He restores your joy. Or better yet, takes it to a higher level.

Prod

Be real. Do you need a break? If so, tell someone today that you might need a few days alone with just you and God. Be brave enough to go and do it.

Praise

 Listen to

"We Need A Miracle"

by Charity Gayle

Pray

Jesus, thank you for creating time and space. Even in this moment, I believe you can hear my thoughts, understand my needs, and heal my soul all at the same time. I really want more time with you. Help me to understand how I can do this. Open up doors, create opportunities, do what ONLY YOU CAN DO! I am willing to seek you, because I know when I do, I always find you! Amen.

Proclaim

"Rejoice in the Lord always. I will say it again: Rejoice! Let your gentleness be evident to all. The Lord is near." (Phil. 4:4-5)

Prompt

When God's joy gets in you, it changes you radically. Like, from the inside out kind of change. Because God is the God who inspires over-the-top devotion and undignified celebration.

Look at someone like King David, who, in 1 Samuel 16, gets so overjoyed with God that he dances like a complete and total fool in front of everyone. And I can relate. Back when I first got sober, I attended a self-improvement workshop every weekend for months. Each Saturday they held a dance and we were encouraged to truly "dance like no one was watching." The more comfortable I got doing this, *the more JOY* I could release. It was freeing to my soul! The more I did, the more I just wanted to let it loose!

That's the kind of joy God gives us—the kind that so consumes us that we just have to express it, even though the rest of the world is full of onlookers who find us both tantalizing and confounding, magnetic and mesmerizing.

In other words: radically changed.

Prod

Are you prepared to demonstrate God's joy to the world? I hope so, because today's PROD is for real: I challenge you to take 30 seconds sometime today and just let it rip! Dance, sing, jump for joy, groove, flex—electric slide if you need to—just let the JOY out!

Praise

 Listen to

"Echo"

by Charity Gayle

Pray

Jesus, let me feel your joy at the life-changing level today. I need you. I want to feel your joy so much that it just comes out in undignified celebration! Today, will you please put YOUR joy deep in my soul? I'm ready to let loose, dance, and get FREE! Amen.

Proclaim

"Rejoice in the Lord always. I will say it again: Rejoice! Let your gentleness be evident to all. The Lord is near." (Phil. 4:4-5)

Prompt

It can be difficult to speak of joy when we look out at the world—or even our own lives—and see hurt, pain, confusion, and turmoil, both within and without.

Fortunately, **GOD'S JOY IS NOT DEPENDENT** on anything other than God. When we live with His joy, He rescues us from looking to sources other than Him to bring us joy. Not laws, not leaders, not even laughter.

In the midst of our bad, God guides our eyes to the good, protecting our hearts while letting them stay soft to the hurt of the world.

Prod

What non-God sources are you trusting for joy? List them out right now and determine to still enjoy them WITHOUT making them be your source of joy. This can be tough! Spend time in prayer, asking God to help you remove your dependence on world-things and full on to Him.

Praise

 Listen to

"I Believe It"

by Jon Reddick

Pray

Jesus, thank you for bringing me joy in the midst of badness. Let me keep my focus on you today. You are my source of strength, my source of hope, and my source of joy. Please help remove my dependence on _____. Instead, I commit to trusting you to fill me with everything I need to persevere, to stay positive, and to keep pursuing the purpose you have put in my heart. Amen.

Proclaim

"Rejoice in the Lord always. I will say it again: Rejoice! Let your gentleness be evident to all. The Lord is near." (Phil. 4:4-5)

Prompt

Scripture gives us a lesson in joy in Romans 12, where we read that we are to "rejoice with those who rejoice." When others have joy, we are called to celebrate alongside them, whether we have our own joy or not!

Why? Because when we do so, we bear joyful witness to God's goodness. We further our status as a family of believers that uplifts our brothers and sisters instead of only rooting for people to fail or lose so we can feel okay.

I'm afraid I have done this way too much in my life, and it really makes me sick. I want to be a person who truly cheers others on. When I can do this, I know it shows that something is different about me and helps others believe this Jesus stuff. It's joyful! But it's hard. Let's take a step towards freedom today by making a real effort to rejoice when others rejoice.

Prod

Who in your circle is celebrating joy today? Send them a text message—or better yet CALL THEM—and let them know you're celebrating right alongside them.

If you want to go further in hopes of deepening this new joy collaborative thing, then send them a gift card, write them a letter, or buy them something they like and ship it!

Praise

 Listen to

"This is Living"

by Hillsong Young & Free

Pray

Jesus, help me take joy in others today. I want to cheer others on with nothing but peace and joy in my heart. God, forgive me for all the times I've rooted for people to lose or fail. Today I want to take a new step to LIVE IN JOY and LIVE IN HOPE. Please help me to see the best in others and to begin to publicly and privately celebrate your children. Amen.

Proclaim

"Rejoice in the Lord always. I will say it again: Rejoice! Let your gentleness be evident to all. The Lord is near." (Phil. 4:4-5)

Prompt

In this passage of scripture, we're instructed to rejoice in the Lord always. Fortunately, when God asks something of us, He gives us the strength and wisdom to do it.

We can love because God loved.

We can hope because God gives us hope through Jesus.

We can forgive because God forgave.

We can rejoice because God rejoices.

And whenever we demonstrate that love and joy to the world, we're showing God just how much we love Him and take joy in Him. This might feel strange, but I promise it's true. When you live your life devoted to loving, celebrating, forgiving, and living in peace with God's children, you are showing God that you love Him.

In short, living a life of love on earth reflects love to God in Heaven.

Prod

In what ways do you take joy in God? Make a list of at least five and meditate on it today. Determine to add five more by week's end.

Praise

 Listen to

"Amadeo (Still My God)"

by Ryan Stevenson

Pray

Jesus, help me demonstrate your love and joy to the world today. I want to embody you in my reactions, my words, my thoughts, and my behavior. I want to be a living sacrifice that is holy and pleasing to you, God. Thank you for loving me, which gives me strength to love others! Fill me with your joy today! Amen.

Proclaim

"Rejoice in the Lord always. I will say it again: Rejoice! Let your gentleness be evident to all. The Lord is near." (Phil. 4:4-5)

Prompt

You want something to be joyful about? God is so gracious that every good gift we have comes from Him. God turns our mourning into dancing and our distress into delight.

Even when we lament, God finds us there and whispers, "I am here." It's up to us to trust the Holy Spirit to open our ears so we can hear God's encouragement, blessing, and promises.

And when we hear Him? Everything turns around into a joyous celebration.

Prod

Stop today. Like, truly stop, right now, and be still.

Now, ask God to reveal to you the gifts you've been given from Him. Write them down.

Now write down the not-so-good gifts, like the tough moments that taught you a lesson, the harsh words that humbled you, the surprise moments of shame that left you feeling weak, and ask the Holy Spirit to reveal their God-authored goodness to you.

Praise

 Listen to

"You Have Made Me Glad"

by Charity Gayle

Pray

Jesus, thank you for turning my mourning into dancing! I know you were with me during all these tough times. Today I can see how you walked with me, how you cried with me, and how you helped me climb out of the pit! Thank you for all the many gifts you have given me in my life, God. Let my feet exalt you today. Amen.

Proclaim

"Rejoice in the Lord always. I will say it again: Rejoice! Let your gentleness be evident to all. The Lord is near." (Phil. 4:4-5)

Prompt

As much as we may not realize it, joy is a choice.

Sometimes we can think that joy should come upon us, like a feeling we don't anticipate, but we can actually *choose* to feel joy—especially when we're talking about God's joy.

That's the power in today's song, "joy." by For King and Country—it's a potent reminder that joy is a choice we can make, and that when we choose joy in the midst of trial, we are taking a stand and declaring the goodness and victory of our God.

Prod

Any time you have to make a choice today—whether it's what to eat, what to wear, where to go—add "joy" to your list of choices and decide to choose it as well.

Praise

 Listen to

"Joy"

by For King and Country

Pray

Jesus, please give me the strength to choose joy today, even when I don't want to. In everything I do and say, I want to choose JOY! Please help me. Amen.

Proclaim

"Rejoice in the Lord always. I will say it again: Rejoice! Let your gentleness be evident to all. The Lord is near." (Phil. 4:4-5)

Prompt

In the Old Testament book of 1 Samuel, we read the love story of Hannah and Elkanah, a husband and wife who could not have children. They went to the temple, and Hannah begged God for a son so intently that the temple priest, Eli, thought she was drunk. But she wasn't—she was just earnestly seeking God.

She was so desperate that she promised she would give her child back to God, and so when her son Samuel was born, she took him back to the temple and left him there to serve.

That's the strength of love. It's a strength that looks to God only as our source and rejoices in whatever cup—***whether bitter, bland, or beautiful***—He asks us to drink.

It's a love that remembers God is our strength. God is our portion. God is our joy.

Prod

Is there a sacrifice God is asking you to make? Of course there is! There's always something God is trying to show us through our sacrifice. What is it?

How can you take steps toward obedience today?

Praise

 Listen to

"Who I Am"

by Ben Fuller

Pray

Jesus, thank you for being my strength and portion. I want to do whatever you ask of me today. Please help me find the courage to say YES to the sacrifice you put on my heart today. I know I've put it off, but today, through the power of your Holy Spirit, I want to step into this and trust you completely! Amen.

Proclaim

"Rejoice in the Lord always. I will say it again: Rejoice! Let your gentleness be evident to all. The Lord is near." (Phil. 4:4-5)

Prompt

God made today. That makes it His.

And because it's His, it's holy.

And because it's holy, it's a day of joy, whether it feels like it or not.

This is a day to fill your lungs with glad tidings and set your heart to meditate on God's goodness. God's spirited life will revive your soul and help you see today as a day of joy, whether it feels like it or not.

So no matter what you are looking at today—big meeting, tough conversation, boring day, life-changing decisions, vacation, whatever it is—*GOD MADE THIS DAY!*

So make today holy. Because it's God's. Because God made it. Like He made you.

Prod

Write down the one or two big things you have in front of you today.

Now, how can you see these things as opportunities to find joy?

Praise

 Listen to

"You Make Me Brave"

by Bethel Music

Pray

Jesus, I bless your name and call this a day of joy. I am choosing joy, knowing full well what I have in front of me today. Make me brave today as I seek to choose joy, no matter what! Amen!

Proclaim

"Rejoice in the Lord always. I will say it again: Rejoice! Let your gentleness be evident to all. The Lord is near." (Phil. 4:4-5)

Prompt

God has touched our lips! God has blotted out our sin! God has shown our guilt the exit!

God has cleaned us up and made us a rags-to-riches story of His grace. What a joy to be His!

Because of this, we can cry out to Him and say: ***"Here we are! Send us! Send us to the broken-hearted, the down-and-out, the poor in spirit, and those who know a mistaken version of God but believe it's the real thing."***

When we pray this prayer, we are acting in joy and sharing it with whomever God sees fit to bring into our orbit.

Prod

Today, I am challenging you to take a step forward in living out this JOY-filled life. Where do you need to go? Where is God sending you? Write down what God has been quietly encouraging you to do.

Praise

 Listen to

"Oceans"

by Hillsong United

Pray

Jesus, put me in front of the right people today. I am ready to spread the joy you have put in my heart to others. Help me find the courage to take a step of faith and share my heart with someone. Open the doors of opportunity, help me to serve, love, give, and inspire those I come in contact with today! And please let me represent you well. Amen.

Proclaim

"Rejoice in the Lord always. I will say it again: Rejoice! Let your gentleness be evident to all. The Lord is near." (Phil. 4:4-5)

Prompt

If the Psalms are any indication, it's okay to get testy with God—to ask Him how long we must struggle with sickness, worry about finances, fight against injustice, tear down unfair systems, and grieve those who die.

God can handle it when we ask how long we must listen without comprehension, look without seeing, and contemplate without conviction.

And yet, with the same wondering mouths, we can also give God thanks, sing God's praise, and proclaim His steadfast love, faithfulness, and soul-strengthening goodness.

But let's be real: none of this is easy. **Why?** Because we are inherently flawed and have no ability to comprehend God's plans! But God is good. His plans are higher than ours, His ways too much for us to understand. But no matter what, He is good. Today, we rest in that and seek joy in the midst of confusion.

Prod

What do you need to complain to God about? Let Him have it! He can take it.

Praise

 Listen to

"Only Jesus For My Pain"

by Cory Asbury

Pray

Jesus, I wish everything was right with the world, but it isn't. I wish I didn't feel pain, loneliness, or depression. I don't know why I keep struggling or why I feel the need to take it out on you. I'm sorry. I need help. Help me persevere and trust your promise that you will make all things right. Amen.

Proclaim

"Rejoice in the Lord always. I will say it again: Rejoice! Let your gentleness be evident to all. The Lord is near." (Phil. 4:4-5)

Prompt

God is the God of Resurrection. Jesus has the final Word: death loses and He triumphs! Think of the seed that falls off the tree, gets buried in the dirt, dies, and rises again as an oak. That's like our resurrection promise.

This is the resurrection we carry with us **today. Tomorrow. This week.** We can rejoice because we're resurrection people who can call out the good in everyone we encounter, speaking the life-giving words of Jesus into them.

What a life!

Prod

Every plant or tree you see started as a seed that had to die before it could sprout. Find a living thing and meditate on this truth. See what God reveals to you and write it down.

Praise

 Listen to

"Glorious Day"

by Kristian Stanfill

Pray

Jesus, help me be a resurrection person today. Let me impart your resurrection spirit on the people I encounter today, whether that's in person or on the internet. Let me be a resurrection light for you! Amen.

Proclaim

"Rejoice in the Lord always. I will say it again: Rejoice! Let your gentleness be evident to all. The Lord is near." (Phil. 4:4-5)

Prompt

Did you know we make God joyful? It's true! He cheers for us! We fill His heart with joy! And that's true whether we're walking in lock-step with His will or we're scattering our potential like it was seed on hard soil. No matter what, God is on our side.

When you make a good decision, **GOD LOVES IT.**

When you give something to someone in need, **GOD IS PLEASED.**

When you stop to pray for someone who needs to feel loved, **GOD IS RIGHT THERE WITH YOU.**

When you pick up this devo and take a moment to meet with God, **GOD IS SO DELIGHTED TO BE WITH YOU!**

God loves YOU. He loves doling out the best He has for you, just like the father who celebrated over the returned prodigal by sacrificing the best animal in his stable.

God takes JOY in you.

Prod

Reflect on the last thing or person you took joy in. Now reflect on how God's joy about you is immeasurably greater! Write about it. What's that feel like today? To know God takes joy in YOU?

Praise

 Listen to

"JOY"

by Ben Rector

Pray

Jesus, thank you for rejoicing over me. Help me to feel the same way about myself that you feel about me. Show me your will and help me walk in it because I know that's the best way to walk. Amen.

Proclaim

"Rejoice in the Lord always. I will say it again: Rejoice! Let your gentleness be evident to all. The Lord is near." (Phil. 4:4-5)

Prompt

Joy is meant to be shared! We receive the spirit of God's joy, the one who advocates for us, and when we do that, we invite that joy to permeate our community—whomever that might be. **Maybe it's our home.** Maybe it's our coworkers. Maybe it's our church community.

God's joy will flow over those in need so that lack becomes provision, tragedy becomes triumph, hurt becomes healing, and death becomes life.

Today, how do you need JOY to overflow your life? Let's get honest with ourselves today: where are you struggling? Need forgiveness? Need to give forgiveness? Need clarity? Let go of a resentment? Do you need to get honest about some sin? CONFESS?!

God longs to give JOY to those who need it. If you've found yourself in a joy rut, be honest about where you need God's joy to overflow in your life today.

Prod

Where in your life do you need God's joy today? Get specific about it. As you pray and listen to the song today, I want you to ask God to invade this area of your life and turn it around!

Praise

 Listen to

"God Turn It Around"

by Church of The City

Pray

God, I need your help today. I want to confess [NAME WHAT YOU WANT TO CONFESS]. I invite the Holy Spirit to invade this area of [NAME A PERSON, RESENTMENT, SITUATION, DECISION, ETC] and bring me clarity, comfort, and ultimately joy! Turn my life around today through the power of your son Jesus! Amen.

Proclaim

"Rejoice in the Lord always. I will say it again: Rejoice! Let your gentleness be evident to all. The Lord is near." (Phil. 4:4-5)

Prompt

This may sound counteractive to joy, but one of the many things we learn from the Cross is that we win by losing. Sounds strange, but it's true.

We win by laying down our lives for our neighbors. By loving our enemies, by turning the other cheek, by going the extra mile, by praying for our persecutors.

When we surrender our will and choose God's, when we give what we think is ours to others, when we do for others what we wish they'd do for us, when we give up our time to spend it with someone who needs it more—when we do these things, we are participating in the counterintuitive joy of the Lord.

All of these seemingly losing propositions always end up in a spiritual win! We follow Jesus when we give of ourselves for others. Our sacrifices lead us to a more surrendered and joy-filled life.

Giving up what we desire *(which can often look like "losing")* always turns into a win in God's world.

Prod

How can you win by losing today? Ask the Holy Spirit for insight on losing greatly. Don't question what He tells you. Write it down and do it! No matter how tough it is. And don't forget, JOY will come from this!

Praise

 Listen to

"Waymaker"

by Leeland

Pray

Jesus, I know I never leave your sturdy hand. Remind me of your faithfulness to always make a way. Help me find the courage to take a step to give up my will, my time, or my money SO THAT I might help others find the joy you have given me. Amen.

Proclaim

"Rejoice in the Lord always. I will say it again: Rejoice! Let your gentleness be evident to all. The Lord is near." (Phil. 4:4-5)

Prompt

What a joy it is to be able to serve an incomparable God! Matchless and wonderful, He always welcomes us. Even in our sin and stupidity, He calls to us and says, "Come as you are."

It's provocative, isn't it? God made and called us, each of us created uniquely, designed exactly as He desired us. Have you ever thought about that?

God made you exactly the way He planned! He knows everything—yes, **EVERYTHING**—about you and He still just loves the heck out of you!

Where else can we find such joy? Whether we're in times of doubt or times of great confidence, He shows us His faithfulness and demonstrates His mercy on us, freely pouring it out on us sinners who can do nothing but come as we are.

Prod

Take a moment to remember who you were when you came to God. How much have you changed since then? Rejoice! Listen to this bop of a song and have some fun. Smile a bit and feel God's love for you!

Praise

 Listen to

"No Greater"

by CeCe Winans

Pray

God, thank you for creating me with no mistakes! And thank you for calling me to you, even after I did make mistakes. Thank you for not leaving me that way. You are my joy-giver. Your love has set me free. Amen.

Proclaim

"Rejoice in the Lord always. I will say it again: Rejoice! Let your gentleness be evident to all. The Lord is near." (Phil. 4:4-5)

Prompt

In 2 Kings 5 we read the story of Naaman, a military man of high esteem who was stricken with leprosy. One of his slaves, a young woman from Israel, suggested he go to her hometown and visit the prophet Elisha there.

Naaman goes, expecting Elisha to emerge and perform some sort of major ceremony to cure him. Elisha doesn't even come out of his house; instead, he sends a messenger who tells Naaman to bathe in the Jordan River.

Mad at this simple cure, Naaman **throws a fit** until his men tell him to give it a shot. And of course, it works.

Often joy comes to us in a way we aren't looking for. We want joy to have something major attached to it, but it is all too often found instead in the simple things.

Like just obeying what God asks you to do.

Prod

What simple joys might you have overlooked while waiting on the big joy? During your prayer time today, ask God to reveal some small ways you can walk in faith today.

Praise

 Listen to

"Rest"

by Kari Jobe

Pray

Jesus, let me see your joy wherever it is today. Open my eyes to experience your JOY in the small ways. I know you can move the mountains and part the seas, but let me see you and feel you in the small things. I want to trust that you can heal me when I just faithfully follow you. Amen.

Proclaim

"Rejoice in the Lord always. I will say it again: Rejoice! Let your gentleness be evident to all. The Lord is near." (Phil. 4:4-5)

Prompt

God's joy is for everyone. And I mean EVERYONE.

But a great thing about God's joy is that WE get to be the ones who share it. We get to go into the world bearing God's reconciling love, being of good courage, holding fast to that which is good, and rendering to no one evil for evil. We get to strengthen the faint-hearted, support the weak, help the afflicted, and honor all people.

Don't forget: **GOD CALLS YOU HIS CO-WORKER.** He has all the power to instill Himself into someone's life in a moment's notice, but oftentimes He wants to use YOU to help lift someone up and to point people to Himself. The cool thing about working alongside God is that YOU get an extra dose of faith, hope, and love at the same time!

But it starts with your JOY. Then your willingness to share that JOY. And then trusting God to do what only He can do through the power of the Holy Spirit.

Prod

God calls you a co-worker. How does that feel?

Who in your life needs the JOY that you have?

What are you going to do about it?

Praise

 Listen to

"Why Not Right Now"

by Jesus Culture

Pray

Jesus, thank you for making me a bearer of your joy. Thank you for giving me the chance to share the joy you have given me with others. I know you have put [NAME OF PERSON YOU LISTED ABOVE] in my life. Please give me the chance today to share my joy with them. Give me the faith, the confidence, and courage to step out, letting your joy overflow! Amen.

Proclaim

"Rejoice in the Lord always. I will say it again: Rejoice! Let your gentleness be evident to all. The Lord is near." (Phil. 4:4-5)

Prompt

I don't get to the beach often, but when I do, I like to see all the different kinds of people who wind up there. Sure, you always have kids with pails and shovels, and families enjoying the tide, and sunbathers working on their tans.

But you know who else you often see? **People with metal detectors,** intently listening to the sand in the hopes of finding some kind of treasure.

These are people who just love to listen, to seek, and to find. They will walk over miles and miles of beach in the hopes of unearthing a coin or two, when usually what they get are hair clips and bottle caps.

It's a little strange, but I kinda dig it. Because it reminds me of how we need to look for joy. We should be on a never-ending journey searching for joy. On a journey to places people aren't going and doing things people aren't doing.

Always listening, always looking, always expecting God to meet us and give us what we need! That's the joy lifestyle!

Prod

Go on a treasure hunt of your own today. Take a walk and keep your eyes on the ground to see what you might find. As you do so, think about looking for joy and ask God to reveal Himself to your spirit.

Praise

 Listen to

"Beauty"

by David Funk

Pray

Jesus, show me your joy today in the beauty of this world. You are beauty! Your presence is the most joy-filled place I can be. I desperately want to experience you today in a new and different way. Help me to find you wherever I go. I'm looking! Amen.

Proclaim

"Rejoice in the Lord always. I will say it again: Rejoice! Let your gentleness be evident to all. The Lord is near." (Phil. 4:4-5)

Prompt

If you keep reading past today's verse, you'll see more of Paul's thoughts on the matter, where, in verses 12 and 13 he famously says, "I know how to be brought low, and I know how to abound. In any and every circumstance, I have learned the secret of facing plenty and hunger, abundance and need. I can do all things through him who strengthens me."

I like to think of these two truths together:

The Lord is near... AND... I can do all things through Him who strengthens me.

They're separated by eight verses, but put them together and you can sense the joy contained within them. You can do anything because God strengthens you. And you can trust in that strength because God is near.

This is critical for you to understand and to get rooted deep in your soul today. I assure you, what you are about to face today will require you to lean on God's strength and to trust that *HE IS NEAR!*

Take joy in these truths: God is here. God is your strength.

Prod

Lie down flat on your bed and intentionally feel the weight of yourself on it. Feel the contact between your body and the bed—starting from your feet, slowly to your head. Think about how God is even nearer.

Praise

 Listen to

"Came To My Rescue"

by Josh Baldwin

Pray

Jesus, thank you for staying with me. Thank you for your strength. Thank you for being my rescue in all kinds of times of trouble. I need you today! I trust you will provide, and I pray that my dependence on you would grow today. Amen.

Proclaim

"Rejoice in the Lord always. I will say it again: Rejoice! Let your gentleness be evident to all. The Lord is near." (Phil. 4:4-5)

Prompt

It can be tough to maintain joy when you're encountering a whole bunch of nonsense. Whether it's your standard temptations to slip back into your old ways or it's the generic difficulties life throws your way like money troubles, sickness, or annoying bosses, joy can sometimes be hard to come by.

But even when you hit those obstacles, you're supposed to count them as joy. Read James 1 if you don't believe me.

Why are we supposed to count these all as JOY? Because they refine your faith. Instead of looking at them as hassles keeping you from living your life, think of them as chisel blows that carve away a little bit of unnecessary stone from the glorious statue God's making you into.

You are on your way to being a masterpiece of JOY.

Disciplined. Hopeful. Kind. Strong. Patient. Resilient. Braced. Powerful. Loving.

But it won't happen if you don't develop the natural reaction to count all the TOUGH stuff of life as joy.

Let's start this training today. Count it all joy, my friend.

Prod

Share all the tough stuff you are up against right now. GO! All of it. Don't hold back.

Praise

 Listen to

"God I Look To You"

by Bethel Music

Pray

Jesus, this is a tall order. I don't know how I can count anything non-joyful as joy, except with your help. So help me, please! I look at you—I won't get overwhelmed. Give me the vision to see things like YOU do. Amen.

Proclaim

"Rejoice in the Lord always. I will say it again: Rejoice! Let your gentleness be evident to all. The Lord is near." (Phil. 4:4-5)

Prompt

February can be a tough month for a lot of people. The excitement of winter is long gone, and now we're just in the doldrums of waiting for spring to arrive. Sometimes it can just feel like stasis, like we're just kind of hanging out, losing forward momentum, weighed down by the seemingly endless winter days.

That's normal. *It's fine to feel that way* and good to acknowledge that feeling.

Because when we acknowledge our labor, when we acknowledge that feeling of being weighed down, then we can take it to Jesus and find the joy we lack.

Don't try to convince yourself you feel anything other than what you feel. Take it to Jesus, give it to Him, and let Him give you joy in return.

Prod

Get a calendar and look ahead to the first day of spring. It's closer than you think!

Hope is looking forward to better days. What do you have HOPE for today?

Praise

 Listen to

"Awake My Soul"

by Hillsong Worship

Pray

Jesus, thank you for giving me joy in the midst of my burdens today. I know better days are coming. I believe that. Sometimes I just need your help in acting like it! Today I want to recommit my life to you. *WAKE ME UP* to your goodness in my life and the purpose you have placed deep in my soul. I want to live this life to the fullest—will you please help me? Amen.

Proclaim

"Rejoice in the Lord always. I will say it again: Rejoice! Let your gentleness be evident to all. The Lord is near." (Phil. 4:4-5)

Prompt

Bonus day!

If you're reading this, then congratulations on living through an extra day in a leap year. Yesterday we talked about the feeling that February drags on and on and how that's a burden we can give to God.

But today we're adding an extra day to February, and instead of a drudge, it feels kind of awesome! Because it's an extra day to love God, to serve God, and to work alongside God to continue building His kingdom!

So don't be lazy—**make this extra day GREAT!**

It's another day God has made! How could we do anything but rejoice and be glad in it?! In fact, how could we do anything but raise a hallelujah to our God for His goodness!

Prod

Treat yourself to a healthy extra something-or-other today. Maybe it's an extra shot in your latte or an extra few minutes of sleep. It's a bonus day—give yourself a bonus. And as you do so, find time to thank God and praise Him for what He is doing in your life.

Praise

 Listen to

"Raise a Hallelujah"

by Bethel Music

Pray

Jesus, you gave everything on the cross. I take everything you want to give me—including bonus days. I sing of your goodness this morning. I rejoice that you have made me new. I praise you for your grace and give you thanks for your provision! Amen.

Proclaim

"Rejoice in the Lord always. I will say it again: Rejoice! Let your gentleness be evident to all. The Lord is near." (Phil. 4:4-5)

Prompt

We all have stories to tell, and a big part of your life of faith is telling people all about yours. So what's your story consist of? Well, it's pretty simple: all you need to do is talk about where you were, what happened, and where you are now. You used to be blind, and now you can see.

As you carry your message, you will have opportunities to tell others your story, which bolsters your faith. Your fortitude, momentum, and passion for life will grow. The end result, **MORE JOY!**

Your story is powerful. It's life-changing! No matter where you have been, what you have gone through, the bad choices you have made, the success you've obtained... ALL OF IT is special and unique just to you. That's a pretty amazing thing to think about.

God has given you the gift of a story. A story that could change the world—if you're willing to share it.

Prod

Write down the three major bullet points of your life story right now. It won't take long, just do it. I promise God will use it if you will prepare it!

Praise

 Listen to

"Graves into Gardens"

by Brandon Lake

Pray

Jesus, thank you for the power of my story. Thank you for walking beside me through ALL OF IT! So much of my past is dark and painful, but God, I believe today that you will use what I have gone through to give someone else hope and to strengthen the joy in my heart. Today I am willing... open the door and give me a chance to share what you've done for me. I'm willing. Amen.

Proclaim

"Rejoice in the Lord always. I will say it again: Rejoice! Let your gentleness be evident to all. The Lord is near." (Phil. 4:4-5)

Prompt

Yesterday, we talked about telling your story, which is extremely important for YOU. It helps to build your commitment to God, maintain your joy, and live in the purpose God built you for.

Your listener is also an important part of the joy of telling your story. How? Because just the act of witnessing you, of hearing where you have been in the past and discovering where you are today, they quickly discover that they are not alone.

Recognizing that you are not alone is *life-changing*. Think about it. Has there been a time when you heard someone say something that perfectly described how you felt or what you had gone through? When that moment hits you, a sense of relief comes with it. Shame begins to unravel as you recognize that what you have done or how you have felt does not disqualify you from God's love, God's joy, or God's plan.

Those who hear your story will find strength and encouragement just from learning how God has changed and shaped your life. That's why you MUST be willing to share it.

Prod

Do you know someone who needs to hear your story? I bet you do... I want to challenge you today to open up, get brave and tell this person YOUR story.

Praise

 Listen to

"My Testimony"

by Elevation Worship

Pray

God, thank you for walking with me as I have journeyed through this life. I praise you for you are faithful, kind and so forgiving. I desperately want others to feel what I have felt when I realized I wasn't alone. Please give me the courage to share what I have been through with others so that my faith will grow, you will be praised, and the captives might be set free! Amen.

Proclaim

"Rejoice in the Lord always. I will say it again: Rejoice! Let your gentleness be evident to all. The Lord is near." (Phil. 4:4-5)

Prompt

To truly experience joy, you have to truly give yourself over to God. You have to truly trust Him wholly and completely.

Which means you have to let go of the control you think you have over your life.

When we still believe we have something to prove, something to add, something we can do in our own strength, we can increase our own doubts, **insecurities**, and hesitance. But when we give ourselves over to God, we can begin to trust that His plans are higher, better, more thought-out, and more meticulously constructed. They're safer yet bolder, harder but healthier, and more challenging but worth every moment.

When we get to that place, then joy becomes attainable no matter how triumphant or tragic the situation.

Our passage this quarter doubles down on its challenge to be joy **full**. Let go, and then let go again and again. There's joy there.

Prod

Today I challenge you to come to God with boldness! A bold surrender that says GOD, YOUR WAYS ARE HIGHER AND YOUR THOUGHTS GREATER!

What do you need to let go of in order to truly experience joy today?

Praise

 Listen to

"My Hands Are Open"

by Josh Baldwin

Pray

Jesus, thank you for taking every part of me, even the parts I'm reluctant to give you. Give me courage to do just that today, and give me joy in return. Amen.

Proclaim

"Rejoice in the Lord always. I will say it again: Rejoice! Let your gentleness be evident to all. The Lord is near." (Phil. 4:4-5)

Prompt

Faith isn't achieved alone. We stay on the road to discipleship through the patient, loving, nurturing support and accountability of trusted mentors. "Hope Partners," you might call them.

As sinners we spent too much time doing things all on our own, so stepping up and reaching out for help can be an intimidating and humbling thought. But life still goes on, and with that comes disappointments, layoffs, **tough financial decisions**, legal battles, loss of a loved one, parenting struggles... you name it.

We need a community around us who will give us wise counsel, encourage us to continue to grow, and be there to pull us up when we're down. Hope Partners are in place for your success, to give you a better chance you have to stay faithful—and joyful.

Prod

Do you have Hope Partners in your life? Pray about who might be a good one for you.

Praise

 Listen to

"Endless Praise"

by Charity Gayle

Pray

Jesus, thank you for putting people in my life to help me achieve my goals and stay as close to you as possible. Amen.

Proclaim

"Rejoice in the Lord always. I will say it again: Rejoice! Let your gentleness be evident to all. The Lord is near." (Phil. 4:4-5)

Prompt

Yesterday we talked about the necessity of having Hope Partners. But how do you get a Hope Partner? If you don't already have any, you probably already have some people in mind. ***Maybe someone who can be a spiritual partner or mentor.*** Someone else who might be a good accountability partner. Someone who would be a good business or industry mentor.

Pray and ask the Lord to identify those people in your life and determine to approach them about becoming a Hope Partner for you.

Ask the Holy Spirit to guide you as you ask these people to step into your life as a Hope Partner, and trust that God will exponentially change your life as you open up to the people He puts in your path. It can be awkward, but it's worth it!

Prod

Determine a new Hope Partner for you and approach them.

Praise

 Listen to

"The Father's House"

by Cory Asbury

Pray

Jesus, guide me in finding and maintaining a stable of Hope Partners. Thank you to the people who want to help me! Thank you to the people who are willing to pray for me. Thank you for people who are willing to hold me accountable. ***Thank you to the people who draw me closer to YOU!*** Amen.

Proclaim

"Rejoice in the Lord always. I will say it again: Rejoice! Let your gentleness be evident to all. The Lord is near." (Phil. 4:4-5)

Prompt

Sorrow is just a part of this life—plain and simple. If you're alive, you're going to feel sorrow at some point. You might be feeling sorrow right now, and that's okay...

But the great thing is, you don't have to *wallow* in sorrow. I know I used to do this so much. When tough things would hit me, they would knock me out for days. This was the enemy trying to hold me back.

There's nothing wrong with feeling sorry, it's good to feel it—**we are, after all, social-emotional beings**—but when you start to hang on to the sorrow, that's when it's time to trade it in. To let it go! To release it!

Trade it for joy. Lay it down for the joy of the Lord. He has something so much better for you.

Prod

What sorrows do you need to lay down today? Pray throughout the day and remind yourself to trade them for joy.

Praise

 Listen to

"Trading My Sorrows"

by Paul Baloche & Lincoln Brewster

Pray

Jesus, you did it. You made a way for me to trade my sorrows for joy! Sometimes I forget this and just allow the sorrow and hurt to take over my life. But not today! Through the power of your Holy Spirit, help me to say "yes" to your trade of joy for sorrow today. I want your joy! I want your love! I want you to lead my life! Amen.

Proclaim

"Rejoice in the Lord always. I will say it again: Rejoice! Let your gentleness be evident to all. The Lord is near." (Phil. 4:4-5)

Prompt

The general wisdom about recovery (getting and staying sober) is that the only thing we really need to change to get sober is... *everything*! And the same holds true when we want to live a life of faith. But changing everything starts with pushing out the inconsistency and impulsivity that fill up our day-to-day living and replacing it with a solid diet of structure, consistency, and accountability. This is the essence of God's joy.

As we track through daily life, we will no doubt come across seasons of sadness, times of loss, and bouts with doubt. But if, as we create our lives of faith, we incorporate times of meditation, scripture, exercise, and prayer, then we restore and maintain the balance we lose when we get outside of God's direction for us.

Prod

Brainstorm some activities you can make into a routine that will help you maintain your sobriety.

Praise

 Listen to

"No Longer Slaves"

by Bethel Music

Pray

Jesus, thank you for the safety of a routine. Help me rely on you! Amen.

Proclaim

"Rejoice in the Lord always. I will say it again: Rejoice! Let your gentleness be evident to all. The Lord is near." (Phil. 4:4-5)

Prompt

Yesterday we talked about the importance of having a routine for maintaining the joy of the Lord as we live lives of faith. So how do you keep that routine? Make appointments with yourself.

Set up a consistent time every day to check off some of the activities you've chosen to do, and keep it up. *As your walk with God grows over time, it can be very common to lose touch with your routine.* That's why scheduling a time every day to check ourselves helps us stay grounded, humbled, and faithful.

The life you're now leading is measurably different... in a great way! Setting yourself up for success and sustaining a life of faithful joy takes creating a routine that stimulates and motivates you to keep going, to keep pushing ahead. The more you stay focused and plugged into your routine, the stronger you will get.

You may be tempted eventually to start skipping your routine, or to think you're strong enough in your faith to break away from it, but I've found that maintaining a routine—even over the past decade-plus—has helped me stay in love with the Lord. And as our strength grows, we will begin to receive the fruits of this labor as we pass along to others what we have learned along our journey. This is the greatest joy of all.

Prod

Make a reminder on your calendar to check in about your daily routine.

Praise

 Listen to

"Spirit Lead Me"

by Influence Music

Pray

Jesus, thank you that my life is getting better and better every day. Thank you for the discipline you are instilling in my spirit. Fill me with the fight to do things right today. I don't want to cut corners, I don't want to give up easy, I don't want to take the easy path. Fill me with the hope to press on! Amen.

Proclaim

"Rejoice in the Lord always. I will say it again: Rejoice! Let your gentleness be evident to all. The Lord is near." (Phil. 4:4-5)

Prompt

Every organization in existence has a mandate. They may call it something different, like a mission or vision statement, or they may wrap it up in a box and call it their core values, but however they describe it, they have a short, easy-to-remember statement they live by, something that guides them toward their end goal.

So if millions of companies and individuals have statements that drive them each and every day, it makes sense that those of us actively working to live lives of God's joy ALSO have one! Our mandates are yet another reinforcing element we must mix into the foundation we are pouring. This critical piece to the puzzle should represent the core of who you are.

And who you are is a joy-filled child of God. We'll talk more about this tomorrow!

Prod

Do you have a mandate? If not, begin brainstorming one. Start jotting down the main themes right now.

Praise

 Listen to

"Breakthrough"

by Red Rocks Worship

Pray

Jesus, I live by what you say about me, and you say I'm yours. That's enough. I'm enough. Be with me today. Amen.

Proclaim

"Rejoice in the Lord always. I will say it again: Rejoice! Let your gentleness be evident to all. The Lord is near." (Phil. 4:4-5)

Prompt

Yesterday we talked about the importance of having a mandate. Today, let's think of some options.

Your mandate can be something like, "I will not leave Jesus, no matter what." Maybe you need a statement that clarifies what you can *not* do.

Or maybe you respond more strongly to: ***"Today I choose to live for Jesus because I am worth it!"*** This keeps your focus on what's healthiest for you physically and emotionally.

Or how about this: "God is not in love with a future version of me—He loves me as I am and will never leave my side." This is a wonderful mandate for those of us who need to be reminded frequently about where we stand spiritually in the light of Christ.

A strong mandate ***acts as a reminder*** of who God says you are. And as our song says today, we can take God at His word!

So write up a mandate that speaks to you, corrects you, challenges you, and beckons you forward!

Prod

Invite the Holy Spirit into the process of determining your mandate so that it's personal and effective and fits you. And then hold that mandate in front of you day and night.

Praise

 Listen to

"Take You At Your Word"

by Cody Carnes

Pray

Jesus, thank you for giving me words to live by. Thank you for being someone I can trust in. I pray you would give me the words to write on my heart, so that I might follow your will for my life, today, tomorrow and the rest of my days. Amen.

Proclaim

"Rejoice in the Lord always. I will say it again: Rejoice! Let your gentleness be evident to all. The Lord is near." (Phil. 4:4-5)

Prompt

Nothing can change a life like blind obedience to God. It's the birthplace of joy. When we put ourselves out there, when we lay our lives down to God, when we take a risk to help another person or call to check on someone... God uses that willingness to bolster our souls and give us momentum to successfully tackle another day.

Obedience comes first in our willingness to surrender our lives to God, then to lay our lives down faithfully to God, and then lastly to start saying YES!

Saying *"yes"* is the attitude of someone completely surrendered to a new way of living.

Saying *"yes"* is the action that your spirit takes to live out your faith.

Saying *"yes"* demonstrates to God that we believe He'll take care of us, no matter what.

I love today's song, it perfectly embodies today's message. The bridge says this..."it will be OUR joy to say, your (God's) will, your way!" May that be true for you today.

Prod

What needs your joyful "yes" today? You never know what's on the other side of a yes. Act on what God is saying to you today! Say "yes!"

Praise

 Listen to

"Lay Me Down"

by Chris Tomlin

Pray

Jesus, I lay me down. I am not my own. I belong to you alone. Hand on my heart, this much is true: there is no life apart from you. I give you my life. Your will, your way. Amen.

Proclaim

"Rejoice in the Lord always. I will say it again: Rejoice! Let your gentleness be evident to all. The Lord is near." (Phil. 4:4-5)

Prompt

Yesterday we talked about the power of saying YES, and I want to dig a little deeper into it today.

I believe when we appear before glory, submitted to the Creator, He will look at us and as ask us these questions:

- *Were you willing?*
- *Were you obedient?*
- *Did you say "yes"?*

When God puts an opportunity your way, saying "yes" breaks down the anxiety that "NO" built up inside you for so long. When you say "yes" to something new or something that challenges you, you take all the power out of the unknown and grab hold of your destiny with both hands.

The outcome doesn't matter: that's God's territory. All you are responsible for is obedience! It's your job to say YES to what He puts in front of you. Say YES today!

Prod

If you think about being obedient to God through the filter of eternity, how does that make you feel? I mean, if you are going to really answer to God about how you responded to His promptings in your life, doesn't that give you some initiative to say YES? How does that feel?

Praise

 Listen to

"Holy Forever"

by Bethel Music

Pray

Jesus, today I recognize that one day I will give an account for what I have done with what you gave me. This is a challenge and tough thought, but it helps me to find the courage to say yes, to be willing and obedient to what the Holy Spirit leads me to do. Today, I just want to please you; help me to take a few steps of obedience.

Proclaim

"Rejoice in the Lord always. I will say it again: Rejoice! Let your gentleness be evident to all. The Lord is near." (Phil. 4:4-5)

Prompt

Joy can be fragile. It must be maintained and guarded with care because eventually, somewhere along the line, **something** will happen to you that threatens your joy. Disappointments are just part of the experience of being human, so you have to have a game plan for the way you're going to handle those disappointments... instead of letting them drive you into regret, resentment, or worse yet, rage.

To ensure we keep a tight grip on our **JOY**, it's important to take steps to identify the emotional risk in our lives. The truth is, guilt, shame, regret, and resentment get sparked during moments of pain. If we don't learn to stay balanced and quickly self-assess what's happening, then when disappointments and conflict come crashing into our lives, joy will get knocked right out of our hands!

Prod

Start thinking of things in your life that rob you of joy. The situation, the emotions, the people, the places, the parents! Who and/or what robs you of your joy? Make a list.

Praise

 Listen to

"A Thousand Hallelujahs"

by Brooke Ligertwood

Pray

Jesus, you are my entire joy. You deserve all the praise! I could sing a thousand hallelujahs, praising you for who you are to me. You are my redeemer, my rescue, my rock, and the source of all my strength. Please help me to keep a tight grip on the joy you have given me today. Amen.

Proclaim

"Rejoice in the Lord always. I will say it again: Rejoice! Let your gentleness be evident to all. The Lord is near." (Phil. 4:4-5)

Prompt

Let's talk a little more about joy and how to maintain it in the midst of life's troubles. Think through the answers to these questions:

What are some ways you respond to disappointment?

Does the prospect of "guarding your heart" feel easy for you? Difficult? Somewhere in between?

Can you name the people and/or situations that might cause you to lose your joy?

The wonderful thing about joy is that it's always available to us through Christ. Making a plan for keeping our joy in the midst of the struggle just keeps us that much closer to Jesus.

One thing I do that helps me is to listen to worship music. That's probably why I'm so passionate about giving you a song each day to listen to. There's something so powerful about connecting to our Good Shepherd through a beautiful song. When I put my headphones on and a song comes on that speaks to my exact situation in life, peace floods my heart, joy begins to flow through my spirit, and the enemy begins to crumble at my feet!

Prod

As you listen to this song today, meditate on the list you made yesterday and the questions in today's PROMPT and ask the Holy Spirit to reveal Himself to you.

Praise

 Listen to

"Shepherd"

by Cece Winans

Pray

Jesus, I give you my heart today. My life is better when I am following you. Please keep me safe and guard me against the joy-robbers and peace stealers. I love you! Amen.

Proclaim

"Rejoice in the Lord always. I will say it again: Rejoice! Let your gentleness be evident to all. The Lord is near." (Phil. 4:4-5)

Prompt

A key part of changing your life in any way is learning to give back. In fact, I think this isn't just one of the most important parts—it's one of my favorites.

One thing is certain: you and I are only here because other people have helped us get here. Yes, you've done a lot of heavy lifting yourself, but others have encouraged you, sat with you in the midst of your despair, worked with and alongside you, and made sacrifices in their own lives so you could get yours back on track.

When's the last time you said a real genuine *THANK YOU* to someone who helped you get to where you are today?

Do you know that when you say thank you to someone—like, really, really say it—YOUR joy increases as much as theirs does?

Prod

Make a list of people who've given to you. Now imagine this: someone else, a year or two or more from now, makes a similar list... and *you're* on it. That's the kind of impact you could have! So pick up the phone today and call at least TWO of the people on your list.

Praise

 Listen to

"I've Witnessed It"

by Passion

Pray

Jesus, thank you for every person who has given to me to get me here today. I'm incredibly, incredibly grateful for them. *Today*, I want to honor them by saying thank you. Give me the courage to reach out and thank them for the investment they made in my life. God, as I do this, please fill both our hearts with your joy! Amen.

Proclaim

"Rejoice in the Lord always. I will say it again: Rejoice! Let your gentleness be evident to all. The Lord is near." (Phil. 4:4-5)

Prompt

Yesterday we talked about giving back, and today I want to dig a little more deeply into it.

How does it feel to know other people have sacrificed for you? It's pretty humbling and joyful at the same time, right? You can bring that feeling to others!

What natural gifts and talents might you be able to give away to others? What aspect of your personal story do you think would benefit someone else? ***How can you give back?***

Maybe you've already begun thinking about ways you can do this. After all, it's a pretty cool thought, right? It's empowering to realize you have something that someone else needs.

That's the power of living a changed life—that we don't do this on our own. You were blessed so you can be a blessing. Someone gave to you. Go and do likewise.

Prod

Ask God to reveal to you the people you should give to today... Make a list, then go down each name and ask God to reveal WHAT you should give to that person. It could be time, talents, treasures, or just a hug!

Praise

 Listen to

"Make a Way"

by Elevation Worship

Pray

Jesus, show me who I can give back to. Make me an instrument of joy in someone's life today. I'm ready to be used for you. Amen.

Proclaim

"Rejoice in the Lord always. I will say it again: Rejoice! Let your gentleness be evident to all. The Lord is near." (Phil. 4:4-5)

Prompt

I love the prayer of St. Patrick because it reminds me about the omnipresence of Jesus. Here's a nutshell summary of it:

Christ with us, Christ before us, Christ behind us,

Christ in us, Christ beneath us, Christ above us,

Christ on our right and left.

When we lie down: Christ.

When we sit: Christ as well.

It's an aspirational prayer, asking God to emanate from us; present in our hearts, edifying in our mouths, visible in our eyes, and audible in our ears. So that when the world looks at us, they see God: one body in infinite parts.

Prod

Pray the Prayer of St. Patrick today.

Praise

 Listen to

"Christ Be With Me"

by The Brilliance

Pray

Jesus, I pray you make me aware of your omnipresence today. I love you. Amen.

Proclaim

"Rejoice in the Lord always. I will say it again: Rejoice! Let your gentleness be evident to all. The Lord is near." (Phil. 4:4-5)

Prompt

There's a blessing found in the book of Numbers that a lot of church traditions use within the context of their services to send people out on a note of joy. Maybe you've heard it before. It goes like this:

"The Lord bless you and keep you; the Lord makes His face to shine upon you and be gracious to you; the Lord lift up His countenance upon you and give you peace."

In just these few sentences, we see God's entire desire for us. God desires to bless us and keep us. God desires to shine upon us and to extend us grace. God desires to smile upon us and bring us peace.

Do you believe this for your life?! Can you see the goodness God has for you through this blessing?!

That's what God wants for you! Let that knowledge fill you with joy today. And start looking for God's joy in every area of your day.

Prod

Take a look in a mirror and say today's blessing over yourself.

Praise

 Listen to

"I Believe"

by Bethel Music

Pray

Jesus, thank you for desiring the best for me. I receive it today! Thank you for helping me get back up time and time again. You give me strength to keep fighting. I believe that you are with me, shining on me, lighting my path for the future, and standing alongside me! Amen.

Proclaim

"Rejoice in the Lord always. I will say it again: Rejoice! Let your gentleness be evident to all. The Lord is near." (Phil. 4:4-5)

Prompt

Waiting for things can be a nightmare. Especially in a culture where we want things now—and we want "now" to happen faster than ever.

But patience is a virtue, and there's a lot that can happen in the midst of waiting. God can do some of His best work as we wait, slowly developing within us a joy that isn't contingent on the springing of a trap or the arrival of some toy.

Instead, through patience and time, God instills in us a joy that is dependent entirely on Him. When we find our joy in the midst of the wait, we can then see our joy over the wait's end as it is: an expression of the love and peace of God.

Don't give up. Choose joy.

Prod

What are you waiting on? Look for the joy to be found in the wait. Write it out and pray for patience.

Praise

 Listen to

"As The Deer"

by Steffany Gretzinger

Pray

Jesus, I trust you to do what you do in the time you want to do it. You are my strength and my shield. I yield to you in every way. Thank you for being my friend and being patient with me during all my ups and downs. I recommit my life to you today and choose joy as I wait for you to answer my prayers. Amen.

Proclaim

"Rejoice in the Lord always. I will say it again: Rejoice! Let your gentleness be evident to all. The Lord is near." (Phil. 4:4-5)

Prompt

Regardless of what the weather's doing outside, on the calendar, today is the final day of winter. As we close out the season, let's take a moment to reflect on the blessing of winter.

Because without the winter, there can't be spring. We need the season of dormancy, the extended time of quiet rest. It's the contrast that allows the colors of spring to pop all the more.

Plus, even though **nothing was happening on the surface**, during these past few months, the earth was preparing, readying for the sudden burst of springtime. Joy may lie under the surface, but it never lies dead for very long.

Joy will come. It's just that sometimes you have to give it time.

Prod

To celebrate the end of winter's long sleep, take a catnap today. For real. Do it. And as you doze off, thank God for this season AND the one to come.

Praise

 Listen to

"I Am Your Beloved"

by Jonathan David Helser & Melissa Helser

Pray

Jesus, thank you for rest. Thank you for loving me so much that you would give me these wonderful moments each day to lay my head down and rest in you. Today, as I prepare my soul for a new season, help my faith grow, my hopes rise, and my love for you to increase! Renew my heart today! Amen.

Proclaim

"Rejoice in the Lord always. I will say it again: Rejoice! Let your gentleness be evident to all. The Lord is near." (Phil. 4:4-5)

Prompt

We made it! Spring is here!

A new season brings new JOY! Today's song is a bop that I've loved for years. It embodies the spirit of springtime. It's happy, upbeat, positive and reminds us that we are living resurrection life!

We were dead in sin, bound in bondage, stuck in shame... **BUT GOD**, in His infinite mercy, sought to give us a lifeline of hope through His son Jesus. He invites us to come away with Him into His eternal springtime.

God opens His mouth and out pours grace upon grace like a spring rain. It's in His grace-filled words, washing over us and changing us into something more like Him.

Where we need repentance, He gives us the strength to turn away from everything that is not Him so that we stay oriented in His direction and in line with the change of His seasons.

Let joy spring forth like the rain and the flower blossoms!

Prod

No matter what the weather is *actually* doing, take a few moments today to go outside. Look for spring's arrival, turn up today's song, and rejoice over it.

Praise

 Listen to

"Resurrection Life"

by C3LA

Pray

Jesus, thank you for bringing new life! Thank you for pulling me out of the grave with you so I can walk in joy and freedom! You are the King of making all things new. Each day, each season, each moment, your mercies are new and filling me with joy! Amen.

Proclaim

"Rejoice in the Lord always. I will say it again: Rejoice! Let your gentleness be evident to all. The Lord is near." (Phil. 4:4-5)

Prompt

Sometimes I just love to read the Psalms. There's something so human and raw about David and the way he isn't afraid to just pour it all out to God, good, bad, and ugly. And the indignance he displays sometimes, like he's saying, "God, this sucks, and I'm mad you aren't doing anything about it!"

But today I want to look at something David writes in Psalm 28, where he says, "The Lord is my strength and my shield; my heart trusts in Him, and He helps me. My heart leaps for joy, and with my song I praise Him."

My heart trusts... ***MY HEART LEAPS FOR JOY.*** Joy and trust go hand in hand. You can't have one without the other.

Today we have another really upbeat jam from C3LA. It talks about how everything we have is God's. This is ultimate TRUST—giving it all to God. Can you do that today?

Prod

Give God everything today. Show Him you trust Him by confessing five things you need to give to Him right now.

Praise

 Listen to

"Yours"

by C3LA

Pray

Jesus, thank you so much for being trustworthy. I wanna give it all to you today. You are calling me closer, and I am coming! It's all yours today. Take my heart, take my mind, take my money, take my life! I'm so grateful to give it all to you because I trust you! Amen.

Proclaim

"Rejoice in the Lord always. I will say it again: Rejoice! Let your gentleness be evident to all. The Lord is near." (Phil. 4:4-5)

Prompt

Yesterday we talked about joy and trust and how they go hand in hand with one another. Today, I want to think through why that's the case.

I think joy can only spring from a place of safety. It's difficult to feel joyful when you feel unstable! You probably already know this. When you aren't sure where your next meal will come from or where you're going to spend the night... that can inhibit your ability to feel joy.

But when you're in a place of complete safety, you can relax and thrive on trust. And when you're in that area of total trust? *That's when joy can come.*

And God? He is absolutely, totally, 100% trustworthy. He will never let you down and never let you go. You can trust Him. You can take joy in Him.

Prod

Think on a time when your life was chaotically unstable. Compare it with where you are today. Has your joy changed between the two? What's made the difference?

Praise

 Listen to

"King of My Heart"

by Bethel Music

Pray

Jesus, I trust you. You are the King of my heart. You are my provider, my rock, my safe place. You are the shadow I hide behind, the source of my joy, and the sword that slays my enemies. God, you are good! And I trust you. Amen.

Proclaim

"Rejoice in the Lord always. I will say it again: Rejoice! Let your gentleness be evident to all. The Lord is near." (Phil. 4:4-5)

Prompt

What's the longest night you've ever spent? I've had a few! Nights when I wasn't sure I would make it to see the next day, nights when my legs kicked for hours as I detoxed from opiates. And many nights when I was distraught with worry over some situation in my life or the life of a loved one.

But one thing I knew I could count on, even if I only knew it in the **back of my head** and not in the moment, is that the morning would come.

Though sorrow may last for a night, joy comes in the morning. That's the promise we have from God—that no matter how dark the night is, you can always count on the sun to rise and dispel the darkness from your life. Sorrow must give way for joy—you can count on it.

Prod

If the weather allows for it, watch the sunset tonight and think about how reliable it is, both to end a day in beauty and to start the next day in joy.

Praise

 Listen to

"Your Love Never Fails"

by Jesus Culture

Pray

Jesus, thank you for the reliability of morning and for the joy that comes with it. Thank you that nothing separates me from your love. Even when I'm stuck watching the clock all night, lonely and hopeless, you are with me. Even when I am riding high with everything going my way, you are with me. Your presence gives me joy, God. Thank you for loving me this much. Amen.

Proclaim

"Rejoice in the Lord always. I will say it again: Rejoice! Let your gentleness be evident to all. The Lord is near." (Phil. 4:4-5)

Prompt

"There's a joy that triumphs over fear."

So says our song for the day, "Love Has a Name" by Jesus Culture. But it doesn't stop there—it also reminds us that "there's a laughter that wipes away all tears."

That's the joy of the Lord! It doesn't just make us happy—*IT COMPLETELY TRANSFORMS OUR LIVES*. It eradicates fear and it erases tears.

That's the transformative power of the joy of our Lord. I didn't always believe this, but I do now. I've seen it at work too many times in my life not to. It really is the case—God's joy really can and does change the way we look at our lives.

When I need to experience God's joy in a profound way, I seek time alone with Him. I've gone on solo retreats, long runs, hikes, road trips, and have even traveled across the country just to be alone with God. Why? Because when I am down, stuck, angry, or hurt, He is the only one who can heal me and renew my joy.

Prod

What fears do you need joy to triumph over today? Write them on a piece of paper and then write the word "joy" at the top to remind yourself that joy is over fear.

Praise

 Listen to

"Love Has a Name"

by Jesus Culture

Pray

Jesus, thank you for conquering my fears with your joy. Thank you for walking with me, sitting with me, weeping with me, and even waiting with me. Your presence gives me joy. Help me to walk in this truth today. Amen.

Proclaim

"Rejoice in the Lord always. I will say it again: Rejoice! Let your gentleness be evident to all. The Lord is near." (Phil. 4:4-5)

Prompt

One of my big Culture Code values is the importance of giving back. I've been given so much—a new life, sobriety, multiple chances to make healthier choices—so it only makes sense to give back what I've been given.

It's also just a part of the work of God's Kingdom. Giving back through giving of our time and energy is crucial for developing ourselves into deeper, richer, more loving, more faithful disciples.

Also? **It feels great!** When you take the time to help out someone in need, you get a little joy boost that can last for hours or even days.

When I go and speak somewhere, I promise you I am the one who leaves the most filled up, grateful, and inspired for God's purpose in my life. I can't tell you how many times I've said this to people, but giving back gives me the best high I've ever found!

What I mean by that is, JOY invades my mind, body and soul when I choose to give to others what God has given to me.

Prod

When was the last time you really gave back?

During your prayer time and as you are listening to today's song, ask God to reveal to you someone who needs what only you have to give.

Praise

 Listen to

"Make Room"

by Community Music

Pray

Jesus, thank you for all I have. I give it all to you. Help me find ways to give back today. Open a door. Create a divine interruption. Make it plain and clear. I'm ready! Amen.

Proclaim

"Rejoice in the Lord always. I will say it again: Rejoice! Let your gentleness be evident to all. The Lord is near." (Phil. 4:4-5)

Prompt

I love how God is the same yesterday, today, and forever because that means God is both richly traditional and radically refreshing. He's extremely reliable and unchanging, yet He always loves to show Himself in new and exciting ways.

This means a lot when it comes to our joy.

I say that because we should live the same way as God. We have our routine that keeps us grounded and produces joy, but we should always be looking for fresh, healthy, new ways to invigorate our lives.

Each year, I pick a big fitness-related event or experience to challenge myself. I've climbed mountains, run half-marathons, and even completed a Spartan Beast race! Each experience offers up a new and unique setting for me to meet with God.

I'm always blown away by how and when God meets me during those experiences. Whether it's on the ride out, the race itself, halfway up the mountain, during the cooldown, or around a campfire after a long hike, ***GOD ALWAYS SHOWS UP WHEN I SEEK HIM.***

So, if you need a little joy in your life—try something new.

Prod

What one challenge or new, tough thing popped into your mind as you were reading today? Sign up for it right now! Go meet God!

Praise

 Listen to

"Champion"

by Bethel Music

Pray

Jesus, thank you for guiding me creatively to serve you in something new. I crave your blessing on my life! Amen.

Proclaim

"Rejoice in the Lord always. I will say it again: Rejoice! Let your gentleness be evident to all. The Lord is near." (Phil. 4:4-5)

Prompt

As this month comes to a close, let's take the last few days to talk about some joy-killers and how we can eradicate them from our lives. First up: **UNFORGIVENESS**.

I say this with no condemnation: unforgiveness makes a lot of sense sometimes. There are people in our lives who might have hurt us in deep, deep ways, and the mere thought of forgiving them can bring up trauma. I get it.

But.

Look, you already know what I'm going to say. We're called to forgive. That doesn't mean you roll out the welcome mat or become a doormat. It just means you give that person (or people!) to God and let God take up the space in your heart you were giving to them.

It's hard, but it's worth it. It will revive your joy.

Prod

Who do you need to forgive? Be real... WHO?

Write down their name RIGHT HERE: _____

Take a second to consider what this person was going through when they hurt you. You might know their situation, or you might not. No matter what, this doesn't excuse their behavior, but it might help you give grace and begin to forgive.

Praise

 Listen to

"Highlands"

by Hillsong UNITED

Pray

Jesus, thank you for forgiving ME. Help me to forgive others, especially [NAME THE PERSON YOU NEED TO FORGIVE]. They really hurt me. I can't do this alone, and I really need your help in this situation. It feels like the hardest thing I'll ever do. Please help me forgive and let it go. Amen.

Proclaim

"Rejoice in the Lord always. I will say it again: Rejoice! Let your gentleness be evident to all. The Lord is near." (Phil. 4:4-5)

Prompt

Today we're going to keep talking about joy-killers as we close out our deep dive on joy, and this time around we're looking at **UNGRATEFULNESS**.

The thing about ungratefulness is that it's not really an attitude you have to cultivate. Like, you rarely go around thinking, "I'm going to be super-ungrateful today." Ungratefulness is, when you think about it, kind of the default way of being a human.

Because really, it's just selfishness. When you lack gratitude, you're just being focused on yourself instead of others. Gratitude demonstrates a sense of awareness that others matter and that you've been given something you don't necessarily deserve.

Having a posture of ungratefulness makes it certain you will be let down at some point. And that kills your joy. Instead, cultivate gratitude, and suddenly, joy will sprout everywhere you look.

Prod

A good way to start choosing gratitude first is by intentionally worshiping God, not yourself. Let's practice. Where's an area of your life where you've stepped into ungratefulness?

As you listen to this song and praise God for all the great things he has given you, place this area of ungratefulness at His feet.

Praise

 Listen to

"I Worship You Almighty God"

by Charity Gayle

Pray

Jesus, thank you for everything good in my life! It's all because of you. I admit that. I choose that. I say that from my heart today. I worship you! You are the King of Kings, Lord of Lords. Lead me today to a place of joy and gratitude! Amen.

Proclaim

"Rejoice in the Lord always. I will say it again: Rejoice! Let your gentleness be evident to all. The Lord is near." (Phil. 4:4-5)

Prompt

The 90-day journey with JOY is almost done. As we close out the month, let's keep looking at some joy-killers. Today, let's talk about **CLUTTER**.

It seems so practical and, in a sense, unspiritual, but I really do mean just plain ol' clutter. Clothes in a pile on the floor, random items stacked on a random surface, or a backseat jammed with fast-food bags.

You'd be surprised at how much of a subtle joy-killer clutter is. It's the kind of thing that you don't even notice until it's gone, and then, *when* it's gone, you realize how much more easily you're breathing and how much joy you're feeling.

Plus, it's scientifically proven that a tidy living space contributes to overall happiness, productivity, and peace of mind. I live by this in a couple of ways: my closet (where I'm writing right now) is always picked up, with the clothes color-coded and generally smelling good!

This small commitment to de-clutter keeps me in a joy-filled place.

Want more joy in your life? Tidy up the place!

Prod

Where do you have clutter in your life?

Don't wait: get to cleaning it up now.

Praise

 Listen to

"Faithful Now"

by Vertical Worship

Pray

Jesus, thank you for cleaning up my life and giving me joy. Let me live all-out 100% for you today. Amen.

Proclaim

"Rejoice in the Lord always. I will say it again: Rejoice! Let your gentleness be evident to all. The Lord is near." (Phil. 4:4-5)

Prompt

As we close out March and our final day of meditation on JOY, we're going to look at one last joy-killer: *DISTRACTION*.

There's a lot going on in our world, and all those things can cause us to look from place to place to place without really stopping to focus on any one thing. We may not even stop and smell the roses because we're too busy hustling from one thing to the next.

That's why we occasionally need to stop, slow down, put our phones on silent and turn off all our notifications, and take a break from the busy-ness. Distance ourselves from distraction, get alone with God, seek His face, pray, walk in nature, meditate on His goodness, SING REALLY LOUD, and just be alone.

I'm a huge proponent of time alone with God. It's the most important way I keep my joy. God has taught me so many lessons, healed so many hurts, and confirmed my calling over and over again each time I get away from being distracted and get alone with Him.

Prod

What's stealing your focus? Screens? Relationships? Social media?

Make a definite plan to get some alone time with God right now. Don't wait: plan it now. It doesn't matter how long it is, just that you take the time to do it.

Praise

 Listen to

"Raise A Hallelujah"

by Bethel Music

Pray

Jesus, thank you that I can focus on you all the time. Thank you for giving me the strength to walk with you, to see you, and to know that you are with me. And thank you for walking with me these last three months. Your joy has filled my heart to overflow! Amen. PRAYER

Proclaim

"Do not be anxious about anything, but in every situation, by prayer and petition, with thanksgiving, present your requests to God." (Phil. 4:6)

Prompt

It's a new day in a new month, and we're turning our attention now to **prayer**. For the next 91 days, we will be working to memorize the Philippians 4:6 and devoting our Prompts each day round the subject of PRAYER. And it's especially appropriate that we're doing that on April Fool's Day, a day which has a passing mention in the Bible (kind of)! Turn to Psalm 14:1 and you'll see what I mean:

"The fool says in his heart, *'There is no God.'*"

Have you ever felt that way? Have you ever felt foolish? That's okay. God loved you even when you didn't believe in him! And He's always, always, *always* been right there with you, wherever you've been or wherever you are right now, inclining His ear toward you and ready to listen when you pray.

That's the wonderful and wise thing about prayer: God is always listening. That's the foundation of your life of prayer, that no matter what you are doing, where you are headed, or how foolish you are acting...

GOD WILL LISTEN TO YOU WHEN YOU PRAY!

Prod

Have you ever felt like a fool? Own it! Tell someone about the "foolish" you today.

Praise

 Listen to

"You Are Good"

by Bethel Music

Pray

Jesus, I love that you listen when I pray and that you've always been with me, even when I was acting foolish. Thank you for blessing me with your wisdom. Thank you, Lord, for being a good Father! I commit my day to you, asking that you would walk with me every step of my day. Amen.

Proclaim

"Do not be anxious about anything, but in every situation, by prayer and petition, with thanksgiving, present your requests to God." (Phil. 4:6)

Prompt

If you're in recovery, you're in a delicate time of life, a time when worries and fears can rear their ugly heads much more easily than normal and a time when your emotions and desires can push and pull you in different directions.

Does that ring true for you?

How can you avoid the anxiety that comes with this stage of life? How can you stay grounded in gratitude and rooted in rest?

It's simple: pray.

Prayer is the key. Saturate yourself in prayer throughout the day, offering your faith-filled requests before God with overflowing gratitude. Tell Him every detail of your life and let him speak to you about it. All of it.

And then watch what happens.

Prod

How can you spend more time in prayer today? Set a reminder on your phone to pray every hour today, even if it's just a simple "breath prayer" like "thank you" or "help me!"

Praise

 Listen to

"Fall Afresh"

by Bethel Music

Pray

Jesus, thank you for listening when I pray to you. Thank you for caring for my soul. Thank you for being there when I need you. I could speak for hours about your goodness in my life. Today, I ask that you would meet with me every hour as I seek to pray throughout the day. Fill me to overflow as my soul connects to you. Amen.

Proclaim

"Do not be anxious about anything, but in every situation, by prayer and petition, with thanksgiving, present your requests to God." (Phil. 4:6)

Prompt

I have a secret. It's a secret about finding longevity in your walk with God. A secret that can help you put down ever-deeper roots in your relationship with your Creator.

That secret is *passion*.

When you serve God with passion, your entire being awakens to your purpose. This is why we're here! We exist to serve Jesus and build His Kingdom on earth—right now—alongside Him!

But you can't just manufacture passion on a whim. It's not a feeling you can just make happen on your own. It takes prayer. It takes time alone with God. It takes building a relationship with your Creator.

Prayer activates your passion. Passion activates your faith. Faith activates the faith in others!

Want to live a passionate life? Live a prayerful life. Let's start today.

Prod

On a scale from 1 to 10, where would you rank your passion today?

How can you activate your passion through prayer today?

Praise

 Listen to

"This Is a Move"

by Brandon Lake

Pray

Jesus, thank you for the purpose you've given me! Activate my passion for you today so that I can give you every part of me. I need you. I confess, I am nothing without you. Today, help me to MOVE in faith. Activate my soul through the power of your Holy Spirit. Amen.

Proclaim

"Do not be anxious about anything, but in every situation, by prayer and petition, with thanksgiving, present your requests to God." (Phil. 4:6)

Prompt

Radios can tune in anywhere. If a radio station is broadcasting on a frequency and you have a radio, you can just turn a knob or punch an arrow button and hear whatever they're sending out.

Radio stations send out their signal on a wave, and you dial it in. **Pretty cool.**

But get this: those radio waves are *always* around us. Whether you have a radio tuned in to a frequency or not, you're always surrounded by those radio waves. That's how your radio can tune them in—because they're always there.

That's like God and our prayers. But kind of backwards. Because like radio waves, God is always with us. But also like a radio, God is always tuned in to our frequency.

Whenever we're ready to broadcast our prayer, God is already listening. Remember, we are establishing a strong foundation of prayer during this quarter, so lean in with everything you got!

Prod

What do you think of the fact that God is always around you, always ready to tune in to your prayers? Does that change the way you'll live your life today?

If you can, as you pray today, get on your knees. See how this changes your heart posture the moment your knees hit the ground.

Praise

 Listen to

"Highest Praise"

by C3LA

Pray

Jesus, thank you for being there for me! Thank you for tuning in to what I have to say to you. I'm so grateful. You are my King, my Savior, and my Lord. You deserve my highest praise, and that's what I am committed to giving you today. I surrender to your will, your way, ALWAYS! Amen.

Proclaim

"Do not be anxious about anything, but in every situation, by prayer and petition, with thanksgiving, present your requests to God." (Phil. 4:6)

Prompt

From the wealthiest CEO to the lowliest gig worker, from a successful performer to the unknown raw talent just starting out, from the smartest among us to those who get by on wits rather than intelligence, one thing is true for everyone:

ANXIETY COMES FOR ALL OF US.

I don't know about you, but I find it comforting to know I'm not alone in feeling anxiety. It's a common experience—so common that Paul wrote about it in Philippians, telling us not to be anxious for anything.

Which is *also* comforting because I know when God gives us a direction in scripture, He also empowers us to live it out. And that power? Is prayer. Maybe not right away, and maybe not all the time, but in due time, we can be free of anxiety through prayer.

Prayer is available to all of us. Prayer is our way to freedom from anxiety.

Prod

What's making you anxious right now? Write it down and set alarms to pray three times today about each of these places of anxiety in your life.

Praise

 Listen to

"Protector"

by Kim Walker-Smith

Pray

Jesus, thank you for caring about the things that make me anxious. I ask you to work in my heart and mind today so that I can be anxious for nothing. Just like this song says, I disconnect from any lies that are keeping me in bondage, keeping me fearful, anxious, or worried! Instead, I claim victory over every area of my life because you are my protector! I cast my cares on you, God, for **you CARE for ME!** Amen!

Proclaim

"Do not be anxious about anything, but in every situation, by prayer and petition, with thanksgiving, present your requests to God." (Phil. 4:6)

Prompt

You know when you move, how you have to pack up everything so you can carry it somehow? If you're like me, it's not too long before you start thinking about all that space, how much room it takes up, and whether you're going to have room in your car/truck/van/Uhaul for it all.

In the same way, people can take up space in our hearts and minds. We can carry them around with us like baggage, always finding room for them, no matter what. Sometimes those people we carry are good—like someone who gave us an encouraging word or a longtime friend or family member who encourages us to be our best selves.

But too often we carry the negative people with us, too. The seventh-grade teacher who wounded us with a callous remark or the parent who told us we'd never measure up.

Instead of carrying those people in your heart and mind, pray them over to Jesus. Let Him carry them for you.

Prod

To be clear, while prayer is integral to letting go of people who are taking up space in your heart and mind, it is part of a larger, longer process of work. Make a list of those people and start to pray for them today. (Bonus: pray for God to bless them.)

Praise

 Listen to

"His Name Is Jesus"

by Jeremy Riddle

Pray

Jesus, I invite you to take up so much room in my heart and mind that there's only you in there. Your name is Wonderful, Counselor, Almighty God, and the Prince of PEACE! Your blood has saved my life! Thank you for meeting with me today and guiding me as I move through the day. Amen.

Proclaim

"Do not be anxious about anything, but in every situation, by prayer and petition, with thanksgiving, present your requests to God." (Phil. 4:6)

Prompt

I know we in the Christian world love to quote Luke 1:37: "For with God, nothing will be impossible." But while that may be true about Mary getting pregnant with Jesus while still a virgin (look it up), I can tell you one thing that actually is impossible:

Changing other people.

I speak from experience on this one because I've tried this in just about every way. Control, manipulation, deception, shame, ignoring... you name it, I've done it! (How about you?)

People only change when they make the decision to change, and there's nothing you or I can do about that. It's the way God set it up when He created the world and gave us all free will.

But you know what we can do? We can pray. It's so hard, but when our hearts are anxious because of this person or that person, we can pray for them and for ourselves.

Prayer can change everything. And as our verse reminds us, after prayer comes peace.

Prod

Who in your life is driving you crazy?! Who are you mad at? Who are you scared for?

Make a list and commit to praying for them every waking hour.

Praise

 Listen to

"One Thing Remains"

by Bethel Music

Pray

Jesus, I thank you for [NAME OF PERSON YOU'RE PRAYING FOR]. You created them, you love them, and you delight in them, just like you do in me. Bless them today. Amen. (Repeat this prayer as many times as you need to.)

Proclaim

"Do not be anxious about anything, but in every situation, by prayer and petition, with thanksgiving, present your requests to God." (Phil. 4:6)

Prompt

When Jesus wanted to show us how to pray, He gave us the perfect template, what has become known as The Lord's Prayer.

Since then, The Lord's Prayer has become a collective prayer that gets prayed aloud in thousands and thousands of churches, **AA clubhouses**, and jail cells every day!

If you're ever stuck, if you ever can't figure out how to pray or what to pray for, you can always turn to The Lord's Prayer as a way of pouring out your heart to the Lord and seeking His work in your life.

Prod

Listen to today's song and meditate on the different parts of The Lord's Prayer.

Praise

 Listen to

"Our Father"

by Bethel Music

Pray

Our Father in heaven, hallowed be your name, your Kingdom come, your will be done, on earth as in heaven. Give us today our daily bread. Forgive us our sins as we forgive those who sin against us. Lead us not into temptation but deliver us from evil. Amen.

Proclaim

"Do not be anxious about anything, but in every situation, by prayer and petition, with thanksgiving, present your requests to God." (Phil. 4:6)

Prompt

I don't know about you, but I am prone to ruminating thoughts. My mind can fixate on a problem, an idea, a strained relationship, an upcoming event, or a conversation I'm dreading, and then I'm toast. This struggle can be really hard for me, even though I've walked with God for years and years now.

This fixation situation has really been challenged as I've meditated on our verse for this quarter. Paul clearly knows a thing or two about being in challenging situations, and he tells us clearly: *don't worry, don't stress, don't get pulled, and don't fixate on anything that can cause anxiety or negativity.*

Pray. Talk to God. Tell Him everything. And do it all with a grateful heart. That's not easy, but it feels good. Turn your fixation onto God and let Him do the rest.

Prod

So how do we do this? We must begin a process of eliminating anything that could trigger a ruminating thought and replacing it with PRAYER and PRAISE. Start right now, crank up the music, get on your knees, and give your thoughts to God!

Praise

 Listen to

"Tremble"

by Mosaic MSC

Pray

Jesus, thank you for being my entire and total fixation today. Help me to see you—and only you—with every part of me. I breathe you in; I breathe you out. Father, as I do this, take the darkness from my mind and replace it with your light. Jesus, you are King! Jesus, you are Lord! Jesus, you are my peace! Amen.

Proclaim

"Do not be anxious about anything, but in every situation, by prayer and petition, with thanksgiving, present your requests to God." (Phil. 4:6)

Prompt

I end every day on my knees with prayer. It's part of a nighttime routine I started when I first got sober and that I now cannot live without.

Each action I take during my nighttime routine builds me toward that final moment with just me and God, the time where I give Him all my burdens, thank Him for all my blessings, ask for help and healing for those I love, and seek His guidance in all my upcoming decisions.

I can say with certainty that I would not be where I am today if not for this routine of nightly prayer. The daily rhythm of seeking an *audience* with God has formed me for the better, and the act of praying has invited God to move on my behalf countless times.

I preach about praying on your knees all the time. But I still think it's hard for people. What about you?

Can you humble yourself today, fall to your knees, and pray to your Creator? I know when I do, I'm instantly reminded that I am not God... and that's really good news!

Prod

Do you have a daily prayer routine? Does it include prayer time on your knees? If not, give it a shot today!

Praise

 Listen to

"Surrendered"

by UPPERROOM

Pray

Jesus, this is how I pledge to fight my battles. On my knees, with my head bowed and my heart surrendered. You are God, and I am not. I need you. Please fight my battles for me today. I give you every single part of me.... ***ALL OF IT***. I surrender. You are KING. Please make me more like you today. Amen.

Proclaim

"Do not be anxious about anything, but in every situation, by prayer and petition, with thanksgiving, present your requests to God." (Phil. 4:6)

Prompt

I can feel when I'm not living like I know God desires. Maybe not instantly, but it doesn't take long. One bad decision, one snappy comment, one negative thought about someone, and within a few days, I am no longer who I want to be.

Whenever I end up here, I find it best to seek out some type of physical activity and push myself: I go for a hard run, a long swim, a tough hike, a bike ride, a long walk... anything physical really. I spend the entire time praying, asking God to help me reposition myself in His hands.

Inevitably, somewhere during mid-exhaustion, I find God again and take my rightful place **UNDER HIS AUTHORITY**. Seeking God in everything we do is an act of prayer.

Today as we meditate on our verse and listen to our song, let us remember the position we must be in to hear God's voice best: under His authority and in His hands.

Prod

What are some concrete steps you can take when you start to feel outside the way God's called you to live? Write them down now.

Praise

 Listen to

"When You Walk Into The Room"

by Bryan & Katie Torwalt

Pray

Jesus, thank you for journeying with me always and for guiding me back to your path when I stray from it. You are always there with me—you never leave my side. I'm so grateful for that! Today, please guide my thoughts and my reactions. Help me to stay in line with your will. Keep me safe. Keep me hopeful. Keep me, GOD! Keep me. Amen.

Proclaim

"Do not be anxious about anything, but in every situation, by prayer and petition, with thanksgiving, present your requests to God." (Phil. 4:6)

Prompt

"Do not be anxious about anything."

I don't know about you, but I think it feels pretty good to hear that God Almighty, the Creator of the Universe, desires that we not be stressed out and fixated on what's to come.

Instead, we get to pray. Rather than furrow our eyebrows with worry or let our hearts get all revved up with anxiety, we get to smile and talk to God. **BECAUSE WE KNOW HE LISTENS.**

But how can you practice this? When you begin to slip into anxiety, sadness, or anger, when you begin to overthink a situation, fixate instead on something within your control... Take a beat. Pause. Breathe for a few moments, and while you breathe, pray and remind yourself that God's Got This.

And then move on. You don't have to be anxious about it anymore! That's not your job!

Prod

Let's practice this right now... let your mind roll through any anxious thoughts you might currently be dealing with. With each one, say out loud, "God's Got This!"

Keep going until the anxiety falls away and a smile comes to your face. Because knowing God is in control feels good!

Praise

 Listen to

"Arms of Jesus"

by Cade Thompson

Pray

Jesus, thank you for taking care of this for me. Thank you for letting me fall into your arms. You give me peace when I'm nervous. You give me mercy when I deserve justice. You give me HOPE when everything seems to be falling apart. Jesus, you've got my burdens! I give it all to you... please give me all smiles in return. Amen.

Proclaim

"Do not be anxious about anything, but in every situation, by prayer and petition, with thanksgiving, present your requests to God." (Phil. 4:6)

Prompt

From the outside, forgiveness can seem pretty foolish. Here's an excerpt from a journal entry I wrote about forgiveness once:

"God, to so many people, forgiving someone who has really hurt me can look foolish. But I trust you that you understand more than anyone what it feels like to be hurt, judged, left out, shamed, and abused. God, you say that our sins have been forgiven as far as the east is from the west. Fill me with the same foolish forgiveness to let everything go and give it all to you. Help me today to fully forgive all those who have harmed me."

One thing that helps me when I know I need to pray to forgive someone is to remember that Jesus was in a position to hold a grudge, and He forgave. After all, His dying words were a prayer for forgiveness:

"Father forgive them..."

Prod

Who do you need to extend foolish forgiveness toward today? Are you willing? Ask God for help today during your prayer time.

Praise

 Listen to

"This is Amazing Grace"

by Bethel Music

Pray

Jesus, thank you for forgiving me! Your amazing grace has freed me from the bondage of my bad decisions, the agony of addictions, and the shame of all my sin. You've forgiven me. Help me to follow your example and to foolishly forgive others. I want freedom, and I know it starts here. ***Help me to FORGIVE!*** Amen.

Proclaim

"Do not be anxious about anything, but in every situation, by prayer and petition, with thanksgiving, present your requests to God." (Phil. 4:6)

Prompt

For years I prayed for friendships. If you have ever seen my life, you would think I have tons of friends. I really don't. And honestly, that's true for most people. Don't let the devil tell you something is wrong with you because you aren't drowning in close friends.

There are millions of people lonely and desperate to be known and needed. That was me for years until God helped me develop into someone who was able to *be* a friend. *Then* He brought me many friends.

We all need people who will stand with us, hang with us, invite us to do stuff on the weekend and be there when we need them. And we need to be those kinds of people for others.

So if this is you, start praying for God to show you how to be a person who can be a friend. And then welcome the relationships He brings into your life.

Prod

If you have friends already, be grateful. And call them today to tell them you love them.

Praise

 Listen to

"Friend in Jesus"

by CAIN

Pray

Jesus, help me to be a good friend. Thanks for being my best friend. You've stuck close to me no matter what. Thank you for showing me how to love others. Today, I ask you to guide me to the right people, to grow into the right person, and for your blessing of rich friendships here on this earth. In the meantime, thank you for being my friend!

Proclaim

"Do not be anxious about anything, but in every situation, by prayer and petition, with thanksgiving, present your requests to God." (Phil. 4:6)

Prompt

Do you ever pray like God is intensely interested in what you have to say? Do you ever talk to God like He's a best friend who can handle whatever you have to throw up on Him?

Check out this prayer I wrote in my journal not too long ago:

"God come invade my life today. I'm needing you to overtake my heart and simultaneously renew my mind. Can you do that?! I know you can. I BELIEVE you can. For so long I've walked mindlessly through my life. But today I woke up needing to WAKE UP! God, please help me today to see you like I once did. Open my eyes to your glory. Stretch me in ways I have never experienced. I will meet you halfway. I pledge to believe today that you are who you say you are and that what your word says is true. You can do all things."

It's kind of all over the place, but it's *honest*. This is what I needed to say to God in that moment, and you know what? Not only can God take it, but God wants YOU to pray like this!

God wants to hear your heart—all of it. Don't be afraid to bare it before Him in prayer.

Prod

Is anything holding you back from praying vulnerably? How can you remove that obstacle today?

Praise

 Listen to

"Single Mind"

by Jeremy Riddle

Pray

Jesus, I find my **delight in you.** You give me joy and hope. And sometimes I just need you to listen to me and let all my fears, doubts, worries and anxieties out! Thanks for being a strong listener who can handle whatever I have to say to you. I trust you. Amen.

Proclaim

"Do not be anxious about anything, but in every situation, by prayer and petition, with thanksgiving, present your requests to God." (Phil. 4:6)

Prompt

I try to start and end my days on my knees. Maybe you were taught this practice or have heard it suggested at church or at meetings.

I've found when I start and end my day on my knees in an act of submission to God, I'm in a much better place throughout the day. I'm more compassionate, more caring, and feel more in tune with what God is doing in and through my life.

It's my way of surrendering **daily**.

You'd be surprised how much a simple routine of morning and evening prayer can do to set the tone for the way your day begins and ends.

But you know this. I've said it before, a few different times. So why are you still not praying on your knees? Today can be the day. Let go of your pride, humble yourself, and position yourself low... then close your eyes, raise your head to God, and just talk to Him.

Prod

As you pray today, ask God to humble you as you walk through your day. A humble and contrite heart honors God. As we make ourselves low, we elevate God to His rightful place as King over our lives.

Praise

 Listen to

"You Satisfy"

by Upper Room Music

Pray

Jesus, you satisfy my heart. You are everything I need. Please forgive me for my arrogance and pride. Keep me away from worldly things that puff up my ego and make me only think about myself. **You are God and I am not.** I can't do life without you anymore. I need you in every area of my life, and today I commit to turning it all over to you and trust that you will provide for ALL my needs! Amen.

Proclaim

"Do not be anxious about anything, but in every situation, by prayer and petition, with thanksgiving, present your requests to God." (Phil. 4:6)

Prompt

When it comes to morning prayer, I literally try to roll out of bed onto my knees.

I start first thing by asking God to help guide me and keep me sober throughout the upcoming day; then I incorporate whatever else might be on my mind, heart, or spirit for that day.

If you have a problem remembering to start your day in prayer, here's a tip: put your phone **UNDER** your side of the bed, so that way you have to roll out of bed to get to it to turn off your alarm. While you're down there: say a prayer!

You could also put a reminder on your phone for the same time you wake up, or tape a reminder to the inside of your bedroom door. Or you can even laminate prayers and stick them to the walls of your shower! Yes, I've done this... a lot, actually!

Morning prayer can change the course of your day. So I'm willing to do whatever it takes to ensure this is a priority in my morning routine. I got no shame in my prayer game.

YOU?

Prod

How's your prayer life in the mornings? Is there anything you need to do to strengthen it? What steps can you take?

Praise

 Listen to

"Faithful Now"

by Vertical Worship

Pray

Jesus, thanks for this wonderful day you made for me. Let me rejoice and be glad in it today. Amen.

Proclaim

"Do not be anxious about anything, but in every situation, by prayer and petition, with thanksgiving, present your requests to God." (Phil. 4:6)

Prompt

Just like I start my day with morning prayer, I end my day with—you guessed it—evening prayer.

It doesn't have to be anything fancy, though my evening prayers have gotten more elaborate as the years have gone on. You can simply just thank God for the day He gave you, that you have had another day of life, let alone with the blessings He's given you.

But one thing I've been working hard to incorporate recently is confession. During my evening routine I've started writing down all the sins, struggles, and doubts I've experienced throughout the day on a whiteboard in my closet. ***This practice of confession is during what I would call my prayer time.*** As I write each of them down, I am asking God to forgive me, heal me, and help me to not repeat the same sin again.

The act of acknowledging my sins in writing helps me give it all to God so that he can lift them off of me instead of me carrying them around in my head and heart.

Prod

Confess your sins to God right now. Write them down on a separate sheet of paper, lift them to God, and then dispose of the paper. They aren't yours anymore!

Praise

 Listen to

"Better Word"

by Leeland

Pray

Jesus, your blood heals my every wound. Jesus, you are making all things new. Thank you for taking my sin and my shame and casting it from east to west. Today, forgive me and heal me as I confess [NAME YOUR CONFESSIONS]. I give this all to you because you're a safe place. Amen.

Proclaim

"Do not be anxious about anything, but in every situation, by prayer and petition, with thanksgiving, present your requests to God." (Phil. 4:6)

Prompt

One of God's promises I find myself leaning on more than I realize is the promise that He's the same yesterday, today, and forever. That means the God who worked on behalf of Jesus, Jacob, Moses, Mary, and David is the same God who loves me!

If God took care of them, then I can trust and remember that He'll take care of me. I may not know when or how, but I know He will. I believe that He will, and I want you to as well. You must believe today that God is **WITH YOU!** This trust will help keep you free as you walk through whatever today has in store for you.

Like our song for today says, He's the same God. We just need to call on Him through prayer and watch what happens.

Prod

What's your favorite story from the Old Testament? Reflect today on how God worked in that story and then ask him to work for you in the same way.

Praise

 Listen to

"Same God"

by Elevation Worship

Pray

Jesus, I'm so grateful that you're always the same! You are the Alpha and the Omega, beginning and the end! You walked with Moses and you walk with me. You spoke through Peter and you will speak through me. You gave strength to Mary and you will give strength to me. You are with me, God... Thank you for your love, thank you for hearing me, thank you for being my solid rock. Amen.

Proclaim

"Do not be anxious about anything, but in every situation, by prayer and petition, with thanksgiving, present your requests to God." (Phil. 4:6)

Prompt

Sometimes we need repetition. Yes, we rely on God to refresh and renew us, but we also can rely on God to be the same yesterday, today, and forever. Routines and repetitions can be lifesavers when used correctly.

I have found that highly successful people in the world have discovered reproducible principles of life; even Jesus gave a tremendous example of consistency and routine: His life was marked by rising early to pray daily.

Educators will also tell you that repetition has great value. Songwriters know the value of repetition, and so do athletes.

Routine in life reveals what we value. If it's true that we succeed in what we celebrate, then let's get on board and celebrate routines that foster daily discipleship.

Prod

Are you avoiding or embracing repetition in your life? Why or why not? What aspects of repetition can be healthy and beneficial for your life right now?

Praise

 Listen to

"Meet With Me"

by Ten Shekel Shirt

Pray

Jesus, I know I say this a lot, but: wow. You're amazing. Let me never get tired of repeating that. Show up in my routine today and reveal yourself in a fresh and new way. Only you can enliven repetition—show me yourself! Amen.

Proclaim

"Do not be anxious about anything, but in every situation, by prayer and petition, with thanksgiving, present your requests to God." (Phil. 4:6)

Prompt

Routine is super-important for a life of discipleship, but all the routines in the world won't help you if you don't first prioritize the various parts of that routine.

And your number-one priority, according to Jesus, is to seek God's Kingdom first and foremost. One way is to follow the instruction found in our verse this quarter and go to God in every situation. ***Not some, not half, not a few—ALL!***

God's invitation to come to Him with everything is sitting in your inbox. Open it!

When you make your relationship with God your first priority, then everything else in your routine falls into place! When you learn to trust Him with every part of your life, then all those parts seem a little less worrisome.

Let the Kingdom of God fill your view.

Prod

Prioritize your routine and make sure God is at the very top of it. And at the bottom. And infused throughout.

Praise

 Listen to

"Upon This Rock"

by The Met Collective

Pray

Jesus, you're my number-one priority in life. Fill my vision today so that I see my world as you see it. Help me stay committed to the spiritual rhythms I implement in my life. You are my light and you are my hope. I commit my day to you. Amen.

Proclaim

"Do not be anxious about anything, but in every situation, by prayer and petition, with thanksgiving, present your requests to God." (Phil. 4:6)

Prompt

Bill Hybels, Pastor of Willow Creek Community Church outside of Chicago, said this about reconciliation:

"The mark of community is not the absence of conflict but the presence of a reconciliatory spirit."

As we seek after this spirit in our lives, God begins to bring about peace in what used to be chaotic and volatile relationships. By taking action toward reconciliation, we become the change agent God uses to restore not only our personal relationships, but also people's relationships with Him.

So how do you get it? For starters, pray. After all, Jesus tells us to do just that in Matthew 5:43-44: "You have heard that it was said, 'You shall love your neighbor and hate your enemy.' But I say to you, 'Love your enemies and pray for those who persecute you.'"

When you pray, you turn your heart toward reconciliation.

Prod

What relationships in your life are in need of reconciliation? Make a list and commit to praying God's peace over those for the next week.

Praise

 Listen to

"Thirsty"

by Chris McClarney

Pray

Jesus, thank you for giving me a spirit of reconciliation. Show me how to use it today. I'm thirsty for freedom. I'm ready to let it all go so I can embrace the peace you long for me to have. Help me to trust you and be an ambassador for you today. Amen.

Proclaim

"Do not be anxious about anything, but in every situation, by prayer and petition, with thanksgiving, present your requests to God." (Phil. 4:6)

Prompt

God is always calling us to go deeper with Him. Deeper in prayer, deeper in dependence, deeper in faith, in generosity, and in boldness.

In Luke 5:4-11, Jesus asks us to launch out into the deep! Because spiritual leadership will never thrive in the shallows. A life going deeper with Jesus requires courage, vulnerability, confession, repentance, and dedication to living in a community.

When you submit to God's call and vow to go deeper, there can be some anxiety! Especially if you look at it with earthly eyes. But when you take it to your knees in prayer, you can look beyond the Big and see what God sees.

The reward is worth it.

Prod

Jesus has written a deep launch on your heart. What is it? What steps do you need to take to make it a reality?

Praise

 Listen to

"Love So Great"

by Hillsong Worship

Pray

Jesus, give me courage to launch out into the deep today because I know that wherever I go, you go with me. There is nothing that compares to your love, there is nothing that compares to your protection, there is nothing that compares to your friendship. Please give me the courage to take my faith deeper with you today. Amen.

Proclaim

"Do not be anxious about anything, but in every situation, by prayer and petition, with thanksgiving, present your requests to God." (Phil. 4:6)

Prompt

We have a lot of areas in our lives where we need to recognize lies. How? Jesus tells us in Luke 21:34-36 that we must be alert. Check this out:

"Watch out! Don't let your hearts be dulled by carousing and drunkenness, and by the worries (or anxieties) of this life. **Don't let that day catch you unaware, like a trap.** For that day will come upon everyone living on the earth. Keep alert at all times. And pray that you might be strong enough to escape these coming horrors and stand before the Son of Man."

What does this mean? It means the enemy wants to lull you to sleep and then place a lie right in front of you. The unaware version of you will snap that lie right on up and give it a good home. But the version of you who is on guard for lies will leave it right there and maybe put a couple of orange cones around it so that you'll remember to leave it alone the next time you encounter it.

Which version of you will you be today?

Prod

What lies have you picked up throughout your life? List five of them and commit to putting them back down where they belong.

Praise

 Listen to

"Sing His Praise Again"

by Bethel Music

Pray

Jesus, help me to recognize the lies of the enemy today. Give me clarity and boldness to renounce the lie. Give me the strength to leave them for you to deal with, not me. Help me to live in focus, freedom, and forgiveness today. Amen.

Proclaim

"Do not be anxious about anything, but in every situation, by prayer and petition, with thanksgiving, present your requests to God." (Phil. 4:6)

Prompt

There are lots of ways to pray. You may be most familiar and practiced with what is called "extemporaneous" prayer, which is just a theological term for praying off the top of your head as the Holy Spirit prompts you.

But you aren't limited to that kind of prayer. Especially when you don't know what to say!

So you can change up your prayer diet by getting a book of prayers and reading through it. There are also tons of pre-written prayers online for just about every circumstance.

Regardless of how you go about it, pray in every situation. There is nothing too shallow, too small, or too silly for you to ask God for. He wants to guide and give you what you need. If you are not already, start giving every situation to God and watch what happens.

Prod

Today, ask God what He wants you to wear. I know this sounds dumb, but it's not. God wants to be involved with your life. Starting the practice of inviting Him into every situation will change your heart. Start today.

Praise

 Listen to

"Trust In You"

by Lauren Daigle

Pray

Jesus, thank you for caring about everything. Thank you that I can TRUST YOU in every situation. Today, I commit to going to you BEFORE I go to the world. I give you my life. Take me, make me, mold me. Set me free! I trust you! Amen.

Proclaim

"Do not be anxious about anything, but in every situation, by prayer and petition, with thanksgiving, present your requests to God." (Phil. 4:6)

Prompt

Several years into Hope is Alive, I began to make huge changes in my prayer life. I still prayed with the same desire as I always had, but I began to take bigger steps and launch out in faith.

I was no longer satisfied with the answered prayers of three years, four years, or seven years ago. I had quit asking God to do the miraculous in my life. I had forgotten that God says to **ASK:** to **ask, seek, knock**...and that His promise is that HE WILL HEAR US!

So, I started making bold declarations over my life, and since then I have made huge decisions, taken steps of faith, and am still believing God will provide for me and answer my prayers.

To me, a declaration is a prayer statement that activates your faith. Here's my favorite:

God, your favor runs to me like a roaring river. What I ask, in Jesus name, will be blessed!

Prod

Write a declaration for your day, right now. What's a statement that will help activate your faith to guide and direct you today?

Praise

 Listen to

"Evidence"

by Josh Baldwin

Pray

Jesus, you're bigger than I could ever imagine, and yet you're closer than my next breath. I know you can—and will—do amazing things in my life, even today. I commit this day—and all my plans—to you. I can't wait to see the evidence all around me of your goodness! Amen.

Proclaim

"Do not be anxious about anything, but in every situation, by prayer and petition, with thanksgiving, present your requests to God." (Phil. 4:6)

Prompt

Okay, in the midst of the bad times, when you're crying out to God over and over, and it seems like he's turned a deaf ear to you, it can be hard to remember, so just really take this in:

God is for you. God is truly, truly *for* you!

Today is a day to remind yourself of this over and over and over again. Say it now!

GOD IS FOR ME!

This can sometimes be hard to believe when it feels like everything sucks, but it's an unchanging truth. God is on your side!

So don't give up. Don't quit calling on Him. Don't abandon prayer and petition just because life is hard. He's still there. Believe it!

Prod

What can you do to remind yourself to keep praying, even when things are tough? Make a plan.

Praise

 Listen to

"Even So Come"

by Passion

Pray

Jesus, just like the sun behind clouds, I know you're there even though I can't see you. Warm me today with your love. I need you today to help get me through. No matter what I'm about to walk into, Jesus come and invade my life. Make me new, make me whole, give me hope! Amen.

Proclaim

"Do not be anxious about anything, but in every situation, by prayer and petition, with thanksgiving, present your requests to God." (Phil. 4:6)

Prompt

When we present our requests to God through prayer, we can sometimes think we need to give God a little help on the fulfillment end of things.

But only God can provide the breakthrough you need! Never lose sight of this.

Because work is such an integral part to faith, it can sometimes feel like my breakthroughs are dependent on me. FALSE! It's ALL in God's hands.

Yes, you and I need to put in work to see breakthrough—that's a key component to discipleship, success, restoration, growth, all the good things—but in the end, we're just watering God's dream and trusting that He'll make it grow and produce fruit.

Prod

Are you waiting on a breakthrough? What can you do to make sure you keep going while waiting? Write it down specifically. Don't give up!

Praise

 Listen to

"Yes & Amen"

by Chris Tomlin

Pray

Jesus, give me the stamina I need to wait for my breakthrough. I trust you will bring it in your best timing because you love me. Through the power of your Holy Spirit, I ask that you fill me with FAITH. Help me to remember all your promises are YES and AMEN! Fill me with hope today to wait for you. Amen.

Proclaim

"Do not be anxious about anything, but in every situation, by prayer and petition, with thanksgiving, present your requests to God." (Phil. 4:6)

Prompt

Can I be honest? I used to hold back in my prayers. I didn't pray for big things because, well, I didn't want to be a pest or ask God for too much.

Deep down, I think I thought God would be offended when I asked Him something that, to my eyes, seemed way too huge.

But guess what? God is NOT offended when I pray for big things. Why would He be? He's God! Nothing is too big or difficult for Him!

God WANTS to do big things on our behalf, just like a good parent wants to do big things for their kids.

Don't be afraid to ask ***BIG. GOD LOVES IT BECAUSE GOD LOVES YOU!***

Prod

Are you holding back from asking God for something big? Write down the big thing you feel God is asking you to pray for and make it a key part of your prayer life.

Praise

 Listen to

"Come Alive"

by Hillsong Worship

Pray

Jesus, help me to dream big. No, bigger than anything I have ever imagined before. Activate my faith and plant dreams in my heart that only you can make possible. Come alive in me and flood my heart with your Holy Spirit! Help me to dream as big as you. Amen.

Proclaim

"Do not be anxious about anything, but in every situation, by prayer and petition, with thanksgiving, present your requests to God." (Phil. 4:6)

Prompt

It may not always seem like it, but prayer works. You and I are living proof.

Try this on. I'm going to tell you something about myself, and you see if it rings true for you:

Every good thing that's ever come to me has been the result of someone's prayers. I am only here on this earth because people prayed for me.

Do you agree? I know my story is full of answered prayers from little old ladies in the church I grew up in. *As I got sober and began to change my life,* many of them sent me messages, letters, and made phone calls to tell me how they prayed for me for years!

God answers prayers. And oftentimes, it starts with your faith!

Prod

If you're here because of others' prayers, who can YOU lift up in prayer today? Ask the Holy Spirit to reveal them to you, then commit to keeping them in prayer as long as God asks you to.

Praise

 Listen to

"Here As In Heaven"

by Elevation Worship

Pray

Jesus, I lift up [NAME OF PERSON] to you today. Bless them wherever they are, and let them feel a tangible presence of your love for them. Thank you for putting them in my life and answering their prayers for me. Help me to see someone today that I can pray for. Amen.

Proclaim

"Do not be anxious about anything, but in every situation, by prayer and petition, with thanksgiving, present your requests to God." (Phil. 4:6)

Prompt

For years, I spent an hour every Sunday night asking God about whatever was in my world for the next day, week, or month. I would follow the instruction of Jesus found in Matthew 7 and would ask, seek, and knock for specific things. Moments, milestones, miracles... you name it.

The point was to be super-intentional about my prayer time, even to the point of keeping a whiteboard near my bed, writing out all this stuff and updating it every Sunday night.

You know what happened? *LOTS OF COOL THINGS!* God answered countless bold prayers when I simply took the time to ask Him.

What might happen if you really took time to present your true requests to God? To ask, seek, and knock? Let God surprise you!

Prod

Set time aside today, turn on today's song, and intentionally ask, seek, and knock—write down your requests and keep them handy to update them as God works on your behalf!

Praise

 Listen to

"Touch The Sky"

by Hillsong United

Pray

Jesus, you are at work! Show me your will in my life, and give me courage to pray bold prayers like this one. I am at your feet, asking for your grace in my life. Your will be done! Amen.

Proclaim

"Do not be anxious about anything, but in every situation, by prayer and petition, with thanksgiving, present your requests to God." (Phil. 4:6)

Prompt

Have you ever used bookends? Better yet, have you ever tried to keep books on a shelf looking good *without* bookends?

Bookends hold things together. They keep things orderly and prevent them from collapsing.

This is why I so heartily recommend bookending your day with morning and evening prayer. By starting and ending on your knees, you're putting bookends in place to keep your world, your life, your *everything* neat, orderly, and chaos-free.

How are your "bookends"?

Prod

Have you incorporated morning and evening prayer into your daily routine? What sort of results are you seeing with your current routine?

Praise

 Listen to

"Breathe"

by Influence Music

Pray

Jesus, help me always to turn to you in times of need, and even in times when I don't need anything. I want to breathe you in and breathe you out. Help me to develop strong spiritual rhythms where I can meet with you each day. Because I always need you. Amen.

Proclaim

"Do not be anxious about anything, but in every situation, by prayer and petition, with thanksgiving, present your requests to God." (Phil. 4:6)

Prompt

It's not a typical fighting stance, but it's one that makes sense for those of us who believe in the power of prayer.

I'm talking **ABOUT BEING ON YOUR KNEES.**

Because that's where our battles are fought—not through our fists but with our hands up in the air, submitted to God in praise and prayer.

Today's song brings this truth home in a powerful way and reminds us that all our battles belong to the Lord, not to us.

Prod

Meditate on the lyrics to today's song. Write down the ones that most stick out to you.

Praise

 Listen to

"Battle Belongs"

by Phil Wickham.

Pray

Jesus, thank you for fighting my battles for me. Help me to remember that when I'm tempted to do things myself, you fight my battles, you fight my battles... THANK YOU... THAT YOU FIGHT MY BATTLES! Amen.

Proclaim

"Do not be anxious about anything, but in every situation, by prayer and petition, with thanksgiving, present your requests to God." (Phil. 4:6)

Prompt

There's an old saying that goes something like this: the best time to plant a tree was 100 years ago. The next-best time is now.

I OFTEN FEEL THE SAME WAY ABOUT PRAYER.

It's easy to despair about past mistakes, but we can't do anything about the trees we didn't plant last century or the prayers we didn't pray yesterday. All we can do is look at the soil we have before us and the seed in our hands, and then kneel down and plant.

So kneel down and pray. There's no better time than now. There's no better day to start than today!

Prod

Don't spend another second worrying about the prayers you didn't pray. Make time to pray right now.

Praise

 Listen to

"More Than Enough"

by Jesus Culture

Pray

Jesus, thank you for hearing me when I pray. Thank you for not holding my past against me and for lifting all the regrets off my shoulders. Meet me here in this soil as I plant this prayer. I commit this day to you. Amen.

Proclaim

"Do not be anxious about anything, but in every situation, by prayer and petition, with thanksgiving, present your requests to God." (Phil. 4:6)

Prompt

What does a posture of prayer look like? Is it kneeling? Is it standing? Arms raised in surrender or hands clasped together? Do your eyebrows have to go down with determination?

Do you have to pace back and forth? Do you have to lie face down, prostrate in surrender? Do you have to lean forward in your chair and clench your fists to demonstrate to God that you mean business?

Or can you just pray however, wherever you are?

Truth is: it's all of them. Sometimes you just want to pray with no outward demonstration at all—maybe because you want to or need to in that moment. And sometimes you just want to make a major change in your posture to signal to God—and yourself—that you're up to something special.

I pray when driving, pray when laying down before bed, pray in meetings, pray while running, pray on my knees, pray standing up, ***pray with my hands held high***, pray with tears in my eyes.

It doesn't matter how you do it. Just pray!

Prod

What's your normal "prayer posture"? Try changing it up today and do something you've never done before. See what happens.

Praise

 Listen to

"Sunday is Coming"

by Phil Wickham

Pray

Jesus, thanks for hearing me when I pray, however I happen to look at the time. I love your grace. Today is yours... Amen.

Proclaim

"Do not be anxious about anything, but in every situation, by prayer and petition, with thanksgiving, present your requests to God." (Phil. 4:6)

Prompt

When you give someone a gift, you expect them to, you know, open it. And if it's the type of gift that's useful to their lives, you hope they use it (though too many of our closets have back corners filled with sweaters we've never worn).

Think about the gift of prayer from God's point of view. Here is an amazing gift He gave us—**THE ABILITY TO HAVE A CONVERSATION WITH HIM!**—and how often do we use it? Is your prayer sitting in the back of your closet next to a Christmas sweater with the price tag still on it?

Prayer is a wonderful gift—a tool—that we get to use as often as we want without ever using it up! Is something keeping you from praying? Are you reading each day but still resisting surrendering? Today is a day to take a step of faith and really PRAY!

Go to God now. Don't wait—operate in your gift TODAY.

Prod

Use your phone to schedule five times today to stop whatever you're doing and pray. Do it! Don't put it off—push yourself into a new rhythm and see what God does!

Praise

 Listen to

"White Flag"

by Chris Tomlin

Pray

Jesus, thank you for the gift of prayer! Thank you that you long to converse with me. I'm opening this wonderful gift and using it! Today, I'm going to cherish our time together! I cherish it. Amen.

Proclaim

"Do not be anxious about anything, but in every situation, by prayer and petition, with thanksgiving, present your requests to God." (Phil. 4:6)

Prompt

Do you use emojis? Personally, I love them. They're a great way to quickly acknowledge or communicate without words.

And one of the emojis I use frequently is—you guessed it—the praying hands emoji.

I like it in text messages because it's a simple way to let the person I'm texting know that I'm praying for them. If someone hits me up with a simple request—I can hit them back with a simple emoji.

It's the simplicity I love (and for the record, if I get a text about a more intense prayer request that requires context or more info, I'll actually text them back). Prayer really is sometimes as simple as an emoji.

When you see something that needs prayer, just lift the need up! Say the person's name, breathe out the request, take a moment to think about the situation, and give it to God.

Don't overthink praying for others—*just do it!*

Prod

Each time you see a person, a need, or a request today, say a quick prayer. Count how many times you do this, if you can. Betcha can't pray 30 times!

Praise

 Listen to

"God of Miracles"

by Chris McClarney

Pray

Jesus, thank you for prayer, and thanks for making it easy. I love that you hear me. Today, help me open my eyes to see the needs in front of me. I want to pray for others and be part of their miracle story. I commit my day to you! Amen.

Proclaim

"Do not be anxious about anything, but in every situation, by prayer and petition, with thanksgiving, present your requests to God." (Phil. 4:6)

Prompt

One of the things I've done a lot since founding Hope is Alive is have conversations. So many conversations. I love it! I love talking with people and telling my story, and I love hearing theirs in return. I love inspiring people and being inspired. I've had countless life-giving conversations over the course of HIA.

You never quite know when you begin a conversation how it will go. **You don't know if it's going to be brief or in-depth, intense or superficial.** But you can't know how a conversation will go if you don't jump into one with both your ears and your mouth.

Prayer is a conversation you have with God, and even though you don't quite know how it's going to go, you have an idea, and it should be a back-and-forth dialogue.

Let's practice both sides of the conversation today—speaking and listening.

Prod

Have a conversation with God, and let it go wherever God directs it. But make time and space to be still, and just listen to what the Holy Spirit says to you.

Praise

 Listen to

"Lean Back"

by Capital City Music

Pray

Jesus, what do you want to talk about today? Here's what's on my mind.... Amen.

Proclaim

"Do not be anxious about anything, but in every situation, by prayer and petition, with thanksgiving, present your requests to God." (Phil. 4:6)

Prompt

We've all been in conversations before with people who are very interested in telling you all about themselves. They don't pay attention to social cues—they just ramble on and on.

Not very interesting, is it?

God wants to hear from you and wants to hear about you—but He also wants to speak to you! *Do you give him the space?* Do you listen?

Yesterday we talked about prayer as a conversation with God, and one aspect that I want to deepen is the idea of listening.

How did you listen to God yesterday? Were you able to hear Him? It can be hard, which is why it's important to develop a way you can best hear God's voice.

Today, let's try one way that really works for me.

Prod

During your prayer time today, get alone, turn on today's song, grab a notebook (a journal would be great), and ask God to speak to you. Then start writing. Whatever comes to mind for the entire six minutes of this song, write it. Just write down whatever the Holy Spirit prompts in your spirit.

Praise

 Listen to

"Like An Avalanche"

by Hillsong UNITED

Pray

Jesus, speak to me. I'm listening! Amen.

Proclaim

"Do not be anxious about anything, but in every situation, by prayer and petition, with thanksgiving, present your requests to God." (Phil. 4:6)

Prompt

As long as we've spent the last couple of days talking about prayer as a conversation, there's another aspect of it we haven't yet touched on: how conversation is usually just talking.

We're conditioned to think of prayer as a time of requests—and that's not wrong! But it's so much *more* than a bunch of **asks**.

Don't misunderstand me: God wants to hear your requests. But He loves to hear the hearts of His children, and if you just want to share what's on your heart and your mind with Him, you're more than welcome to do that.

You don't have to come to God with your hand out. You can come just as you are and share your heart.

Prod

What's on your mind? Tell it to God today. Practice today by just sharing like you would with a friend, at an AA meeting, or with a therapist. Let it all go... ALL OF IT!

Praise

 Listen to

"Bones"

by Hillsong UNITED

Pray

Jesus, thanks for listening to my heart, here's what's really going on in my life.... Amen.

Proclaim

"Do not be anxious about anything, but in every situation, by prayer and petition, with thanksgiving, present your requests to God." (Phil. 4:6)

Prompt

You know who I think about sometimes when it comes to prayer? Not the normal person you'd imagine: Zacchaeus.

You remember him, right? He's the tax-collecting guy who climbed a tree to get above the crowd and take a look at Jesus. He's up there, gaping, and Jesus sees him and calls him out. It changes Zacchaeus's life.

I feel like prayer is the same way sometimes. Like, I just have to change up what I'm doing when it comes to praying. I have to **DO SOMETHING DIFFERENT** so I can get a better look at what Jesus is up to in my world and what He wants to do with me. I have to go somewhere different, do something different with my body, or say something different.

You can get in a rut with prayer. Don't be afraid to Zacchaeus your prayer routine. Who knows? Jesus might call you out and change your life!

Prod

The weather should be pretty good today. If so, go on a walk and listen to this song with headphones on. Soak in every word. Thank God for what He did for you as this song plays.

Praise

 Listen to

"Beautiful Exchange"

by Hillsong Worship

Pray

Jesus, thank you for making a way for me. You gave your life to me! To me... a sinner, broken, hurt, lonely, tired, depressed, anxious, addicted, judgmental, mean, prideful, lustful, hopeless... you gave your life to me SO THAT I might get everything in return! Freedom on earth and freedom with you forever in eternity. Thank you!! AMEN!

Proclaim

"Do not be anxious about anything, but in every situation, by prayer and petition, with thanksgiving, present your requests to God." (Phil. 4:6)

Prompt

Big things rarely just happen. Small stuff can happen anytime but the big stuff? That gets planned and prepared for, with groundwork laid for days or months or years in advance.

And this is where the big stuff happens: *in prayer. In solitude.*

Do you want something big in your life? Do you have big dreams, big goals, big plans? They won't happen without some effort on your part, and that effort is powered by prayer.

I want to urge you to spend daily, private time alone with God. Sharing your dreams, pouring out your heart and asking God to reveal Himself to you. As you begin to present your requests to God in prayer, your relationship will grow stronger as God begins to provide in ways you could've never imagined.

Prod

What's a big goal or plan you've been working on? Write it down now. During your prayer time, ask God to open your eyes to how to take your next steps.

Praise

 Listen to

"Open The Eyes Of My Heart"

by Michael W. Smith

Pray

Jesus, nothing can be bigger than what you did for me on the cross. I'm in awe. Thank you for your sacrifice. Today, I present a request to help guide me to fulfilling this dream of [SAY YOUR DREAM] that has been on my heart. Please open my eyes to see how I can begin to make this happen. Guide me today! Amen.

Proclaim

"Do not be anxious about anything, but in every situation, by prayer and petition, with thanksgiving, present your requests to God." (Phil. 4:6)

Prompt

If you're anything like me, praying for yourself comes naturally. We tend to pray for ourselves easily because, after all, we have a lot of concerns, and it makes sense to take those to the Lord so that, at best, He can move on our behalf and we can at least feel some measure of peace that, no matter what, we prayed about it.

BUT WHAT ABOUT OTHERS?

Are you praying for others in your life? I think it's good practice to occasionally have a time of prayer when you pray only for others and not at all for yourself. This helps us get outside ourselves and remember that there's an entire world of hurting people in need out there.

But let's be honest, this is not easy. So let's practice together today.

Prod

Who are you praying for? Send them a text message today and let them know they're in your prayers.

Praise

 Listen to

"Let It Rain"

by Michael W. Smith

Pray

Jesus, thank you for listening to my prayers about others. Work in their lives today. May your blessings rain down on them today. Today, I want to spend time praying for [SAY THEIR NAME]. Amen.

Proclaim

"Do not be anxious about anything, but in every situation, by prayer and petition, with thanksgiving, present your requests to God." (Phil. 4:6)

Prompt

Yesterday we talked about praying for others, and I'd like to dig into that a little more today.

You are only where you are right now because other people prayed for you. Throughout your life, you've had at least one person praying for you, whether they knew it or not. Even today, people are praying for you, whether you know it or not.

Have you returned the favor?

Today I want you to think specifically about the people who you know prayed for you in the recent past. Maybe it's one or both of your parents, a sibling or spouse, person from back then, or whomever.

And now I want you to pray for them. Commit to praying for them daily for the next week. Not to repay a debt you owe—prayer doesn't work that way—but just to honor the time they spent praying for you. Will you do it?

Prod

Make a list of the people you're going to pray for, then set a reminder on your phone to pray every day for the next week.

Praise

 Listen to

"You Hold It All Together"

by All Sons & Daughters

Pray

Jesus, I'm so grateful for all the people who prayed for me when I needed it. I'm here because of them! And so I lift them up to you today. Bless [NAME THEM] in every way, bring them joy and comfort, mercy and peace, and make a way for them where there is no way, Lord. Thank you. Amen.

Proclaim

"Do not be anxious about anything, but in every situation, by prayer and petition, with thanksgiving, present your requests to God." (Phil. 4:6)

Prompt

As long as we're on the topic of praying for others, here's a fun exercise:

Pray for others... but don't let them know. Let it be a secret between you and God.

Personally, I love knowing when people are praying for me, so it's good to do that (as we talked about yesterday), but sometimes there's a lot of fun in having a little secret with the Almighty. Just to put up your prayers with no expectation other than obedience and then sit back and see what God does in that person's life.

This is a good practice of humility as well. This prayer practice deepens our relationship path with God because it creates a conversation *JUST WITH HIM!*

Prod

Ask God who you should pray for in secret, and then make a commitment to lift them up in prayer regularly.

Praise

Listen to

"King Of Glory"

by Michael W. Smith

Pray

Jesus, thank you for all those who prayed for me that I'll never know about. Let me be that person for someone else today. Today, let's spend some time praying for [NAME THE PERSON AND ANY CONCERNS THEY MIGHT HAVE]. Amen.

Proclaim

"Do not be anxious about anything, but in every situation, by prayer and petition, with thanksgiving, present your requests to God." (Phil. 4:6)

Prompt

Prayer can be a lot of things, and one of my favorite things is when it's still. If you know me, you know there are lots of times when I pray big and loud, but I do enjoy the times when it feels like it's best to be quiet and still.

There's a word for this practice (though it's been corrupted by a lot of non-Christians), and that word is *meditation*.

All I mean by meditation is the act of being still, being calm, and being attentive to whatever the Holy Spirit may want to speak to you in that moment. This kind of receptivity is a form of prayer, and it's one I try to practice regularly.

You'd be surprised what might happen. Today, find a space and time to sit in solitude, turn on today's song, ask God to speak, and listen for His voice.

Prod

Make time to interact meditatively with the Lord today. Start with five minutes of silence and then turn on today's song.

Praise

 Listen to

"More Than Amazing"

by Lincoln Brewster

Pray

Jesus, thank you for calming the storm of my heart. I look for you in the quiet. Speak to me today! Amen.

Proclaim

"Do not be anxious about anything, but in every situation, by prayer and petition, with thanksgiving, present your requests to God." (Phil. 4:6)

Prompt

In addition to the Lord's Prayer, we have another key example of prayer from Jesus, this one found in Luke 22, where Jesus prays on the eve of His arrest and eventually crucifixion that The Father remove this burden from Him.

But then He has a crucial addition: ***"Not my will, but yours be done."***

Jesus was fully God and fully human, and in this moment, His humanity shone through: "I really don't wanna do this, God, but nevertheless, I'm going to because you want me to."

WHAT POWER!

What Jesus demonstrated in that moment is something we all face every day. Moments when we don't want to go forward with something even though we know it's the right thing. It's in these moments that personal, private, quick prayers of FAITH help get us through.

Here are some of mine:

- · God I need you in this moment
- · God you go before me, you stand beside me
- · God I trust you—do your thing

Prod

What are some short, powerful, faith-building prayers you can pray when you need them? Write them down so you can have them handy!

Praise

 Listen to

"Great is Thy Faithfulness"

by Carrie Underwood & CeCe Winans

Pray

Jesus, thank you for following God's will and going to the cross. I'm forever grateful! Help plant these personal, private prayers in my heart so I can recall them when I need them! Amen.

Proclaim

"Do not be anxious about anything, but in every situation, by prayer and petition, with thanksgiving, present your requests to God." (Phil. 4:6)

Prompt

I want to spend one more day thinking about Jesus' prayer in the Garden of Gethsemane, where He prayed, **"NOT MY WILL, BUT YOURS BE DONE."**

At the cornerstone of this prayer is the idea of submission. We can think of submission through prayer as an act of weakness, but I think it's the other way around:

Submission through prayer is one of the most powerful things we can do.

Because when we submit, we lay aside our own pitiful strength so that God can fill us with His immense strength. That's the power of prayerfully submitting to God's will.

Just like it says in today's song, when you come to God fully submitted He **"gives grace without condition / as you are / nothing else / just come."**

Prod

What do you need to lay down so you can pick up God's will? Give it up to God today. Come to Him and get honest. Today's a great day to get free through the power of submission and confession.

Praise

 Listen to

"As You Are"

by Life.Church Worship

Pray

Jesus, thank you for having a plan for my life. Thank you for giving me grace. Thank you for loving me just as I am. Today, I bring all of me to you. I'm not hiding anything! I fully submit to your will for my life and ask that you would fill me with hope today! Amen.

Proclaim

"Do not be anxious about anything, but in every situation, by prayer and petition, with thanksgiving, present your requests to God." (Phil. 4:6)

Prompt

In the 1800s, George Müller ran an orphanage in England. Müller was a major, major proponent of prayer, to the point where one morning, when there was nothing for breakfast, he simply had all the children sit at the table to pray.

Moments later, there was a knock at the door. It was the town baker, who told Müller that God had laid it on his heart the night before to bring enough bread for all the children to eat.

Then, another knock. It was the milkman, whose cart had a broken wheel. All the milk would spoil before he could get the wheel fixed, so could the orphanage use it? There was just enough for the children to drink.

God loves to do big things in our lives, **often just in time.**

Have you asked God to show up in your life today? In that one area where you keep trying to do it on your own? Manipulate it, control it, white knuckle it?

Back off, let it go, invite GOD in to do what only He can.

Prod

How can you pray like George Müller today?

Praise

 Listen to

"Greater Things"

by Mack Brock

Pray

Jesus, please provide for my every need today. I know I can trust you. Amen.

Proclaim

"Do not be anxious about anything, but in every situation, by prayer and petition, with thanksgiving, present your requests to God." (Phil. 4:6)

Prompt

The Grand Canyon is an amazing sight that pictures don't do justice to. All the big adjectives pale in comparison to it—jaw-dropping, awe-inspiring—you name it, it applies.

And yet this immense, amazing thing was carved by water. Year after year after year, the Colorado River eroded the sandstone and carved the canyon deeper and deeper and deeper.

It didn't happen all at once. It didn't happen in big chunks. It was just persistence.

This is the power of prayer. Don't give up. Stay persistent. Keep praying. Keep believing. Keep trusting that God will hear you and answer your prayers. He's working, even though it might not look like it yet.

Prod

Are you tempted to give up on a Grand Canyon-sized prayer? Keep going!

Praise

 Listen to

"Do It Again"

by Elevation Worship

Pray

Jesus, I trust you to fulfill your will in my life in your time. Give me strength for today. Help me to trust that you are enough for me. Keep me focused on your will and filled with your love! Amen.

Proclaim

"Do not be anxious about anything, but in every situation, by prayer and petition, with thanksgiving, present your requests to God." (Phil. 4:6)

Prompt

We talked about the Grand Canyon yesterday and the power of persistence in prayer, but I want to take that thought in a different direction today:

WHAT IF YOU ARE THE GRAND CANYON?

Here's what I mean: sometimes God uses prayer—the daily routine of submission and petition—to change US. Slowly wearing our flat, desert selves into a magnificent and breathtaking creation of God.

You're being changed. You really are. You may not know it just yet, and you may not notice it until a lot of time has passed and you can look back at who you used to be, but prayer is changing you.

Magnificent. Spend extra time today journaling about how you've grown and changed as you've focused on PRAYER for the past seven weeks and how you might change more over the next month.

Prod

How has your life changed as you've focused on prayer? Your rhythms? Your faith? Your daily time talking with God? Write it all down!

Praise

 Listen to

"Set a Fire"

by Michael W. Smith

Pray

Jesus, I've submitted to your will in my life. Keep changing me as you see fit. I want more of you! I want a fire lit that's so bright and burning so hot that everyone can see your presence in my life. Thank you for what you've done so far in my life. I want more! Amen.

Proclaim

"Do not be anxious about anything, but in every situation, by prayer and petition, with thanksgiving, present your requests to God." (Phil. 4:6)

Prompt

Continuing our discussion about the ways God uses prayer to change us, there's another way in addition to the Grand Canyon-style slow change.

While the Grand Canyon eroded over a scale of geologic time, there are other ways to shape a landscape more quickly. I'm talking about lightning.

And sometimes, just like lightning, God uses our prayers to change us in an instant.

God's going to do what God wants to do; our job is to be ready to let Him do it in our lives, whether that's in an instant like lightning or over a lifetime like the Grand Canyon. *Do you need a dynamic touch from God today?* Do you need a miracle? Do you need an answer?

You can come to God with whatever is on your heart! He loves you and desires to hear from you. Believe enough today to ask for what you need!

Prod

Where in your life do you need a dynamic touch from God? A person? A situation? Sickness? Mental health? Write about it so you can bring it to the Lord during your prayer time.

Praise

 Listen to

"Miracles"

by Jesus Culture

Pray

Jesus, I need you to touch my life today! This is what I am facing [PRAY ABOUT WHAT YOU WROTE DOWN]. Amen.

Proclaim

"Do not be anxious about anything, but in every situation, by prayer and petition, with thanksgiving, present your requests to God." (Phil. 4:6)

Prompt

Back in the Old Testament days, the priests had a particular blessing they'd say over the people, and you can read it in Numbers 6:24-26. Or you can listen to a version of it in today's song, "The Blessing" by Kari Jobe.

This is a great blessing to say as a prayer over others or even over yourself. It goes like this:

May the Lord bless you and keep you.
May the Lord make His face to shine upon you and be gracious to you.
May the Lord turn His face toward you and give you peace.

What a prayer! And it's just as relevant today as it was when it was written.

Be blessed.

Prod

Write down this blessing and whisper it over yourself throughout the day.

Praise

 Listen to

"The Blessing"

by Kari Jobe

Pray

Jesus, thank you for making your face shine upon me! What a glorious image that is. Thank you for loving me so personally. You are my King and my Savior, I dedicate my day to you, Jesus! Amen.

Proclaim

"Do not be anxious about anything, but in every situation, by prayer and petition, with thanksgiving, present your requests to God." (Phil. 4:6)

Prompt

Ours is a culture that doesn't quite honor the virtue of humility anymore, but that's no reason not to have it. Here's what I mean: it's good to be humble.

But just because it's GOOD to be humble, that doesn't mean it's EASY. In fact, it can be pretty darn difficult, just because of who we are! We are self-focused people, so humility is a discipline we usually have to learn, not a default we can just revert to.

Fortunately, *God gave us prayer.* When we pray, we practice lowering ourselves. We practice humility.

This is why we pray on our knees at least once a day. This is why we bow our heads. This is why our posture, our passion, and our tone matters.

We are not God, and when we pray, we remind ourselves of that!

Prod

Define one area of your life where you need to practice humility. Focus on that area during your prayer time this week.

Praise

 Listen to

"Home"

by Jeremy Riddle

Pray

Jesus, I need you to help me be humble. Show me the way to live. Guide me back to you. You are my home. When I am living in you, and you are living in me, I can feel your presence. Fill me with this all day today. I want to feel at home **SO THAT** humility will pour out, love will pour out, and YOU will pour out on those around me. Amen.

Proclaim

"Do not be anxious about anything, but in every situation, by prayer and petition, with thanksgiving, present your requests to God." (Phil. 4:6)

Prompt

How's your attitude? Feeling good? Feeling rotten? Feeling numb? Feeling just kinda... whatever?

Our emotions are a complex part of us, and they aren't always easily swayed. But regardless of how our attitude is, we can bring it more into line with God's will for our lives when we pray.

Prayer changes our attitude, simple as that. When we pray, when we go before God, our hurts can be healed, our snarls can become smiles, and our losses can become laughter.

Don't wait for the situation to get better for your attitude to adjust. Pray first and invite the Holy Spirit to work in you.

Prod

What sorts of attitudes can you stand to see changed in prayer? Make a list and take that list before the Lord.

Praise

 Listen to

"Broken Vessels"

by Hillsong Worship

Pray

Jesus, thank you for being the constant in my life, regardless of how I feel. Let my emotions line up with your will for me today. I give my all to you. Amen.

Proclaim

"Do not be anxious about anything, but in every situation, by prayer and petition, with thanksgiving, present your requests to God." (Phil. 4:6)

Prompt

A lot of words have been written over a lot of years about prayer, but Christian author Anne Lamott contends that there are really only three kinds of prayer, the first of which is Help.

This is one I'm sure you're familiar with—I know I am! The great thing is that God loves to help us, even if we're turning to Him as a last-ditch effort when nothing else has worked. Even then—God loves to help. That's just the kind of God we serve.

But sometimes, even though we need help, we can feel ashamed to ask or embarrassed that we need it. Worse yet, we can hide behind the fear that God doesn't want to help us.

Let me be clear. **God loves to help His children.** He's our Good Shepherd, who leaves the ninety-nine to chase the one gone astray, who found themselves needing **HELP!** Ask Him!

Prod

Today, as you walk through your world today, try to be aware of the times you need HELP from God. In those moments, just ask.

Praise

 Listen to

"Fear Is A Liar"

by Zach Williams

Pray

Jesus, I need your help! I know you'll come through—help me to believe it. I'm committed to bringing all my needs to you TODAY. No fear, no shame, no embarrassment will hold me back. Thank you for your willingness to be there when I need help. Amen.

Proclaim

"Do not be anxious about anything, but in every situation, by prayer and petition, with thanksgiving, present your requests to God." (Phil. 4:6)

Prompt

Yesterday we learned about *Help*, the first kind of prayer according to author Anne Lamott. Today we learn about the second one: *Thanks*.

This is a powerful kind of prayer (and we'll dig deeply into the concept of gratitude later this year) because it places us in a proactive place. ***Instead of asking, we're thanking.***

Sometimes we thank God because of what He's done in our lives. And sometimes we can thank God for what we believe He's going to do in our lives (but hasn't quite yet). Regardless, a posture of gratitude is a powerful one when it comes to prayer.

A posture of Thanks is often displayed by holding your hands out in front of you, with your palms up. As you pray, think about all that God has done for you and receive His love as you give Him praise.

It's powerful.

Prod

What do you need to thank God for? Make a list, turn on today's song, and spend time THANKING God as you pray.

Praise

 Listen to

"I Could Sing Of Your Love"

by Delirious?

Pray

Jesus, thanks for everything. Literally. *Everything.* Thank you for your love and how I feel it when I'm praying to you. Thank you for this song and how its peaceful melody reminds me of the peace you fill my heart with every time I sing to you. Amen.

Proclaim

"Do not be anxious about anything, but in every situation, by prayer and petition, with thanksgiving, present your requests to God." (Phil. 4:6)

Prompt

So we've had *Help*. Then we've had *Thanks*. And now, the final kind of prayer according to author Anne Lamott. This is one that doesn't seem to offer anything in return, but that may be the most important: *Wow*.

It's good to be in awe! It's good to let our hearts and souls be overwhelmed by what we've seen God do in this world, whether it's in our personal lives, in the lives of someone we love, or just the world in general.

God moved on your behalf? *Wow*.
God healed a coworker? *Wow*.
God created the stars you're looking at right now? *Wow*.
God took away your addiction? *Wow*.

Give yourself capacity for awe, and then turn that awe toward the One who made it in the first place.

Prod

When's the last time you felt like saying *Wow* to God? Think of five reasons to say it and pray them as part of your prayer time today.

Praise

 Listen to
"Glorious"
by Jesus Culture

Pray

Jesus: WOW. You are the God of WOW! What you've done in my life is worthy of a WOW. Thank you for seeing me in my most desperate place and seeing fit to save me! You are glorious, you are holy, and the heavens declare that you are worthy. You are WORTHY OF MY WOW! Amen.

Proclaim

"Do not be anxious about anything, but in every situation, by prayer and petition, with thanksgiving, present your requests to God." (Phil. 4:6)

Prompt

Help.
Thanks.
Wow.

Those are the three categories that pretty much every prayer breaks down into.

When you can truly see this, it opens up your prayer life. Because you stop turning to God for one thing or another, and you start to turn to God in a more well-rounded way.

You turn to God for help.
You turn to God for thanks.
You turn to God just because He's God. Wow!

Open up your prayer life and you just might find yourself being transformed in ways you didn't expect. Be intentional with how you spend your time with God and the way you enter this sacred and holy time.

Be thoughtful and aware. Are you seeking help, saying thanks, or sitting in wonder and WOW?

Prod

Which of these three types of prayers do you practice the least? Make an effort to pray that type of prayer more over the next month.

Praise

 Listen to

"Light of the World"

by Jesus Culture

Pray

Jesus, thank you for helping. Thank you for gratitude. Thank you for being you. Please help my prayer life grow with you today. I commit this sacred and holy time to you. Help me see you fully, light up my world, and give me strength to live in your will today. Amen.

Proclaim

"Do not be anxious about anything, but in every situation, by prayer and petition, with thanksgiving, present your requests to God." (Phil. 4:6)

Prompt

One of the things Paul tells us to do in 1 Thessalonians 5 is to *"pray without ceasing."* How can we go about doing that, though? We can't just stay on our knees all day long, right?

I think a way we can accomplish this is to carry an attitude of prayer into the world with us wherever we go. We can sort of put on **"prayer glasses"** and make Jesus the lens through which we view the world.

When we do this, we adjust the way we look at things—now we're seeing them prayerfully. And that can change everything.

Prod

Today, I want you to work really hard on staying in an attitude of prayer ALL DAY. Pray for people you come into contact with, pray for challenging situations, pray when you are in your car, pray right now for your family. In all things today, connect with God and pray.

Praise

 Listen to

"Great Is Our God"

by Young Oceans

Pray

Jesus, thank you for being my sight as I go through the world today. Let me see people as you see them. Let me see the problems the way you do. Let me see my purpose in this world as you do. Let me see through YOU, Jesus. Amen.

Proclaim

"Do not be anxious about anything, but in every situation, by prayer and petition, with thanksgiving, present your requests to God." (Phil. 4:6)

Prompt

Prayer isn't just a way of changing you or changing the world—prayer can also change the way you interact with the world.

What I mean is this: when you develop a lifestyle of prayer, **you begin to notice.**

You notice when people seem off, like they need a helping hand or an encouraging word.

You notice God's creative handiwork in the vein of a leaf or the warmth of a ray of sunshine.

You notice your own self, the way you carry God's love into the world.

Prayer works outwardly. Pray it out!

Prod

Take a notice-heavy attitude into the world with you today, and write down everything you notice. Attitudes, demeanors, body language, spoken language. Review your list at the end of the day and spend time praying for each thing you wrote down.

Praise

 Listen to

"When I Say Jesus"

by Life.Church

Pray

Jesus, let me notice what you would have me notice today, and if I need to, act on what I see. You are my compass, you are my rock, you are the one who fills my heart with joy. Help me to connect with your Holy Spirit today and see things I've never seen before. Amen.

Proclaim

"Do not be anxious about anything, but in every situation, by prayer and petition, with thanksgiving, present your requests to God." (Phil. 4:6)

Prompt

God knows us so much better than we know ourselves. He created us! And not only did He create us, but He created us *the way He created us*. That means He knows what makes you smile, what makes you laugh, what inspires you, what motivates you, and what challenges you. That also means He knows what gets you down, what you are struggling with, and where you need Him to step in.

God is on your team. Sometimes it may feel like you're fighting God, but you never are. He is pushing, pulling, guiding, and steering you to better days. **That is who He is.** That is what He does. He's good!

Knowing this totally opens up the way you pray. If you haven't internalized this truth, you'll pray small prayers rooted in worry and fear that God may not want you to have what you pray for. But once you grab this realization, you will pray unafraid. You'll pray huge prayers, prayers that will change your life AND impact the lives of others!

Prod

When's the last time you prayed unafraid? Commit today to praying huge, life-changing prayers. Write down the biggest, boldest prayer you can think of now.

Praise

 Listen to

"King of My Heart / Pieces / No Longer Slaves"

by Mass Anthem

Pray

Jesus, help me to follow you in praying something huge today because I know that, whatever happens, you're on my side. I claim the victory! Today's song says that you split the seas so I could walk right through them. You are a sea-splitter! **You are GOOD!** And you are FOR me. Today, I ask that [PRAY A BIG PRAYER]. Amen.

Proclaim

"Do not be anxious about anything, but in every situation, by prayer and petition, with thanksgiving, present your requests to God." (Phil. 4:6)

Prompt

For doers like me, trusting God to provide a breakthrough is a tough truth to soak in. I am so ready to credit what I accomplish as evidence of my abilities, my skills, or my strategy. I think, *See that? I did that.* I'm so quick to puff up my chest and walk around like I did something.

But the reality is, on my own, I fall short. I have not provided a solution to any problems, overcome any obstacles, or done anything good on my own—it's all been what God has done *through* me. When I believe the lie that I have done something, then it's only a very short walk to thinking that the breakthroughs I need today can be found through my own strength.

But I can't provide a breakthrough. Only God can! And you know what? That's such a relief. I am so weak on my own. **My strength runs out.** My will gets beaten down. My mind begins to spiral. But when I can fully surrender in prayer and give all my requests to God, then PEACE comes flooding back to me.

And when peace is the foremost feeling in my life, everything makes more sense.

Prod

Do you need to repent of *doing?* Take five minutes today to sit quietly and do absolutely nothing except let God do what He wants in your heart. Fully surrender.

Praise

 Listen to

"Love You More"

by Harvest

Pray

Jesus, sometimes I get so caught up in doing that I forget it's your job to do! Give me the strength to let go today. Fill me with your peace; help me let go of my anxiety. Fill me with joy; help me let go of depression. I give my day to you because you are so great. I love you. Amen.

Proclaim

"Do not be anxious about anything, but in every situation, by prayer and petition, with thanksgiving, present your requests to God." (Phil. 4:6)

Prompt

So many times, our prayers fall short of what God can really do. God loves it when we pray big prayers—when we get to the end of ourselves and admit, "Okay, God, I really need you to take over on this one." God gave you those giant desires, and one reason why is this: so that He can fulfill those desires.

Early in my sobriety, I spent a lot of time praying big prayers. Night after night after night, I prayed and prayed and prayed for what would become Hope is Alive.

The background music for many of these prayer sessions was today's song. I would sit and listen to these words and follow the instructions to **"Come Away"** with God. As I meditated and prayed, God would fill me with hopes and dreams.

It was through those prayer sessions that God developed the vision of what this organization could look like, how it could operate, and what my role would be in the middle of it. I am where I am today—and hundreds of residents and graduates of HIA are where they are today—because of big prayers. What a testimony to God's faithfulness!

Prod

Turn on today's song and **CRANK IT!** As you listen to the lyrics, follow the instructions. Let your heart and mind float away to a place where only God lives. Ask Him to fill you with new dreams, new visions, and new hopes!

Praise

 Listen to

"Come Away"

by Jesus Culture

Pray

Jesus, give me a big, big vision for building your Kingdom on this earth today. Make it as big as the next person I encounter today. Let me share your love with them in a way they can receive it. Thank you for creating a plan just for my life; I receive it today. Amen.

Proclaim

"Do not be anxious about anything, but in every situation, by prayer and petition, with thanksgiving, present your requests to God." (Phil. 4:6)

Prompt

I've had people praying for me for years, in all the forms my life has taken. My mom, my wife, friends, and other relatives... I could go on and on.

These are people who prayed for me not just when I was in the depths of my addiction, but also when I was in treatment, when I was working that first job out of rehab, when I was back at my parents' house, when I was launching Hope is Alive, when I was riding the wave of those first few months, when I was getting a vision for expanding the reach of this ministry, and even today.

Every step of the way, I've had people praying obstinate prayers for me.

I am only alive today because someone was bold enough to pray for me, and God was kind enough to answer them.

Prod

Who is God putting on your heart to pray for? Follow through for the next week and let them know you're praying for them all week. Ask how you can agree with them and see what happens.

Praise

 Listen to

"Hand of God"

by Ernstly Etienne

Pray

Jesus, I just can't believe I get to talk with you like this. Prayer truly is amazing. I claim the victory that you have given me today. Nothing is too hard for you. That's why I commit [NAME A PERSON YOU'RE PRAYING FOR] to you today. May your right hand guide them as they journey out into this world. Help them live a life of boldness, power, and prayer. Amen.

Proclaim

"Do not be anxious about anything, but in every situation, by prayer and petition, with thanksgiving, present your requests to God." (Phil. 4:6)

Prompt

In the last few years, I have had four realizations about prayer that led to some major action on my part, and my faith is so much stronger as a result.

1. I wasn't praying big enough, so I started.
2. I wasn't praying desperately enough, so I started.
3. I wasn't praying often enough, so I started.
4. I was quitting before the miracle, so I stopped.

God can do anything, and part of the anything God can do is this: God wants to do something in your life that you've always thought in the back of your mind was just a dream, something you thought would never come true.

So many of us need God to move in a way that's radical. We need God to do the impossible.

I believe He can and He will!

Prod

Which of these four realizations do you respond the most strongly to? Incorporate it into your prayer journey.

Praise

 Listen to

"Awaken Me"

by Jesus Culture

Pray

Jesus, help me to pray big enough, desperately enough, and often enough, and when I'm almost to the miracle, help me to keep going. Fill my heart with the rhythm of joy that this song has today, Jesus. May my praise be a fragrant offering to you, and may my faithfulness ignite a revival in those I come in contact with. Wake me up today, Jesus! Amen.

Proclaim

"Do not be anxious about anything, but in every situation, by prayer and petition, with thanksgiving, present your requests to God." (Phil. 4:6)

Prompt

God's worked on your behalf before, right? Of course He has—you're reading this devotional.

God will work on your behalf again, right? Of course He will—He's the same today as He was yesterday.

So why not right now?

What do you need in your life? Where do you lack? Where do you hunger or thirst? Why not trust that God will meet you where you are *right now?*

He did it before.

He'll do it again.

Maybe even today, this moment, right now. It starts with your belief, and you exercise your belief when you pray. Do it now.

Prod

Do you feel like anything you're doing is holding God back from working in your life right now? What can you do to adjust that?

Praise

 Listen to

"Why Not Now?"

by Influence Music

Pray

Jesus, I believe you'll act on my behalf today, right now. Show me yourself! I'm asking you to show up in my life and help me through this season. I need a fresh touch, a renewing of my heart, a FIRE LIT in my soul. I need you, Jesus. I need you right now! Amen.

Proclaim

"Do not be anxious about anything, but in every situation, by prayer and petition, with thanksgiving, present your requests to God." (Phil. 4:6)

Prompt

Are you familiar with the concept of the *"breath prayer"*?

It's pretty much what it sounds like: saying a prayer in the space of a single breath. I like breath prayers because they free me from the act of trying to sound especially theological in a moment of prayer.

Breath prayers are a great way to bring prayer into your everyday, workaday world. You can whisper them at work, in line for your morning coffee, while you're reheating your lunch, or whenever.

All it takes is a breath and an open heart. Here are a couple I use daily.

Breathe in: Thank you, God...

Breathe out: ...for everything you've given me

Breathe in: I trust you, God...

Breathe out: ...with my life

Prod

Make a reminder to say ten breath prayers about whatever God leads you to pray today in that moment. Write down a couple of examples you will use, or feel free to use mine.

Praise

 Listen to

"Nothing New"

by Brandon Lake

Pray

Jesus, thank you for being there at the end of this breath and the beginning of the next one. I love you. Amen.

Proclaim

"Do not be anxious about anything, but in every situation, by prayer and petition, with thanksgiving, present your requests to God." (Phil. 4:6)

Prompt

What's your perspective?

When you look at the world outside yourself, how do you perceive it?

Do you see it as angry? Do you see it in pain? Do you see people hurting?

Or do you look at the world through the perspective of prayer? Do you see the things that need to change in order to make the world a better place and commit to praying about those things? Do you see yourself as a potential agent of that change?

I do. And I hope you do as well.

Committing to making the world a better place is not just a thing to say. It's real. God wants to use it. He wants to use ALL of us!

And that ALL begins in prayer. Your commitment to impacting this world and finding your purpose in God's greater plan starts with prayer. And that can start today.

Prod

Take a moment during your prayer time to set a timer for 60 seconds, just listening to God as you ask this question: God, how can I bring your hope and light into my world today?

Praise

 Listen to

"Look To The Lamb"

by Jesus Culture

Pray

Jesus, let me see the world through your prayerful eyes. Give me the strength to act where I need to. Give me the faith to believe that what YOU can do through ME will make a difference. Give me the courage to take my first steps. Amen.

Proclaim

"Do not be anxious about anything, but in every situation, by prayer and petition, with thanksgiving, present your requests to God." (Phil. 4:6)

Prompt

Yesterday we talked about prayer being a perspective on the world. Now, let's turn the lens the other way:

How do you see *yourself* prayerfully? When you look at your own thoughts, desires, and actions, do you look at them through prayer? Do you submit them to God through prayer and ask Him to bless them and keep them in line with His will for your life?

Do you see yourself as an agent of change for your innermost thoughts and desires?

Submit yourself to the Lord in prayer and bring that prayerful perspective to yourself.

Prod

Ask God to give you a prayerful perspective on yourself today. Practice renewing your mind in prayer by focusing on presenting all your needs to God today as soon as you recognize them.

Praise

 Listen to

"Coat of Many Colors"

by Brandon Lake

Pray

Jesus, let me see the world through your prayerful eyes. Give me the clarity today to submit ALL my requests to you. Renew my mind, fill me with wisdom, take my burdens, take my pain... I present everything to you today! Amen.

Proclaim

"Do not be anxious about anything, but in every situation, by prayer and petition, with thanksgiving, present your requests to God." (Phil. 4:6)

Prompt

Prayer can open up the world to you in ways you never before imagined. Regular communion with God through prayer especially opens up the world to become a place of awe.

Prayer taps you into the divine, and once you're there, you see God's handiwork everywhere—especially in the beautiful people He's placed all around you. Every person is a work of art.

And just for the record: that includes *you*, too.

Open your eyes through prayer to see the world with awe, especially the people that surround you. This is how God sees, after all. He sees us all equally beautiful, unique, powerful, gifted, worthy, lovable, precious, and strong.

And again, that includes *YOU!*

Prod

Take the prayer-powered awe mindset into your day. Write reflections throughout the day on what you see that brings you awe.

Praise

 Listen to

"Refresh Me"

by Leeland

Pray

Jesus, show me your awe today. Let me see my fellow humans as your special creations. As I feel your presence in my life today and I see your wonder in the lives of others around me, please refresh me. Amen.

Proclaim

"Do not be anxious about anything, but in every situation, by prayer and petition, with thanksgiving, present your requests to God." (Phil. 4:6)

Prompt

The cornerstone of every good and healthy relationship is simple: time.

You want a good relationship with someone? *You spend time with them.*

You want to know someone deeply? *You spend time with them.*

You want to be able to know someone's character? *You spend time with them.*

You want to learn what a person cares about? *You spend time with them.*

Without the benefit of time deepening your bonds through time spent, that's just a person you kinda know.

I think you probably already know where I'm going with this.

You want a good relationship with God? Spend time with Him... in prayer! Quiet solitude with God is one of the most life-giving and soul-healing times you can give yourself.

Without the benefit of time deepening your bonds, that's just a God you kinda know. And we don't want to KINDA know God, we want to know Him deeply, intimately, fully!

Prod

How much time do you spend with God daily? Is that enough? If so, great! If not, examine your schedule and determine what needs to go so that God can have more of you.

Praise

 Listen to

"Show Me Your Ways"

by Thrive Worship & Leeland

Pray

Jesus, I love you. Speak to me now in this quiet place. Tell me things that only you can. Father, all your ways are good, and I claim that over my life today. Guide me to a deeper understanding of who you are and what you would have for my life. Amen.

Proclaim

"Do not be anxious about anything, but in every situation, by prayer and petition, with thanksgiving, present your requests to God." (Phil. 4:6)

Prompt

If you work out, you know how to build strength: a little bit at a time.

Sometimes those strength-building exercises come easily—you can knock out those pushups, no big deal. And sometimes those strength-building exercises feel a little harder than they usually do—*you struggle to get even half the pushups* you ordinarily would do.

That's just the nature of the game when it comes to getting stronger.

And the same holds true for prayer. Sometimes prayer comes easily; sometimes it's a battle.

The point isn't how easy or hard the exercise is—the point is to do it consistently.

That's when you start building strength.

Prod

How has your prayer life been lately? Easy or difficult? Commit to keeping it up no matter what. Go to God today no matter how you feel and thank Him for His love and His provision in your life, then present all your requests.

Praise

 Listen to

"You're Not Done"

by Leeland & Charity Gayle

Pray

Jesus, thank you for always being right by my side. Thank you for faithfully giving me everything I need in this world. I've struggled, but you've given me strength. I've failed, but you've been there to love me. Today, I pray for the strength to get through this day today and to help me keep praying to you regardless of how I feel about it. Amen.

Proclaim

"Do not be anxious about anything, but in every situation, by prayer and petition, with thanksgiving, present your requests to God." (Phil. 4:6)

Prompt

Happy Birthday to my wife, the Queen.... **Ally Lang**.

God is the Lord of all creation. The earth is His, along with everything in it. Every person, young and old; every living thing, from the single cell to the intricate and complex.

God made my wife. He made her perfectly for me. That doesn't mean she's perfect, but she's perfect for me.

But I don't think this is a cosmic accident. I think finding a partner so perfectly created to be strong when I am weak, to be positive when I am negative, to be kind when I am hateful, to chase after Jesus when I want to run away... is all the product of prayer.

For years, I prayed for my wife. In fact, I wrote a list of qualities, characteristics, gifts and talents that I wanted my wife to possess. And guess what: God did not answer that prayer—He gave me more!

God wants to hear the desires of our hearts. There is nothing you can't take to God. Today, I celebrate my wife, **MY QUEEN**, and how perfect she is for me. Thank you, God, for answering my prayers!

Prod

Is there a partner you need to pray for? A project? A purpose? Take time today to write out specifically what you want and present your requests to God during your prayer time.

Praise

 Listen to

"Living In The Overflow"

by Charity Gayle

Pray

Jesus, today I want to share my heart with you. This is what I really want [SHARE YOUR DESIRES WITH GOD]. Amen.

Proclaim

"Do not be anxious about anything, but in every situation, by prayer and petition, with thanksgiving, present your requests to God." (Phil. 4:6)

Prompt

Even though God is good to us, we often tend to get in our own way. God wants to work in our lives, but sometimes we elbow Him out of the way, close our ears to His voice, and look at the world with our own eyes instead of His.

The good news is that if we seek God, we'll find Him in the small and big of the world we live in. When we pray, we find the strength to let God in and let go of both our idea of control and our passivity.

When we pray and acknowledge God as our ultimate provider, *we right-size ourselves*, finding contentment and, ultimately, joy.

Prod

Are you in God's way? Determine to move out of it!

Praise

 Listen to

"Jireh"

by Maverick City Music

Pray

Jesus, I give up control and give it all to you. You are my provider. You are enough. You are all I need and MORE. Help me to be content in all circumstances, fully embracing you as Jehovah Jireh, my ultimate provider! Amen.

Proclaim

"Do not be anxious about anything, but in every situation, by prayer and petition, with thanksgiving, present your requests to God." (Phil. 4:6)

Prompt

God is all about big ideas, big dreams, big plans. But you know what? He's also the God of the small. "Go big or go home" is a cultural mindset, but for us, it's a choice, and we can choose to go home to God.

Instead of being swayed by the next big thing, when we pray we can find God in the small as well. Because while God loves to work unmistakably big, He also loves to work atomically small.

Like in a handful of loaves or a couple of fish. *Or in you and me.*

God is HOME. Home is where your heart is. Home is where you feel safe. Home is where all your small things have a place. Seek God today in your prayer time as you would your home. Find your joy and peace there with Him.

Prod

What do you have that's small? Offer it to God today so He can magnify it in your life.

Praise

 Listen to

"Home"

by Jeremy Riddle

Pray

Jesus, big or small, you're my home. Thank you for embracing me. Thank you for protecting me. Thank you for letting me be myself. I know I am safe with you. Thank you Jesus for your presence in my life today. Amen.

Proclaim

"Do not be anxious about anything, but in every situation, by prayer and petition, with thanksgiving, present your requests to God." (Phil. 4:6)

Prompt

God's default setting is mercy. Even though He's the King over all, He deals gently with us because that's His nature—even when we turn God's mission to our own self-serving ends.

Mercy means showing compassion to someone who is in trouble, especially when it is within the person's power to punish or harm them. God's mercy is even more powerful than this definition.

God's mercy doesn't just show compassion, it forgives sin! *Sin is forgiven through the mercy of God and the sacrifice of His son Jesus.*

Just like today's song says, I thank God that our freedom was not based on what I have done but on the goodness and mercy of God and the power of Jesus's blood.

As I sit with Jesus in prayer moments, I often think FIRST of God's mercy on my life. I reflect on how I don't deserve anything I've been given, much less to be alive. When I start my prayers speaking through the filter of mercy, everything seems to fall into place.

Prod

Write down ways God has shown you mercy today.

Praise

 Listen to

"Mercy"

by Elevation Worship

Pray

Jesus, thank you for your mercy. Thank you that I have a story to tell of how your mercy saved my life. I rely on you to face today. Thank you for showing your mercy on me and setting me free to be who you've created me to be. Help me make you proud today. Amen.

Proclaim

"Do not be anxious about anything, but in every situation, by prayer and petition, with thanksgiving, present your requests to God." (Phil. 4:6)

Prompt

We can be certain that God is our provider of everything, but even so: it can be easy to forget. We know it in our heads but doubt in our hearts that God provides us everything we need.

There was a time in the Old Testament when the prophet Elijah was starving and prayed that God would just take him to heaven already. You know what God did? He fed Elijah instead.

Sometimes **God answers the prayers of our mouths, and sometimes He answers the prayers of our hearts.** And feeds us anyway.

God's an awesome God that way. He knows our wants and our needs. Our focus verse for this quarter reminds us to bring it ALL to Him in prayer.

Whatever you need to say or ask of God today, do it. He's an awesome God who gives generously and faithfully to His children.

Prod

Are you fed up with God somewhere? That's fine—He can take it! Tell Him about it today.

Praise

 Listen to

"Such An Awesome God"

by Maverick City Music

Pray

Jesus, thanks for feeding me even when I was a punk about it. Thank you for healing my heart when I was embarrassed and humiliated. You're so great. You give and give and give, both what I want and what I need. Thank you for your love! Fill me with it today so I might share it with others! Amen.

Proclaim

"Do not be anxious about anything, but in every situation, by prayer and petition, with thanksgiving, present your requests to God." (Phil. 4:6)

Prompt

Things are not always as they seem. We don't always have a spiritual perspective on what's going on in our lives.

It may look like we're surrounded, but in actuality, we're surrounded by the Lord.

This is the gist of today's powerful, powerful song, **"Surrounded (Fight my Battles)" by UPPERROOM.**

We don't have to get caught up in the way things look because we know we have an Advocate on our side when we go to the Lord in prayer. We can let God fight on our behalf—all we have to do is remember that we are infused with God and that He surrounds us on all sides.

This is how we fight our battles.

Prod

What surrounds you? Look at it through spiritual eyes and look for the Lord instead. He's all around you.

Praise

 Listen to

"Surrounded (Fight my Battles)"

by UPPERROOM.

Pray

Jesus, thank you for surrounding me with your peace, joy, and love. Wrap me in your arms today. Help me to walk in your will with confidence, love, and humility. Amen.

Proclaim

"Do not be anxious about anything, but in every situation, by prayer and petition, with thanksgiving, present your requests to God." (Phil. 4:6)

Prompt

When we pray, we submit to God and give Him the entrance to show us not just how to live, but also that He is *Life Itself*. He frees us to live out of that life, free from anxiety and fear, confident in His promises.

But God does love to see you take the step of faith and give your fears, anxieties, and requests to Him.

I don't know about you, but I've had several bouts of depression throughout my adulthood. Depression is such a tricky illness. It's hard to self-diagnose, so it is rare that we can begin to give it to God as soon as we start to identify the symptoms.

But through the power of prayer and a steady routine of spending time alone with God, we can constantly present all the requests and situations where we find ourselves. As we do this, we are asking God to remove anything holding us back, like depression, before we even start to recognize its impact.

Prod

Write out the signs that might show you that you are heading down a wrong path. Spend time praying over them and asking God to remove all the roots of these struggles, in Jesus' name.

Praise

 Listen to

"What I See"

by Elevation Worship

Pray

Jesus, may I demonstrate you today in all that I think, say, and do. I proclaim today that you are Lord of my life. You died for my sins so that I might live free. Not just feeling good and happy, but fully free! So God please take [NAME A RECURRING STRUGGLE]. I give it all to you and ask that you would keep the devil away from me today and instead fill my heart with your love, your grace, and your joy! Amen.

Proclaim

"Do not be anxious about anything, but in every situation, by prayer and petition, with thanksgiving, present your requests to God." (Phil. 4:6)

Prompt

One of the things prayer breaks us of... is our fallback reliance on the usual, on *"the way things are supposed to be."* Sometimes those things are there for a reason, but sometimes we need prayer to prod us to look deeper and see God beneath our traditions, to see the Why, not just the What.

Prayer works on us in this way, changing us from within, molding our hearts so that our hands will act and our mouths will speak only in love. So that we'll respond to God's Why with our YES.

Prod

What sorts of "usuals" in your life are holding you back? Think about the basics, like food, shows, people, and traditions. Look for God underneath them. Pray for God to reveal what you are relying on that's empty and shallow. Write down what you find.

Praise

 Listen to

"Honey In The Rock"

by Brooke Ligertwood & Brandon Lake

Pray

Jesus, help me see you behind what I'm used to. Show me yourself. Reveal to me WHY I am going through this season of my life. Give me wisdom today so I might learn to rely on you even more for my daily bread. Amen.

Proclaim

"Do not be anxious about anything, but in every situation, by prayer and petition, with thanksgiving, present your requests to God." (Phil. 4:6)

Prompt

It's no secret: this is a crazy world we inhabit. It can get loud, but as we go through the busy-ness of living, prayer gives us ears to hear God calling through the chaos.

Tuning into God's wavelength like this helps us hold this life loosely, with open hands, always ready to receive whatever He chooses to give us. This is why reserving time to just be alone with God is so important.

In one recent year, I took two separate three-day SOLO retreats. On these retreats, I tried my best to do only what the Holy Spirit told me to do. I would ask and He would answer.

What to do... What to eat... What to read... How to exercise.

It didn't matter what it was: if I felt the Holy Spirit telling me to do, read it, pray it, sing it... I DID IT!

As the days went on, my ability to hear God speak, to tune into His wavelength, got better and better. And the revelations got stronger and stronger!

I learned that I must take these times to quiet the noise of my life, to remove myself from the business, and focus only on God.

Prod

Find a quiet place to pray in the midst of your chaos today. What do you hear? Make a note of it and hold it close.

Praise

 Listen to

"Lost In Your Love"

by Brandon Lake & Sarah Reeves

Pray

Jesus, help me to hear you. Speak to me. I'm listening. Amen.

Proclaim

"Do not be anxious about anything, but in every situation, by prayer and petition, with thanksgiving, present your requests to God." (Phil. 4:6)

Prompt

God loves words. I don't know if you've noticed that or not, but He does. At the beginning of it all, God spoke and everything was. In the Garden of Gethsemane and at the cross, *Jesus only said the words that would get Him killed.*

This is why it's important to choose our words in God's wisdom and to hold our tongues in peace, letting them loose only when necessary. We can pray for life and then model that by speaking life and only life when we're out in the world.

Is that a tall order? Sure. But God is more than capable. And because He is capable, YOU are capable. You can be a truth-teller, a hope dealer, a grace-giver, a messenger of mercy, and a beacon of light.

You can speak words that set people free. It can happen. But it starts with honestly admitting where you are with this and asking God to prune you, preserve you, and protect you!

Prod

How are your words lately?

Are you speaking as Jesus spoke?

What are your favorite words Jesus spoke?

Take an inventory of the life-giving words you speak today and ask God to help you increase it tomorrow.

Praise

 Listen to

"Reign Above It All"

by Bethel Music

Pray

Jesus, guide me in my words today. Help me have wisdom in all I say. You reign above all things. You are the King of my life, but sometimes I act like I am. I use words as weapons and I hurt people. Jesus, please forgive me! Please remove the darkness from my life and wash me white as snow. Amen.

Proclaim

"Do not be anxious about anything, but in every situation, by prayer and petition, with thanksgiving, present your requests to God." (Phil. 4:6)

Prompt

Does your heart stir for injustice? Have you ever been inspired to make a difference?

I know I have. It first hit me when I was in rehab during the summer of 2011. God activated this fire in my spirit during a specific moment of prayer. As I knelt next to my twin bed, with tears streaming down my face, I pleaded with God to understand why I was where I was... but importantly: WHAT WAS NEXT?

He quietly answered, *"Lance, I've called you to make an impact."*

Yesterday we talked about God's words; today it's time to talk about our own. Because sometimes we need to speak! We can see areas where those who cannot speak for themselves need an advocate to expose the corruption of this world and call forth salvation, redemption, and resurrection.

But we can't speak those words without first speaking words to God in prayer. If we want our hearts to be alight with Holy Fire to call out injustice where we see it, to make an impact, we must be people of prayer. That's how we can bring restoration and be the unpredictable fire of healing in a cold and calculated world.

If you want to be an agent for change, it starts with prayer. Dedicated, sincere, alone time with God, seeking His face and His will.

Prod

Where do you see a need in this world? Somewhere that needs your voice? Pray over that need and ask God for the words you need to speak, when you need to speak them.

Praise

 Listen to

"Fresh Fire"

by Maverick City Music

Pray

Jesus, let me speak with your wisdom today. Give me courage to speak up when I need to. Fill me with a fresh fire today. Amen.

Proclaim

"Do not be anxious about anything, but in every situation, by prayer and petition, with thanksgiving, present your requests to God." (Phil. 4:6)

Prompt

When we look at our lives, it is so easy to get swept up in the **now**. In the daily struggle, in the planning for today, for tomorrow, the next year, the next five years.

But God is a Forever God, so it helps to take a step back and pray for His eternal perspective, to let it be the engine behind our everyday choices. When we pray for that perspective, we can then revel in God's eternal present and begin to grasp what C.S. Lewis called God's "unbounded now."

Ask God for His eternal perspective and see how that might change your plans for today and for tomorrow.

Spend more time today writing and praying than you did yesterday.

Prod

What are your future plans? Let your mind go and just write.

During your prayer time, submit them to God's unbounded now, one at a time.

Praise

 Listen to

"Make Room"

by Community Music

Pray

Jesus, thank you for journeying with me yesterday, today, and forever. Thank you for knowing the beginning from the end. You know my heart and have seen everything I just wrote down. I invite you to completely consume my plans. Make them YOUR plans. Take my will and knit it tightly to yours. I trust you and only want what you would have for me... today, tomorrow, and in the future. Amen.

Proclaim

"Do not be anxious about anything, but in every situation, by prayer and petition, with thanksgiving, present your requests to God." (Phil. 4:6)

Prompt

God is a God of mercy. Even though we often relive our suffering week after week and day after day, God is still merciful. Those personal, private, painful wounds we bear in silence? He hears them. And He heals them.

This is the power of prayer. We can bring those to our community, from the prayer warriors to those who call it a victory just making it through the day. We can carry one another's burdens in prayer and, in so doing, show God's mercy to one another.

Today I want you to practice carrying another's burdens. To spend actual time praying for someone else. We must practice this, building the rhythm of our knees hitting the floor and our hearts extending to others. We must work to get our eyes constantly off of our pains and to begin to lift them to see others.

This is a practice of prayer that will change your heart.

Prod

Whose burdens do you need to carry?

Who in your life is hurting right now?

Who is in trouble?

Who is lost and searching?

Praise

 Listen to

"His Mercy Is More"

by Matt Boswell & Matt Papa

Pray

Jesus, thank you for those who carry my burdens. Help me to be a good burden-carrier, too. Today, I want to pray for [NAME SOMEONE WHOSE BURDENS YOU WISH TO CARRY AND HOW YOU WANT TO CARRY THEM.] Amen.

Proclaim

"Do not be anxious about anything, but in every situation, by prayer and petition, with thanksgiving, present your requests to God." (Phil. 4:6)

Prompt

The thing about prayer is that none of it takes God by surprise. He knows our transgressions already, and yet He still awaits us, a patient listener as we pour out all our complaints and the things that make us crazy!

But He doesn't stop at just listening. He brings tranquility to turmoil. He brings harmony to havoc. **He brings PEACE to pain.**

And where there is nothing, He fills it with His everything. Doesn't that feel good to know? When you are depleted, GOD can fill you. Where you are lonely, God can comfort you. Where you made a mistake, God's grace is enough to free you from any guilt or shame.

But He wants to hear from you. He wants to heal you. He wants to hear your confession and all your complaints. Give them to God today.

Prod

What are you holding back from God? Journal about it and give it to Him.

Praise

 Listen to

"YET"

by Maverick City Music

Pray

Jesus, thanks for listening. I believe you heal me—every part of me. Today I want to tell you what I'm upset about. I want to express my concerns. I want to tell you what's hurting me. And I ask that you would begin to heal me and make me new. Amen.

Proclaim

"Do not be anxious about anything, but in every situation, by prayer and petition, with thanksgiving, present your requests to God." (Phil. 4:6)

Prompt

Do you ever think about how God is so patient with us in our prayers? We come to Him with our limited imagination, thinking it's the sum total of the world, and He just looks back at us with kind eyes and says, "You don't know what you're asking."

When we're overzealous, He graciously reins us in, even while being pleased with our enthusiasm. When we're lackadaisical, He tenderly spurs us on while being gratified with our perseverance.

When we need a door to open, **He quietly opens it.** When we need a door to close, He *can slam it shut.*

But sometimes our world is so LOUD that we can barely hear from God, and when we do, we sometimes think we hear Him through a critiquing voice of someone who used to hurt us, shame us, or was just rude to us.

That's not God. God loves YOU. He will give to you what you need, but sometimes to receive it fully, it requires you to get quiet and listen.

Prod

Reflect on times when God lovingly corrected your attitude. Write them down with gratitude.

Praise

 Listen to

"Quiet"

by Hillside Recording

Pray

Jesus, guide my prayers. Help me quiet my mind. I want to trust you with my future and with my day today. Thank you for walking with me. Cut out the distractions of my life today and help me to just hear from you. As I sit here in the quiet, fill my mind with your voice. Amen.

Proclaim

"Do not be anxious about anything, but in every situation, by prayer and petition, with thanksgiving, present your requests to God." (Phil. 4:6)

Prompt

"Do not be anxious." How can we obey this command? Perhaps we can do it through a prayer of calm and peace. Try praying this prayer today and see if it helps with any anxiety you might feel:

God of Light,
We cannot make you love us more;
We cannot make you love us less.
So we are content to serve you,
wherever You would have us.

Where we need light, show us the way;
where we need hope, send us help;
where we need healing, be our balm.
All this we ask through Jesus Christ, Our Lord.
Amen.

Prod

Pray this prayer three times today.

Praise

 Listen to

"Praise Him Forever"

by Jervis Campbell

Pray

Jesus, here's a bonus prayer, just to say how much I love you. Thank you, thank you, thank you. Amen.

Proclaim

"Do not be anxious about anything, but in every situation, by prayer and petition, with thanksgiving, present your requests to God." (Phil. 4:6)

Prompt

Where else can we go but God? In all situations, He listens.

When all seems lost and when our lives are upended by choices we've made or choices others have made without us, God cares for us, fashioning us into His continual family.

HE KEEPS HOPE ALIVE.

When all seems well, when our lives are smooth, harvests are bountiful, and all our loved ones are healthy, God reminds us of those He loves whose lives are not the same.

HE KEEPS HOPE ALIVE.

When we see mental health, homelessness, financial lack, and complete upheaval in those we love and all around our world.

HE KEEPS HOPE ALIVE.

Against all logic, God keeps HOPE alive in the hearts of those who seek Him in prayer.

Prod

When's the last time you prayed for the hungry, the imprisoned, the blind, the stranger, the orphan, or the widow? When's the last time you asked God to fill you with a new HOPE? Do so today.

Praise

 Listen to

"You Keep Hope Alive"

by Jon Reddick

Pray

Jesus, renew my hope today as I pray. Amen.

Proclaim

"Do not be anxious about anything, but in every situation, by prayer and petition, with thanksgiving, present your requests to God." (Phil. 4:6)

Prompt

Sometimes it's good just to pray a simple prayer of love. We often think about how much we love God, but we may not say it. Even though He knows our innermost thoughts, it still feels right to say, *"I love you."*

And then it's good to demonstrate that love.
To love God with all our hearts, even when our hearts are wayward and fickle.
To love God with all our souls, even when our souls are troubled and despondent.
To love God with all our might, even when our might is weak and sore.
To love God with all our mind, even when our minds are divided and despairing.

As we close out this season focused on prayer, pour out your heart to God.

Pray. Love. Trust.

Prod

Tell God how much you love Him today. Multiple times today. Make it a practice when you see something that reminds you of His love for you, tell Him!

Praise

 Listen to

"Heaven Is Where You Are"

by Erik Nieder

Pray

Jesus, I love you! Simple as that. I love you! I really do. Amen.

Proclaim

"And the peace of God, which transcends all understanding, will guard your hearts and your minds in Christ Jesus." (Phil. 4:7)

Prompt

Today is our first day beginning to focus on **PEACE.** As you just read, our verse for the next 90 days has changed as well.

Peace is one of my favorite words. Just saying it oftentimes connects my soul to God. But because peace is often associated with serenity, we tend to think of it as something that comes to us. Like, if you want peace, you should just sit still and meditate all day.

But that's not true. Like, at all.

Peace takes action. *A ton of it.*
Peace is the fruit of labor. *Mountains of it.*

Peace is found on the side of tough conversations.
Peace is found when you actively listen and apply what your spouse, boss, or mentor asks.
Peace is found when you simply accept what God asks you to do—and then do it.
Peace is found when you make good on the promises you make to yourself.
Peace is found when you look for it.

Peace is the result of taking proactive steps to clear your heart and invite God to fill you.

Prod

What actions are you taking today to find peace?

Praise

 Listen to

"No Longer Slaves"

by Bethel Music

Pray

Jesus, thank you that the promises of today's song ring true. I am no longer a slave to fear. Please guide my steps and the work of my hands, my heart, and my mind to seek peace today. Because I know when I look for it with your eyes, I'll find it. Amen.

Proclaim

"And the peace of God, which transcends all understanding, will guard your hearts and your minds in Christ Jesus." (Phil. 4:7)

Prompt

It's tempting to ignore difficult conversations that need to be had or situations that weigh heavily on us. It's easier to just expect them to go away on their own and call that "hope."

But that's not hope. That's bad strategy and an invitation for peace-blockers.

Peace comes when we acknowledge something isn't right, take steps to protect ourselves and our feelings, and let go of whatever blocks peace from reaching us.

Peace is: texting someone you need to forgive.

Peace is: picking up the phone and apologizing when you were wrong.

Peace is: setting a boundary and not allowing certain persons or groups of people to be in your life anymore.

Peace moves heavy into our life when *we remove the peace-blockers.* But those peace-blockers won't magically float away—you have to be proactive in letting them go and guarding the peace God has given you.

Prod

Who or what is blocking your peace? What steps can you take to remove the peace-blocker(s) in your life?

Praise

 Listen to

"More Than Able"

by Elevation Worship

Pray

Jesus, thank you for being my peace. Show me the peace-blockers in my life and give me the courage to let go of them so I can guard your gracious gift of peace. Amen.

Proclaim

"And the peace of God, which transcends all understanding, will guard your hearts and your minds in Christ Jesus." (Phil. 4:7)

Prompt

Everyone gets off course sometimes. When that happens in my life, you know what recenters me and restores my peace?

Helping others. Serving others. Encouraging others.

Each time I answer the phone to a hurting mother of an addict or step on stage to share my story, I always walk away from the encounter so much more peaceful.

There's something about helping others that brings out God in such a tangible and real way, as if God sends you peace as a blessing.

It's no wonder that a lot of addicts love serving others and do it religiously. Each time you serve, you get a little stronger, a little more confident, and a whole lot more peaceful.

I know there's someone on your mind right now that you can serve today. Do it.

Prod

Who can you serve today? How will you do it?

Praise

 Listen to

"Rescue"

by High Street Worship

Pray

Jesus, thank you for the blessing of peace. Show me how I can be a help to others today, and give me the strength to act. I want to be used by you today to help someone else. Please show me how. Thank you for loving me! Amen.

Proclaim

"And the peace of God, which transcends all understanding, will guard your hearts and your minds in Christ Jesus." (Phil. 4:7)

Prompt

Today is a day we celebrate a country's freedom, but an even more important freedom is the freedom we have in Christ. He gave himself to the chains of death so that we might receive the *freedom of life!*

Jesus wants to deliver every prisoner, whether they're captive to power-hungry regimes, money-hungry traffickers, or self-hungry desires.

And so, on this day we celebrate freedom in the USA, let's renew our commitment to being ambassadors of God's freedom, letting Him guide our every step, confident in the calling He's put on our lives and willing to do whatever we can to help others experience what we have.

Prod

Post on social media about the freedom you've found in your relationship with Jesus. Share with boldness and bravery.

Praise

 Listen to

"Fear Is Not My Future"

by Maverick City Music

Pray

Jesus, thank you for freeing me from the chains of sin and death! Thank you that FEAR is not my future. That bondage is not my future. That shame is not my future. You've set me free to live in peace and joy today. I rejoice! I claim my victory over sin, and I pray you would use my boldness to help others find this same freedom. Amen.

Proclaim

"And the peace of God, which transcends all understanding, will guard your hearts and your minds in Christ Jesus." (Phil. 4:7)

Prompt

"The peace of God will guard your hearts and minds."

What does that mean?

Think of guards on vigil, like those at Buckingham Palace. **Always on alert,** *always ready.*

When we pray, Jesus gives us a shield of peace just like that.

Peace can be a guard. When the world rises up against us, peace can be the shield that rebukes it, ready to work whether you are or not. Because we can rest in the peaceful knowledge that we are in God's hands and that God's plans are better than ours.

That's a guard like no other.

Prod

Take a moment to visualize Jesus holding a shield in front of you, on each side and behind you. He's got you! What a feeling!

Now, write out what Jesus is guarding you against lately.

Praise

 Listen to

"Prince of Peace"

by Hillsong United

Pray

Jesus, thank you for your peace in my life. Thank you for meeting me every time I seek you. Thank you for a peace that guards my heart, my mind, and my eyes. Thank you for having my back and walking by my side. You are my Prince of Peace. I love you. I trust you. Amen.

Proclaim

"And the peace of God, which transcends all understanding, will guard your hearts and your minds in Christ Jesus." (Phil. 4:7)

Prompt

How have you been sleeping lately?

Sleep is critical. It's a life requirement.

You can't live without sleep, even though someone tried for awhile—they lasted just over eleven days and set a world record.

That sounds insane to me! I'm a wreck after one all-nighter or overseas flight. I can't imagine who I would be after eleven days!

Sleep is a tangible act of transcendent peace. Even if you're only getting a couple of hours each night, even if your sleep is troubled by nightmares or some other disruption, every time you sleep, you are practicing peace.

Perhaps you can practice resting in **God's peace** a little longer the next time you lie down.

One way that's helped me fall into **God's peace** before I completely fall asleep is the 4-7-8 breathing technique, with a slight "LL" modification. Let's practice it!

Prod

Close your mouth and quietly inhale through your nose to a mental count of four. Hold your breath for a count of seven. Exhale through your mouth, whisper "God I trust you" for a count of eight. Repeat the process three more times for a total of four breath cycles.

Praise

 Listen to

"Hosanna"

by The Belonging Co.

Pray

Jesus, I thank you for the gift of sleep. Thank you for providing for me wherever I have lack, including in my sleep. Guard my sleeping and guard my waking. Amen.

Proclaim

"And the peace of God, which transcends all understanding, will guard your hearts and your minds in Christ Jesus." (Phil. 4:7)

Prompt

What do you do when old thoughts, old temptations, and old traumas come back to you? I've had this happen recently. I thought I had dealt with one particular issue, only to have it show up again in my mind, trying to steal my peace.

And when I say "particular issue," *I mean one particular PERSON!* You know the one. The one who hurt you, blindsided you, did something that's tough to forgive and near impossible to forget?

Do you have that person in mind now?

What's really helped me is our verse for this quarter. Speaking this biblical truth out loud over and over: "And the peace of God..." "And the peace of God..."

Slowly, this has helped take away the sting and fill my heart with love and hope to press on.

I can't always control the thoughts, temptations, or traumas that try to rear their ugly heads, but I can control the truth I speak over myself each morning. The truth that the peace of God, which transcends all understanding, will guard my heart and my mind in Christ Jesus.

Let it be so, Lord. Let it be with THAT person... In Jesus' Name.

Prod

Practice the peace process now. Say this out loud: "And the peace of God, GUARDS MY HEART & MIND!"

Praise

 Listen to

"Better Word"

by Leeland

Pray

Jesus, I'm so grateful that you guard my heart with your peace. Remind me of it when my past tries to come back to haunt me. You're so good. Amen.

Proclaim

"And the peace of God, which transcends all understanding, will guard your hearts and your minds in Christ Jesus." (Phil. 4:7)

Prompt

The devil is a liar. Always.

It's not just a one-time, black-hole-moment type of lying. He's an every day, all day, any way he can, using anyone he can kind of liar.

That's why we must start today and every day by reciting our scripture. So let's practice doubling down on the *"peace process"* we learned yesterday.

Take the time to remind yourself in your head and your heart that, no matter the situation you give to God, His gift back is peace.

When you take action on this good news and present your struggles, your pain, your worries, your decisions, the people who bother you, the issues you don't understand, the deal that won't close, the kid who keeps making bad decisions—ALL OF IT—God gives you back a big deep breath full of peace.

Prod

Take in God's peace with a big deep breath, then breathe out all of the situations and struggles you are facing today. Say this out loud as you breathe out: "And the peace of God, GUARDS MY HEART & MIND!"

Praise

 Listen to

"Tremble"

by Mosaic MSC

Pray

Jesus, I'm so grateful that you make the darkness tremble. That you give peace in the midst of chaos. That you bring hope when we find ourselves stuck in despair. Your shoulders are broad enough to carry all my burdens. Thank you for filling me with PEACE today. Amen.

Proclaim

"And the peace of God, which transcends all understanding, will guard your hearts and your minds in Christ Jesus." (Phil. 4:7)

Prompt

Everything you have, every good gift you've received—it's all God's.

When you give your life back to God, you're not giving God anything you've earned. You're just giving back what was already His.

I find great peace in this truth. Because it takes the pressure off. None of this is on me. ***It's all on Him.***

Every interaction with every person, every word I write, every phone call I take, every text message I send—those are God's gifts, and I'm just giving them back to Him.

And in return, God gives me peace. Peace that transcends all understanding.

Prod

What can you give back to God today? Remember, you don't have to carry it all, just give it up and get some PEACE!

Praise

 Listen to

"For All My Life"

by TAYA

Pray

Jesus, I'm blown away by your gifts. Help me to see them for what they are and then give me strength to give them back to you. I turn to you. I turn to you. I TURN TO YOU! I'm letting go and trusting you with everything. Thank you for carrying my burdens today! Amen.

Proclaim

"And the peace of God, which transcends all understanding, will guard your hearts and your minds in Christ Jesus." (Phil. 4:7)

Prompt

There is immense power in just the name of Jesus.

And there is peace within God's presence.

Today's song, *"I Speak Jesus" by Charity Gayle,* gets at this truth from the very beginning, reminding us that the name of Jesus is above all names and that when we find ourselves in a place other than a peaceful one, we can call on that name and retreat to God's presence to find the peace we need.

There's power over fear.
Power over depression and anxiety.
Power over addiction and insecurity.
Power over everything that troubles us in our hearts and minds.

Just call on His name and retreat to His presence.

If you need a surge of peace today. **Ask for it!**
If you need healing today. **Ask for it!**
If you need a stronghold broken. **Ask for it!**

Just call on His name and retreat to His presence.

Prod

What line(s) from the song "I Speak Jesus" speak to you today? Jot them down and ponder them.

Praise

 Listen to

"I Speak Jesus"

by Charity Gayle

Pray

Jesus, your name is so powerful. Remind me of that truth and help me declare your name over my life. Amen.

Proclaim

"And the peace of God, which transcends all understanding, will guard your hearts and your minds in Christ Jesus." (Phil. 4:7)

Prompt

"Every faculty you have, your power of thinking or of moving your limbs from moment to moment, is given you by God. If you devoted every moment of your whole life exclusively to His service you could not give Him anything that was not in a sense His own already."

What C.S. Lewis wrote in *Mere Christianity* back in 1952 still has resonance today. Because there's an immense peace that comes when we wake up to the fact that our every breath is a gift God has given to us.

And there's an even greater peace when we commit to the not-so-radical notion of giving those breaths—**and the life they indicate**—right back to God for His service.

Experience peace. Give back. It was never yours anyway.

Prod

What parts of your life are you keeping for yourself today?

How can you give those back to God?

Praise

 Listen to

"Yahweh"

by Elevation Worship

Pray

Jesus, thank you for giving me life and for the peace that comes with it. Help me serve you with every part of me today. Take my breath and use it, take my mind and use it, take my heart and use it, take my mouth and use it, take my hands and use them! They're all yours! USE ME! Amen.

Proclaim

"And the peace of God, which transcends all understanding, will guard your hearts and your minds in Christ Jesus." (Phil. 4:7)

Prompt

Surrender is a complicated concept—until it isn't.

Let me explain: as an addict, I surrendered a lot of things. I surrendered my money, my relationships, and my very life so I could get a temporary high. This is a complicated kind of surrender that requires a lot of self-convincing and deviousness.

In recovery, I found that peace comes through an entirely different kind of surrender: *a surrender to God's will and to the love of Jesus.*

This is a simple surrender, the kind that just looks at Jesus and says, "Not my will but yours be done."

It was a shift in my heart from me to HIM. A change from everything being run through a selfish filter to now looking at the world *self-LESS-ly.*

And that's where we find peace, leaving behind the complicated surrender of selfishness for the simple surrender of following Jesus.

Prod

What parts of your life do you still need to surrender? Get honest right now!

How can you trade those for peace today?

Praise

 Listen to

"Resurrender"

by Hillsong Worship

Pray

Jesus, thank you for making me capable of surrender. When I want to hold on to the old me, give me strength to surrender to you. Take away my sinful, selfish, self-centered motivations and fill me with your love and peace. Help me get my eyes off me and onto you. I surrender all to you today. Amen.

Proclaim

"And the peace of God, which transcends all understanding, will guard your hearts and your minds in Christ Jesus." (Phil. 4:7)

Prompt

Turn on today's song as you read today's prompt.

When's the last time you really thought about the miracle that is breathing?

Take a moment to breathe. Really breathe. Close your eyes (after you read this sentence, obviously), and take a slow, deep breath, in through your nose and out through your mouth. Feel your lungs inflate, feel the air rush through your nasal passages, feel the expansion of your chest.

All of that is A MIRACLE.

It's a miracle we all take for granted.

But the greater miracle is the supernatural transfer of peace in our lives and in our hearts through our breath. Because as our song today reminds us, with each breath we take, our lungs fill with the presence of God, our bodies are filled with the daily bread we **desperately** need, and our soul is encouraged by the words the Holy Spirit speaks to us.

YES! All of that within a single breath!

The next time you're in need of peace, the next time you are in need of God's presence, PAUSE whatever you're doing and focus on the miracle of your next breath. And the next one.

Prod

Did you do the breathing exercise mentioned above? Set a timer for three minutes and just focus on your breathing, thanking God the entire time for each breath.

Praise

 Listen to

"Breathe"

by Michael W. Smith

Pray

Jesus, thank you for the breath that fills my lungs and brings me life. It reminds me of you. I am desperate for you today. Amen.

LANCE LANG

Proclaim

"And the peace of God, which transcends all understanding, will guard your hearts and your minds in Christ Jesus." (Phil. 4:7)

Prompt

Even though our pasts are in the past, the effects of our past actions can linger far into the future. This is a universal truth, not just a truth for those with addiction, legal troubles, or marriage issues, but for all people with ALL issues.

Which means YOU.

Those of us who are addicts learn on our recovery journey that it is good and necessary to make amends for those we've hurt in our past. But you know what's neither good nor necessary? Beating ourselves up for our past mistakes.

We need to *learn* from our mistakes, yes. But we don't need to *relive* those mistakes, and we definitely don't need to *continually punish ourselves* for those mistakes.

Instead, we find peace when we let go. You aren't meant to hold them anyway—that's Jesus' job. You're a new creation! The old you has gone away! Let it stay back there, in the crucified arms of Jesus, and move forward in peace today.

Prod

What past mistakes are you still holding? Get on your knees this morning, lay out what you need to let go of, and ask Jesus to cast them as far as the east is to the west!

Praise

 Listen to

"Arms of Jesus"

by Cade Thompson

Pray

Jesus, show me where I'm not trusting you enough with my past. Today, I give you everything that I'm struggling to let go of, including [NAME WHAT YOU NEED TO LET GO OF]. Amen.

Proclaim

"And the peace of God, which transcends all understanding, will guard your hearts and your minds in Christ Jesus." (Phil. 4:7)

Prompt

You know what makes me anxious? Regret.

You know what brings me peace? Acceptance.

Peace comes when I accept that everything Jesus did on the cross is enough. Peace comes when I accept that there's nothing I can do better, *no harder I can work*, no level I can achieve where Jesus will love me more than He already does and already has.

When my identity is rightly placed, rightly sized, and rightly prioritized—inside Jesus—*peace floods my soul*.

In the light of that peace, my regrets fall away. I might still need to make amends, I might still make mistakes, I might still have behaviors that can be improved. BUT, I can live from a place of health and wholeness, from a deep, peaceful understanding that I am loved fully and completely by my Savior.

Prod

What do you regret? Write it down and then prayerfully put it in the arms of Jesus.

Praise

 Listen to

"You Say"

by Lauren Daigle

Pray

Jesus, your peace is everything to me. Help me to rest in my place of peace in your arms and in your will. I want to believe what you say about me. Help me to find my worth in you, my identity in you, my strength in you, my calling in you, and my HOPE in you Jesus. Amen.

Proclaim

"And the peace of God, which transcends all understanding, will guard your hearts and your minds in Christ Jesus." (Phil. 4:7)

Prompt

Struggles make us stronger.

Not long ago, I felt God take me on a journey of pain, but I trusted He had a purpose. He saw me through my suffering, and it made me stronger. Here's something I wrote at the time:

"I'm often confused and hurt, but you comfort and heal. God, you sent your Holy Spirit to walk with me, encourage me, build me, and comfort me. Today I need it more than ever. When I get knocked down, PULL ME BACK UP! I know I get stronger through the struggle. I need your presence today, your power today, your protection today, your provisions today. *I NEED YOU.*"

I was stronger after that struggle. And then when the next struggle came, I had peace, because I knew it would make me stronger, just like last time.

If you are in a struggle right now, I promise God will pull you through. Give it to Him today and grab hold of the peace that comes when you know that, by God's power, your struggles will make you stronger,

Prod

What's your greatest struggle today? How is God using that struggle to make you stronger? Take peace in that.

Praise

 Listen to

"Upper Room"

by Hillsong United

Pray

Jesus, thank you for staying right with me throughout all my struggles. Strengthen me in this one and in the next one. Amen.

Proclaim

"And the peace of God, which transcends all understanding, will guard your hearts and your minds in Christ Jesus." (Phil. 4:7)

Prompt

Sometimes peace can only come when we come fully to the end of ourselves. Take this journal entry I wrote a few months ago:

"God, fortify my faith. Help me believe the invisible and feel the intangible. I choose to trust you 100% with my life. I know this will come with testing, and I am ready. I choose to seek you with all my heart. I believe you will restore my peace, heal my mind, and make me something new. My only hope is in you and I know you will never fail."

As you can tell, I was in need when I wrote that, and the thing I needed most was the ***PEACE THAT COMES FROM COMING TO THE END OF MYSELF*** and surrendering, once again, completely to the Lord.

For me, this happens most profoundly when I get away with God. It's in these times of soulful solitude, when I can pour out my heart to Jesus and ask Him to refill me, where real transformation happens.

Prod

Have you come to the end of yourself today? What do you need to surrender today? As you listen to today's song, think about how you can get away with God. Even today!

Praise

 Listen to
"Getaway"
by TAYA

Pray

Jesus, thank you for meeting me at the end of myself and for taking over from there. Help me rely entirely on you today. Amen.

Proclaim

"And the peace of God, which transcends all understanding, will guard your hearts and your minds in Christ Jesus." (Phil. 4:7)

Prompt

Bitterness is a weight that holds you back and keeps you down. It's an anchor that ties you to your pain and keeps a mask over your face. That's why it's so important to learn to forgive.

Your pain may have been inflicted by another person or it may have been the result of your own choices, but either way, you have to forgive. I know it's hard. I know it can feel like giving up or letting the other person win.

I also know that **forgiveness is necessary for peace, happiness, and hope.**

When you forgive, you're acknowledging the power of your pain, you're recognizing what it is doing within you, and you're intentionally cutting off that power in order to get out of that debilitating cycle you're stuck in. Forgiveness brings freedom with it, but sometimes to get there you have to forgive over and over again, probably for the rest of your life.

Prod

Is there anyone in your life you need to forgive (again) today? As you listen to today's song, think about how much YOU'VE been forgiven. That might help you as you work to forgive others.

Praise

 Listen to

"Forgiven"

by Crowder

Pray

Jesus, thank you for your grace for me. Thank you for forgiving ME! Help me to forgive [NAME A PERSON (OR YOURSELF)] today. I give them to you; let me walk with open hands throughout the rest of my day. Amen.

Proclaim

"And the peace of God, which transcends all understanding, will guard your hearts and your minds in Christ Jesus." (Phil. 4:7)

Prompt

As an addict in recovery, I still have strong tendencies toward depression, anxiety, and general discontentedness. **SO HOW DO I MAINTAIN PEACE?**

One peace-giving remedy I have found to help counteract depression, ruminating thoughts, and honestly, just general negativity, is exercise. I've found that a good beat down of my body keeps me balanced.

I discovered very early on in my recovery process how much I actually enjoyed running. It's a great way to clear your mind, and it's an easy, cheap, healthy way to still get high (*a runner's high, that is!*).

I love it, so I make sure to get a few miles in each week.

Peace is something you have to work for sometimes, and connecting with God through balance and exercise is a great way to do that work.

Today's song is a great one to crank up, get outside, and exercise. It doesn't matter what you do really—just get outside today, see God's wonder in nature and through your body, and seek PEACE!

Prod

How can you get outside today and get your body moving?

Praise

 Listen to

"Wonder"

by Hillsong United

Pray

Jesus, I need your peace. Guide me toward healthy ways to achieve that peace today. Let me run my race for you! Amen.

Proclaim

"And the peace of God, which transcends all understanding, will guard your hearts and your minds in Christ Jesus." (Phil. 4:7)

Prompt

Think of your life as a beautiful, peace-filled mansion. A place where you feel at ease, serene, and comfortable. It's taken you a long time to build this mansion. Many years of heartache, worldly trouble, and fraught relationships may have threatened it, but you finally did it. You worked hard, tried some new tactics, and were able to construct a place where you finally feel at peace.

But every morning you look out the window and see robbers waiting outside, just hoping to catch you at a weak moment so they can invade your mansion and steal your peace.

They want some of it for themselves, or worse yet, they can't stand to see anyone else with it because they've never attained it. That's sad and unfortunate for them, but *their lack of peace has nothing to do with you.*

As bringers of peace, we want to see God's peace imparted to everyone we meet, but we can't always do that, and we especially can't give away peace until we learn to keep it ourselves. Sometimes we have to let go.

Prod

How is your peace today? How will you guard your peace?

Praise

 Listen to

"Build My Life"

by Housefires

Pray

Jesus, your name is the name above all names. You are my peace in this world. Thank you for the peace you have given to me. Help me maintain that peace through whatever storms I experience today. Keep me safe, fill my heart, and build my life on your love! Amen.

Proclaim

"And the peace of God, which transcends all understanding, will guard your hearts and your minds in Christ Jesus." (Phil. 4:7)

Prompt

Just like we learned yesterday, there are forces out there who want you to lose your peace.

Understanding and identifying who and what robs you of your peace is the first step towards maintaining that peace. We must force ourselves to recognize what circumstances cause us to fear, have anxiety, or be disappointed or hurt.

We need to name the individuals who evoke feelings we aren't fully capable of dealing with yet. **Not to exact justice upon them or get revenge on them,** but just to know them and understand them.

Remember, there is nothing wrong with proactively protecting your peace. And that starts with identifying who and what is robbing you of this precious peace.

The more we understand this, the more we understand ourselves.

And then God can do the work within us to lavish us with His understanding-transcending peace.

Prod

Do you have an inventory of your "peace-robbers"? Make a list of any people or situations that steal your peace, then commit those names to prayer.

Praise

 Listen to

"P E A C E"

by Hillsong Young & Free

Pray

Jesus, your peace is amazing. I love that I don't have to understand it to experience it. Guide me past my peace-robbers today and let me revel in your peace. Amen.

Proclaim

"And the peace of God, which transcends all understanding, will guard your hearts and your minds in Christ Jesus." (Phil. 4:7)

Prompt

As long as we're talking about peace-robbers, sometimes you have robbers in your life who need some special attention. Simply pursuing them or distancing yourself from the situation just won't be enough.

Maybe you have a family member you must learn to live with or a co-worker who's not going anywhere anytime soon. These kinds of robbers must be dealt with head-on.

This is where you bring in outside help—name your robbers and then share those names with a trusted friend or mentor, someone who can provide you with the kind of accountability you need to maintain your peace in the midst of turmoil.

The Bible says this in Ecclesiastes 4:12: *"Though one may be overpowered, two can defend themselves. A cord of three strands is not quickly broken."* In this verse, Solomon emphasizes the truth that there is strength in numbers. So don't try to keep the peace in your heart by yourself—pull in others to help you set up a stronger perimeter around the precious gift of peace.

Prod

Who are the peace-robbers you must deal with head-on? Make a plan to discuss them with a trusted partner today.

Praise

 Listen to

"The Stand"

by Hillsong UNITED

Pray

Jesus, I thank you for the people you've put in my life who are helping me stay on track with living fully for you. Bless them—and me—today. I want to honor you in everything I do today. Amen.

Proclaim

"And the peace of God, which transcends all understanding, will guard your hearts and your minds in Christ Jesus." (Phil. 4:7)

Prompt

Another way peace can guard your heart is when God guides you to remove the risk of future heartaches.

As Christians, we must try to be proactive about our discipleship, proactive about our peace, and proactive about our state of mind. We all want to be successful, and removing the risk of future disappointments is just another way to engage the environment around us before **IT engages US**.

A few years back, I had to make a really tough decision to separate myself from people who were destroying my peace. The hard part about this was that I truly loved these people. They were not my enemies; they were my friends. In fact, I had journeyed with them for years and had the privilege of watching as God changed their lives.

But... whether they knew it or not, whether they were doing it on purpose or not, they were robbing me of my PEACE.

God has used this experience to help me grow and depend on Him more. His love has patiently guided me as I've stumbled my way through this peace-keeping, boundary-setting season.

Prod

How did this example make you feel? May it inspire you to let the peace of God guard your hearts today.

Praise

 Listen to

"This Is Love"

by New Wine Worship

Pray

Jesus, I'm so grateful you love me no matter what. Help me to honor you in my future. Guide me and lead me as I do my best to protect my heart. Amen.

Proclaim

"And the peace of God, which transcends all understanding, will guard your hearts and your minds in Christ Jesus." (Phil. 4:7)

Prompt

There are few natural things on this earth as transcendent as a mountain, let alone a mountain river.

If you've ever lived in a part of the country that has mountains, you know those mountains are never something you lose track of. You're always aware of where they are, and sometimes you just look at them in awe.

That's what God's peace is like—a strong mountain that occupies the landscape of our lives, a rushing river that revives our souls.

When we think of God like that, then we can trust His abundance and rest in His lovingkindness, knowing that He looks upon us with favor.

Prod

What's something in your life that you're always aware of? Imagine it as God. Does it fill you with peace or anxiety to know that God is always near like that?

Praise

 Listen to

"Those Who Trust"

by Enter the Worship Circle

Pray

Jesus, I trust your loving, grace-filled abundance in my life. Let me live in it! You're the immovable mountain in my life, so I know I can rest in you! Today is your day, I rejoice in it, I find peace in it, I give it to you! Amen.

Proclaim

"And the peace of God, which transcends all understanding, will guard your hearts and your minds in Christ Jesus." (Phil. 4:7)

Prompt

I used to try to just gut it out and have good days. I would tell myself every morning that the day was going to be great and peaceful, but often by lunchtime, I wasn't feeling all that great and peaceful anymore.

Then it hit me: if I desired to live a more peace-filled life, I had to begin every day by casting *a powerful vision of grace and peace.*

If I desired to live a more forgiving life, I had to begin to forgive people—***out loud***—each morning. I know this might sound really crazy, but that's ME! I need radical things to find radical peace.

So if I desired to push through fear and overcome things that had held me back, I had to begin speaking faith, courage, and confidence over myself each morning to get there.

How you start often determines how you finish.

Prod

How are you starting your days? Make a plan to begin every day the next week with a declaration of peace, forgiveness, and confidence. Forgive people OUT LOUD, pray that peace would flood your heart, and ask God to fill you with boldness!

Praise

 Listen to

"Touch of Heaven"

by Bethel Music

Pray

Jesus, this is a day that you made. Let me rejoice and be glad in it. Guide my tongue to speak GOOD things, to DECLARE peace, to DELIVER forgiveness, and to DARE to walk in confidence! Amen.

Proclaim

"And the peace of God, which transcends all understanding, will guard your hearts and your minds in Christ Jesus." (Phil. 4:7)

Prompt

Our scripture tells us God will guard our hearts. You know what you can't do when you're trying to guard your OWN heart?

Surrender.

Surrendering is the act of laying down your weapons. Weapons you use to push people away, avoid intimacy with God, and run away from your purpose.

I know because I did this for years. I fought everything, everyone, and every good plan God had for my life. It was only when I finally came to the end of myself, fell to my knees *(literally and figuratively),* and surrendered it ALL to God that peace came in.

We have a choice: we can either keep running, fighting, and avoiding God's plan for our lives OR we can surrender.

The act of surrendering supernaturally shifts our perspective and opens the floodgates of peace into our hearts and minds.

Surrender ALL to God today...

Prod

Where does God want to take you? Why are you still fighting? Write down what you're laying down for the Lord today.

Praise

 Listen to

"I Surrender All"

by Phil Wickham

Pray

Jesus, I surrender to you, trusting that your peace will guard my heart and mind when I lay down my weapons. I believe you and take you at your word. Amen.

Proclaim

"And the peace of God, which transcends all understanding, will guard your hearts and your minds in Christ Jesus." (Phil. 4:7)

Prompt

Play today's song while you read this...

"Perfect submission, all is at rest." So go the lyrics in the hymn "Blessed Assurance," a long-lasting and time-honored piece of music that has lasted as long as it has and been as honored over time because of the ageless truths it contains.

When we can be perfectly submitted to God's will, then we're acting in complete trust. And when we do THAT, we find ourselves with the immense rest and peace that comes with that trust.

Elevation Worship borrowed some of the lyrics to "Blessed Assurance" for their song "Trust in God," emphasizing the need to trust in a God who has proven Himself trustworthy over and over.

No matter where you find yourself today, seek God with **ALL OF YOUR HEART.** Take action to believe enough to seek God with your prayers, petitions, and problems.

You can trust—and rest in—Him. He takes care of you.

Prod

Do you have areas where you have difficulty trusting God? How can you give those back?

Praise

 Listen to "Trust in God" by Elevation Worship.

Pray

Jesus, thanks for being so trustworthy. I give you my will today. I submit to you. Thank you for rest. Thank you for your protection. Thank you for ordering my steps. Thank you that you never fail. In you, I'm happy and blessed. Amen.

Proclaim

"And the peace of God, which transcends all understanding, will guard your hearts and your minds in Christ Jesus." (Phil. 4:7)

Prompt

God is our refuge, and His loving arms are the only true calm amidst our chaos. Down here in the tangible stuff of this earth, where we see pain and destruction, ruin and devastation, God brings peace to our hearts, minds, and souls.

Even in the middle of the worst of it, we can rest in the knowledge that God upholds all who fall.

We can lament even while we trust and weep.
We can grieve the loss of someone we love.
We can persevere while we wait for the blessed ending that God has ordained for every one of His children.

God is near. **He is our peace.** Where else can we go?

Prod

What is causing you grief or distress today? Write it down and commit to praying for it daily until God brings you peace—however long that takes.

Praise

 Listen to

"Even When It Hurts"

by Hillsong United

Pray

Jesus, thank you for listening to my laments. I'm so grateful to know that you can handle my grief and sadness. I don't have to pretend to be happy all the time—help me be myself in all my uniqueness, acknowledging the less-than-perfect parts of this world while you provide your peace and joy in my life. Amen.

Proclaim

"And the peace of God, which transcends all understanding, will guard your hearts and your minds in Christ Jesus." (Phil. 4:7)

Prompt

I had a pretty great childhood, and I've said before that my dad is my biggest hero.

Maybe you can say the same thing, or maybe, like my dad's childhood, yours was just the opposite.

Maybe you had a really challenging childhood. An absent father, unstable home, or an upbringing where you never felt safe or secure.

Regardless of how we got here, one thing God makes clear in scripture is that He is our Father. Our earthly role models may have embodied that truth, or they may have turned their backs on it—neither of those actions changes the fact that God calls us beloved children.

He's the Great Parent, the One who cares for us. The One who feeds us with everlasting life and provides a home for us under the shadow of His wings.

He's a **Peaceful** Father.

Prod

In what ways was your father like God? In what ways was he unlike God? Compare and contrast them and let it open up your own relationship with God.

Praise

 Listen to

"Good Good Father"

by Chris Tomlin

Pray

Jesus, thanks for always being here with me, no matter what. Thank you for loving me, never leaving me or forgetting about me. You are my faithful, good Father! Amen.

Proclaim

"And the peace of God, which transcends all understanding, will guard your hearts and your minds in Christ Jesus." (Phil. 4:7)

Prompt

With peace comes goodness. God's gifts are good. God's ways are good. God's posture toward us is always good. **God is unfiltered, unimpeded, unbounded, uninhibited Goodness.**

The problem comes when we confuse OUR IDEA of good with God's pure, actual Good. Sometimes, in the name of pragmatism or idealism, we call evil good, but God's peaceful wisdom looks past those worldly values and adds more and more and more of his REAL Good to our world.

And that feels a lot like peace.

Prod

Are there worldly ideals you've confused with God's goodness? Identify them and lift them to God in repentance.

Praise

 Listen to

"God, You're So Good"

by Passion

Pray

Jesus, you are good, good, good. Show me your Good instead of mine. Let me call things "good" that are actually good as you know it, not as I do. Don't let me get confused on what is your Real Good when I encounter it today! Amen.

Proclaim

"And the peace of God, which transcends all understanding, will guard your hearts and your minds in Christ Jesus." (Phil. 4:7)

Prompt

God is a God of Comfort. He permeates the universe with His peace. It can be tough to remember this, but it's true: God is not a part of the world—He IS the world. **He is the whole thing.** It is all God, so His comforting presence is ALWAYS here.

We can trust this truth. When we ask for God's comfort to be felt in a real and tangible way, we can believe He'll do it. He won't give us the concept of comfort; He won't show us a PowerPoint presentation about comfort.

He'll give us the real thing—real comfort—present in every breath.

As today's updated version of a classic worship song says, God is our strong tower. He is our comfort, our shelter, our strength!

Prod

As you pray and worship today, write down how you see God present everywhere, in everything, at all times. Write a reflection on this truth and what it means for your peace.

Praise

 Listen to

"Shout to the Lord"

by Influence Music

Pray

Jesus, I take comfort in knowing you're with me right here, right now, all the time. Help me relax in your peace today. Let me know your comfort even when it doesn't feel available to me. Amen.

Proclaim

"And the peace of God, which transcends all understanding, will guard your hearts and your minds in Christ Jesus." (Phil. 4:7)

Prompt

When there seems to be no way, God provides a way. Whenever I think of this principle, I think of the story of Esther, where she was so filled with God's peace that she knew, whatever might happen, she'd be okay. After all, God had opened an avenue for her "for such a time as this."

Esther knew something wasn't right, and she knew she was the only one who could stop it—even if it cost her her life. And yet she walked in such perfect peace that she had no doubt speaking to the king about the genocidal plot against her people. Whatever happened afterward, she knew she was doing what God had called her to do.

Sometimes we have to face tough things (but probably not as tough as that!). If God's peace was there for Esther, then we can trust it'll be there for us, too.

Prod

What major life thing do you need peace to face TODAY?

Praise

 Listen to

"God Will Make A Way"

City First Worship

Pray

Jesus, give me the peace I need today to face the major obstacles in my life. You are trustworthy, and just like Esther, I'm made for such a time as this. Nothing in my life is taking you by surprise, so help me follow you. Amen.

Proclaim

"And the peace of God, which transcends all understanding, will guard your hearts and your minds in Christ Jesus." (Phil. 4:7)

Prompt

Sometimes we get outside of God's peace, and that's when we make mistakes. Take, for example, the mistake of pragmatism—looking to practicality as our be-all, end-all. We can start to believe that the logical and sensible are the same thing as the godly.

Which, don't get me wrong, it often is. God made logic, so sometimes—oftentimes—God operates within logic.

But also, a lot of times... He doesn't! And that's where we can get off track, by trying to cram everything God does into our little boxes of logic. *He doesn't always fit there!*

God is GOD! He is beyond our wildest imaginations. And I believe we miss out on experiencing the amazingly absurd by playing it safe. Refusing to move when He says MOVE. Sitting, soaking, and souring in what seems sensible instead of saying YES to the spirit of the living God.

Today could be the first day of the rest of your life. A new life! Beyond anything you could imagine! But it starts with you saying YES!

Prod

Where have you fallen prey to world-logic instead of God-logic? Spend time asking God to show you what COULD BE and fill you with the confidence to say YES!

Praise

 Listen to

"Dare You To Move"

by Switchfoot

Pray

Jesus, thank you for showing me a different way to live. Help me to follow your footsteps today, wherever they might lead—even if I don't understand where you're taking me. I trust you! My answer to YOU is YES! Amen.

Proclaim

"And the peace of God, which transcends all understanding, will guard your hearts and your minds in Christ Jesus." (Phil. 4:7)

Prompt

Have you ever seen a Sequoia tree in person? These are the trees found in the great Redwood Forest in the western part of the United States. If you ever go to view them in real life, you go there knowing they're going to be big, and you've seen pictures of how big they get, but until you stand in front of them, you really aren't prepared for their *actual bigness*.

And yet, as awe-inspiring as the trees are, being in the Redwood Forest is incredibly peaceful.

You know how those Sequoias can grow so tall and peaceful? Because they put down deep, deep roots, and they steadily, **faithfully grow.**

Which is exactly how we need to be with God. When we abide in God and put our roots deeper, deeper still into His eternal earth, we can grow impractically tall, a towering testament to God's peace.

Prod

Look up some pictures online of Sequoias and meditate momentarily on how they got to be so tall.

Praise

 Listen to

"Glory, Honor, Power"

by Influence Music

Pray

Jesus, I pray you'll show me how to go deeper and deeper and deeper with you. I want my faith to be as tall as a Sequoia tree! Feed me, water me, shine on me, and care for me so that I can grow as tall as you'll let me be! Amen.

Proclaim

"And the peace of God, which transcends all understanding, will guard your hearts and your minds in Christ Jesus." (Phil. 4:7)

Prompt

God is a Just Judge who makes all things right. He doesn't do that to balance out the ledgers of punishment—He wouldn't be God if He had to do that—but He makes all things right in order to restore everyone to grace.

A way we can walk in peace with God is to seek this same kind of restoration: to keep our sights on the good, the wholesome, the renewed, on Christ as He hides in the world. When we practice God's restorative grace among everyone we encounter, we also enact His peace.

This has been a personal challenge for me. I'm naturally a judger! I hate to admit that, but it's true. I've worked on it a lot, but I still find myself judging others in my mind all the time.

I know God is healing me daily as I bring this to Him. Thank God for His grace. And thank God that He is not like me (or like you).

He is kind, He is loving, He is accepting, He is the giver of all grace and peace: that's God's way.

Prod

Who needs to receive restorative grace from you today? Write their name down here and let them know with a phone call, FaceTime, or text message. Don't wimp out—do it!

Praise

 Listen to

"Good Grace"

by Hillsong United

Pray

Jesus, thank you for your grace toward me. I know I don't deserve it, but I love it all the same. Thank you for restoring my life. I want that restoration to flow out of me like water today so that I drench everyone I meet! Only you can make it happen, Jesus! Amen.

Proclaim

"And the peace of God, which transcends all understanding, will guard your hearts and your minds in Christ Jesus." (Phil. 4:7)

Prompt

As long as we're talking about transcending understanding, here's a bit about the economy of God that doesn't seem to track with our achievement-oriented brains: in God's reckoning, the last shall be first and the first shall be last.

Here's what I think, though: this passage from the Sermon on the Mount doesn't mean that the standings get flipped upside down and winners become losers while losers become winners. I think it means we stop playing the game and just get welcomed into an extreme equality, *a radical ratio where there IS no ranking and we just ARE.*

Take peace in this: you're not in competition with anyone. The last shall be first, the first shall be last, and all shall be well.

I know, for all the naturally uber-competitive people out there—like ME—this is a tough pill to swallow. But it's God. It's the Radical Kingdom where all are welcome and all are loved. It's HIS victory that we are after anyway.

Our goal should never be to win at everything, to promote our agenda, or push our platform. It should always be to partner with God to set the captives free.

Prod

Where are you feeling competition within God's Kingdom? Name it to yourself and give it to the Lord.

Praise

 Listen to

"Victory Is Yours"

by Bethel Music

Pray

Jesus, thank you for freeing me from the obstacle of competition with my fellow human beings. Give me peace right where you have me. Teach me to stop playing games and just to serve you with all I have because YOU are my ultimate goal! Amen.

Proclaim

"And the peace of God, which transcends all understanding, will guard your hearts and your minds in Christ Jesus." (Phil. 4:7)

Prompt

There's peace in sacrifice. After all, God calls us to sacrifice the comforts that make our hearts too careful.

But hear me on this: **God doesn't ask us to do things He hasn't equipped us for!** He gives us the strength to let go, to empty our hands of whatever we clutch too tightly. God grants us the grace to drop our burdens of safety and security so we can fully embrace Him and His call.

We can do this in peace because we know that, with God, all things are possible.

Is there a dream welling up in your heart that seems scary? *Does it feel like it's going to take unusual sacrifice and increased faith?!*

GREAT! It sounds like God is moving in you, and if He is, He will equip you with what you need for this new adventure. And more peace awaits on the other side.

Prod

Is there a thing you're holding onto out of a sense of security? How can you drop that and offer it to God?

Praise

 Listen to

"Open The Heavens"

by Gateway Worship

Pray

Jesus, give me the strength to drop everything and follow you. Peter did it, and so I know I can too! I just need your help and your strength! Let's gooooo! Amen.

Proclaim

"And the peace of God, which transcends all understanding, will guard your hearts and your minds in Christ Jesus." (Phil. 4:7)

Prompt

One way to rely on God's peace is to remember that the Holy Spirit is with us always.

The Holy Spirit is the presence within us, animating and motivating us to do our best for God's Kingdom. Always present, always available.

Much like the air we breathe or the warming rays of the sun, we cannot go away from the Holy Spirit's presence—all we can do is become more or less aware of it. It's this level of *awareness adjustment* that can also strengthen or lessen the level of peace we feel.

The world is so busy and LOUD! It's annoying at times, right? This is why worship music, solitude with God, fasting, and fully surrendered prayer are so important for discipleship.

We must pursue God's presence with incredible intentionality. It must be our priority every single day.

Tune your heart to the presence of the Holy Spirit right now and see what God does for your peace.

Prod

How aware are you of the ongoing presence of the Holy Spirit? Take some time today to reflect on it.

Praise

 Listen to

"Holy Spirit"

by Kari Jobe & Cody Carnes

Pray

Jesus, fill me with your presence right now. Speak to my soul, fill me with your PEACE. Holy Spirit, you are welcome in my life. Amen.

Proclaim

"And the peace of God, which transcends all understanding, will guard your hearts and your minds in Christ Jesus." (Phil. 4:7)

Prompt

You know a surefire way to lose your peace? Look too far ahead in anxiety. That's why God tells us He will guard our hearts with His peace so that we don't get caught up in prediction and looking ahead to figure it all out.

I love how today's song speaks to this. **The writers say that God doesn't give His heart to us in pieces. He doesn't hide Himself to tease us.** But yet, at the same time, He protects our hearts by giving us what we need for each day.

So we can relax in peace, trusting in God TODAY, knowing full well that He will bring us into TOMORROW in the ways that only He knows how.

Rest. Let your heart be guarded.

God will bring you through. Enjoy today for what it is!

Prod

It's good to have vision, but not to try to predict the future. How does this statement resonate with you? Write a brief reflection on it.

Praise

 Listen to

"Pieces"

by Bethel Music

Pray

Jesus, I trust you. You're with me and will never let me down. I rest in you. You will take care of tomorrow as much as you took care of today, so I know I can relax because you're in charge. Give me the rest I need. Amen.

Proclaim

"And the peace of God, which transcends all understanding, will guard your hearts and your minds in Christ Jesus." (Phil. 4:7)

Prompt

Yesterday we talked about the anxiety that can come when we look ahead and try to predict the future. Today, let's reflect on what we can do when that happens.

God is the ultimate reality, the one and only Truth. It's God and only God. So when we're tempted to look for confidence and confirmation in anything that's not God, well, we can get pretty messed up.

But fortunately, we can also rely on the fact that, when we keep our hearts soft toward God, He will gently nudge us back into alignment with His plans for our lives.

You'll get off track. You'll get worried. You'll get impatient. But that's okay. Because if you stay soft to God's voice, He'll always guide you back to peace.

Prod

What have you tried to predict in the past, and how did it work out for you? Make a plan for avoiding this pitfall the next time you approach it.

Praise

 Listen to

"Wait For You"

by Leeland

Pray

Jesus, thanks for the grace of putting me back on the right path when I stop trusting you. Keep my feet following after yours so that I can always be right behind you every step of the way. Amen.

Proclaim

"And the peace of God, which transcends all understanding, will guard your hearts and your minds in Christ Jesus." (Phil. 4:7)

Prompt

God's peace transcends understanding, but maybe the most understanding-transcending aspect of His peace is how it can completely transform relationships and turn foes into friends.

Jesus said, *"He who does not follow me, cannot be my disciple."* God sent His Son, the Prince of Peace, to bring peace to this world. He also sends His sons and daughters, you and me, to make peace, too.

We read in Proverbs 16:7 what the result of peacemaking can be: *"When a man's ways please the Lord, He makes even His enemies to be at peace with Him."*

There is no doubt that coming off years of addiction, I had some enemies. I imagine you do too. But the Bible makes it clear that peace is attainable, and that formerly volatile relationships can be restored. All I'm saying is: *give peace a chance.*

Prod

Who do you need to restore peace with? Pray and ask God to reveal just one name to you, then pray about how God would most like you to handle the situation. Then act.

Praise

 Listen to

"Brother"

by The Brilliance

Pray

Jesus, thank you for being the Prince of Peace in my life. I submit my will to yours. Amen.

Proclaim

"And the peace of God, which transcends all understanding, will guard your hearts and your minds in Christ Jesus." (Phil. 4:7)

Prompt

What could be more peaceful than knowing you are the beloved child of an all-giving, all-caring, all-powerful Parent?

Such is the truth we find in today's song, "Who I Am" by Ben Fuller.

"I'm a child of the Most-High God and the Most-High God's for me," goes a line in the bridge of the song. You're not an orphan! You're a child whose Heavenly Father is on your side and is actively championing you!

How much more peaceful can you get?!

Rest in this knowledge today—that the all-powerful, Creator of the Universe loves you unconditionally as His child and is for you. *For you!*

Amen!

Prod

How have your relationship(s) with your parent(s) had an impact on the way you view God? Are there any adjustments you need to make as a result? Write about it.

Praise

 Listen to

"Who I Am"

by Ben Fuller

Pray

Jesus, I sometimes can't even comprehend that you're for me. Help me internalize that today. Remind me everywhere I look of who I am, and remind me that I'm your child, Lord. Amen.

Proclaim

"And the peace of God, which transcends all understanding, will guard your hearts and your minds in Christ Jesus." (Phil. 4:7)

Prompt

God is unchanging—we can count on that. Look at the world around you or even just watch a nature documentary and you'll discover that God has an unfettered imagination of limitless variety, all while remaining singularly Himself.

In the same way, God calls us to reflect Him to the world in all our different ways. **He wants unity but NOT uniformity.**

This is the work of peace—to honor our individuality while still finding togetherness with our fellow believers. We do that by submitting ourselves—each of us—to God's will.

One way I've tried to practice this is by honoring those I once disagreed with or even those relationships that ended poorly. Instead of ducking them in shame or annihilating them in my head with evil thoughts (don't act like you've never done that), I try to think positive thoughts about them, even praying for blessings to fall on their life.

And when I see them publicly, I try to make a point to say hello and greet them with a smile. This can be tough, but I find peace sticks with me after I do it.

There can be peace in disagreement and peace within our differences.

Prod

How does this PROMPT hit you today? Is there someone who comes to mind? Write out some God-honoring ways to approach them in public.

Praise

 Listen to

"Homecoming"

by Bethel Music

Pray

Jesus, thank you for making me me. Help me be a great embodiment of you to the world today. Help me to show love to those who might not look like me, act like me, believe like me, or even LIKE ME! May peace be the blessing I pass on. Amen.

Proclaim

"And the peace of God, which transcends all understanding, will guard your hearts and your minds in Christ Jesus." (Phil. 4:7)

Prompt

The first time Jesus met Peter, the man was fishing. Well, specifically, he was *trying* to fish and failing. Peter had spent the whole night trying to bring in a catch and had nothing to show for it. Nevertheless, Jesus told him to cast his net one more time, which Peter did... and then he hauled in so much fish his boat almost capsized.

Sometimes life just feels like a long, long night of catching nothing. But if we can listen to Jesus, we can know that sometimes we just need to cast our nets in courage one more time to see God bring the increase.

Imagine the peace Peter felt in that moment. All his anxiety, all his worry of going home empty-handed—alleviated in one toss. *Jesus.*

This story reminds me of when I was fired from what I thought was my dream job. A job I thought God had specifically created for ME! I cried, sulked, and pouted for six months until God told me to get up and try again.

When I did, God birthed Hope is Alive.

Sometimes, God's "one more time" is when the breakthrough happens!

Prod

Do you need to keep casting? Ask God for the courage to keep going! TRUST HIM!

Praise

 Listen to

"Won't Stop Now"

by Elevation Worship

Pray

Jesus, you are so unexpected! Help me to obey you when you tell me to do something outrageous, trusting that you're going to come through. You are mighty! You are faithful! You are a promise-keeper and a miracle-worker! Amen.

Proclaim

"And the peace of God, which transcends all understanding, will guard your hearts and your minds in Christ Jesus." (Phil. 4:7)

Prompt

God wants to give us peace, no matter what. Even when we choose to fret over circumstances that seem unfair or things we cannot control (and even those we can), God wants to hand us His patient peace instead.

If we let Him, God will give us the peace we've been learning about, the peace that transcends all our understanding. It will be a *peace* that either soothes our rage or shakes us out of apathy... all so we can act with confidence that we are walking with Him.

Peace can be an active force in our lives if we let it. Let God's peace do its work in you!

Prod

Do you need your rage to be soothed or your apathy to be shaken? Try these three peace-activating steps this morning:

1. Confess your sins to God and ask Him for full forgiveness.
2. Journal about the things that are scary, confusing, or painful in your life today.
3. Spend the four and a half minutes of today's song meditating on the lyrics.

Praise

 Listen to

"Peace"

by Robbie Seay Band

Pray

Jesus, convict me where I need it. I crave your peace in my life. Fill me to overflowing today. I love you, I give my life to you. Amen.

Proclaim

"And the peace of God, which transcends all understanding, will guard your hearts and your minds in Christ Jesus." (Phil. 4:7)

Prompt

God's commands are easy to uphold when we are called to love the lovely. But what about other kinds of commands? The difficult commands are the ones that transcend all understanding. *To pull those off, we need God's help.*

We need God's help to love those who hate us, to bless those who curse us, to pray for those who cry out against us, to offer our other cheek for striking, and to hand everything over to the thief.

Are these difficult commands? You bet they are! But we can believe God when He calls us to mercy and forgiveness. Even though it goes against what we understand, we can extend God's peace to our families, our workplaces, our social media profiles, our city, and our world.

Because He calls us to.

The result of obedience to God always, ultimately, results in **PEACE.**

Prod

Think of a person in your life who is hard to love. Ask God to give you love for them every day this week.

Praise

 Listen to

"Obedience"

by Lindy Cofer

Pray

Jesus, let me be a person of peace everywhere at all times. That's a difficult request that doesn't make a whole lot of sense, but I know you can do it! Shine through me and let others see your peace in me today! Help me take the action I need today. Amen.

Proclaim

"And the peace of God, which transcends all understanding, will guard your hearts and your minds in Christ Jesus." (Phil. 4:7)

Prompt

God is an almighty God who knows us like no other. He knows, in great empathy, how we feel, ESPECIALLY when we're tempted. After all, Jesus was led by the Spirit into the wilderness and was tempted just like WE get tempted.

Since He knows what it's like to be vulnerable in the wilderness, He can find us in our own wildernesses. He comes quickly to help us when we are assaulted by many temptations. He knows our weaknesses, so He knows exactly how to give us strength in the midst of them. He is mighty to save.

Call on Him. Let Him find you in your wilderness and bring peace to you right then and there.

Prod

What's an area of great temptation for you? Make a physical marker—whether that's a bracelet, another piece of jewelry, a sticky note, a phone wallpaper, or whatever—to remind you to call on Jesus when you're tempted.

Praise

 Listen to

"Mighty To Save"

by Hillsong Worship

Pray

Jesus, thank you for finding me in the wilderness. Guide me out! I need your help! Help me avoid this wilderness in the future and just stay right next to your side instead of straying away on my own! Amen.

Proclaim

"And the peace of God, which transcends all understanding, will guard your hearts and your minds in Christ Jesus." (Phil. 4:7)

Prompt

Have you ever participated in a fast? It's pretty eye-opening. You experience hunger (or thirst, depending on the kind of fast you do) while God calls you to refresh yourself at the table of His peace, love, and joy.

I've always found that fasting food is one of the most effective ways to snap me back into a right relationship with God. Food is such a natural way we soothe ourselves, so any time you take it away, you fairly quickly begin to NEED GOD to fill you!

That said, fasting becomes a way to partake in God's restorative food. He is the **"Bread of Life"** after all, and when we feast on His goodness, it helps us forsake our wicked ways, take captive our unrighteous thoughts, and repent of our inaction.

It's God's way of feeding us with His higher ways.

Fasting is hard, but it's so worth it.

Prod

What can you fast today to actively enhance your relationship with God? I know you weren't expecting this, so spend the prayer time asking God to reveal what you can cut away to make room for God to fill you and sustain you.

Praise

 Listen to

"Bread of Life"

by Citipointe Worship

Pray

Jesus, you're my source of everything. Sustain me today. I give you all I have and know you will give me all you have in return. YOU are everything I need! Amen.

Proclaim

"And the peace of God, which transcends all understanding, will guard your hearts and your minds in Christ Jesus." (Phil. 4:7)

Prompt

In Psalm 63, David writes that God's steadfast love is better than life itself. Better than life!

WOW. Bold but true.

God is constant, always satisfying our thirsty souls and reviving our weary bodies. What kind of response can we have to that kind of peace other than just praising God for as long as we draw breath?!

But we also have to be on guard and be grounded in God's humility so that when we think we are standing, we do not fall. It's this level of humility, brought about by God's constant peace, that allows us to receive every situation, every disappointment, every mountaintop, and every person we encounter as the gifts from God that they are.

Prod

What can you thank God for today? Do it! Give it all to God...

Praise

 Listen to

"Better Than Life"

by Phil Wickham

Pray

Jesus, I give everything I have to you. You are the King of my life. Please help me receive what you have for me today. Give me courage and wisdom to accept it. Give me humility so that I can stand without falling and stay strong in you. Amen.

Proclaim

"And the peace of God, which transcends all understanding, will guard your hearts and your minds in Christ Jesus." (Phil. 4:7)

Prompt

God is a Master Caretaker who has raised us up from seeds and saplings. And even beyond that, His grace is so great that even when we bear no fruit, He still says, "Give it time. Let Me do My work."

It's a holy stubbornness—the kind God wants us to emulate as we build His Kingdom, wherever we are in the world. God calls us to be persistent and patient, tender and trepidatious, wise and courageous.

When we follow through on this, we do our part and plant what we have so that we can bear fruit in God's great orchard.

Then we wait. We wait and watch God do His thing. Yes, waiting for God to move, to speak, and to act can be tough. But it's in the season of waiting and wondering where your peace builds its roots and prepares to push through the dirt, ready to take on the earth.

Prod

Get a piece of fruit and consider its humble beginnings as you eat it.

Praise

 Listen to

"Waiting Here For You"

by Passion

Pray

Jesus, you care for me. Show me how to love you and others today. Plant me in the right place and let me grow so I can bear your fruit in my life and the lives of those I encounter. As I wait, I will reach my hands to you! I adore you and I will wait for you. Amen.

Proclaim

"And the peace of God, which transcends all understanding, will guard your hearts and your minds in Christ Jesus." (Phil. 4:7)

Prompt

Today's my Dad's birthday. Happy birthday, Wendell Lang. I love you so much! You are my hero, every good thing about me I learned from you.

My dad's a super peaceful guy. Loved by everyone, rarely riled up, and he's never met a stranger. He carries a peace that gives him confidence that he can do anything.

Have you ever felt that way?

Maybe you could walk on water? Or maybe even you could walk on water so confidently that you could dance on it?

This is the image conjured in today's song, ***"Peace Be Still"*** by The Belonging Co. It reimagines the story of Peter walking on the water as a complete and total triumph—to the point where he dances on the waves in complete trust and peace that Jesus knows what He's doing.

What a concept! Dancing on the waves! Yes, please! Stop what you're doing and do a little dance while you listen to today's song, and imagine you're dancing on waves!

Prod

What "waves" do you need to dance on today? Trust God in the midst of those waves!

Praise

 Listen to

"Peace Be Still"

by The Belonging Co.

Pray

Jesus, thanks for calling me to walk on water. Let me trust you, even in the waves—trust you so much that I can dance on them like David danced before you. I believe you! Amen.

Proclaim

"And the peace of God, which transcends all understanding, will guard your hearts and your minds in Christ Jesus." (Phil. 4:7)

Prompt

Have you ever been far from God, yet you felt His peace in a moment? This happened to me the day I was intervened on and **shipped off to rehab**. My life was a chase, yet peace flooded my heart when I knew it was over.

Regardless of our level of closeness to God, He wants to bring peace to our lives. When we are near, His desire is to hold us even closer so that we may know His heart. When we are far, His desire is to remind us of His unconditional love so that we will turn around and come home.

Who can understand this?! As conditionally loving human beings, this doesn't make much sense. But God is God, and we aren't. *Can I get an AMEN?!* He wants to pour out His peace on us when we're near *and* when we're far.

Prod

Where are you today? Near to God? Far from God? Use your prayer time today to recenter your life around God's peace.

Praise

 Listen to

"Cannons"

by Phil Wickham

Pray

Jesus, thank you for the peace of your presence. Thank you for pouring out your peace on me unconditionally—draw me even closer to you today so that I can know your heart even more greatly. Amen.

Proclaim

"And the peace of God, which transcends all understanding, will guard your hearts and your minds in Christ Jesus." (Phil. 4:7)

Prompt

Today's song is super peaceful. It's a vibe and I love it!

It's a bit of a blast from the past, but the lyrics are such a vivid reminder for our feeble human minds of the incredible love God has for us.

It's true, God's love for us is extravagant and His friendship is intimate. *He is both immeasurably vast and sitting right next to you at this very moment.*

So here's something peaceful to ponder the next time you take communion: God the Father sent His son to earth from heaven to be the true bread that feeds and gives life to the world. That's the sacrifice He made for our sins.

How can we do anything but live sacrificially in our world? How can we carry anything but the peace of Jesus? At work, at school, at church, at home—everywhere we go, we are called to be people of peace, the kind of people who always carry a communion grace with us.

Prod

Reflect and write about God's extravagant love for you.

Reflect and write about God's intimate friendship with you.

Praise

 Listen to

"Your Love Is Extravagant"

by Darrell Evans

Pray

Jesus, thank you for your sacrifice. Thank you for your love. Thank you for your friendship. Amen.

Proclaim

"And the peace of God, which transcends all understanding, will guard your hearts and your minds in Christ Jesus." (Phil. 4:7)

Prompt

Sometimes God's peace gets misrepresented. Perhaps you're a person who believed—or even still believes—that God is someone other than who He really is.

Maybe your perception of God's peace has been obscured by pain, suffering, financial lack, bad news, loss, or the intentionally hurtful actions of others.

These are wounds. But the good news is: God's in the wound-healing business. He loves it! Because when He does, He shows His peace more clearly, not just to the person whose wounds He healed but also to everyone else.

Prod

Do you have wounds that need healing today? Are you willing to allow God to heal them?

If so, take a moment to listen to today's song, recite (or sing!) the lyrics with Kari, and BELIEVE them in your heart!

Praise

 Listen to

"Healer"

by Kari Jobe

Pray

Jesus, nothing is impossible for you. Take my wounds and heal them. I trust you. I believe in you. I need you! Heal the places in my life that are keeping me from living in your peace and keeping me from living the purpose you've created me for. Amen.

Proclaim

"And the peace of God, which transcends all understanding, will guard your hearts and your minds in Christ Jesus." (Phil. 4:7)

Prompt

Today we're going to look at a quote from Julian of Norwich, an English woman in the late 1300s who lived a solitary life spent studying theology, praying, and writing. She was truly remarkable and brought incredible, divine insight to her reflections, including this one:

"Some of us believe that God is almighty and may do everything, and that He is all-wisdom and can do everything; but that He is all-love and wishes to do everything—there we stop short. It is this ignorance, it seems to me, that hinders most of God's lovers."

Are you willing to go all the way and believe that God wishes to do everything?

Prod

What viewpoint on God hinders you—and limits God? How can you give that back to God today?

Praise

 Listen to

"Everlasting God"

by Chris Tomlin

Pray

Jesus, you want to help everyone! I believe it! Help me today. Help me past my doubts and despair. Help me past my unbelief and unawareness. Help me trust you farther, deeper, and wider today! Amen.

Proclaim

"And the peace of God, which transcends all understanding, will guard your hearts and your minds in Christ Jesus." (Phil. 4:7)

Prompt

Where do you look for your identity? Do you look to others to tell you who you are?

Do you look in the mirror to tell yourself? Or do you look to the peace of God?

When you finally get to the place where you accept that you are fully KNOWN by God, peace comes running.

I call this a *spiritual identity shift.* It might require you to hit rock bottom or have some kind of moment of desperation. But it doesn't have to!

Today, right now, you can accept that God fully knows you.

When you accept this, you can smile and not hide in shame.

When you receive this, you can breathe and unclench your fists.

When you live this, you can walk in freedom and live in peace.

Prod

If you are fully known and loved by God, then what does God say about you? Write down your reflections.

Praise

Listen to

"Known"

by Tauren Wells

Pray

Jesus, help me believe you when you call me "blessed." I don't always feel that way, but I know that what you say and what I feel aren't always the same thing. So please give me the strength I need today to believe you and to trust that I AM BLESSED in Jesus' name! Amen.

Proclaim

"And the peace of God, which transcends all understanding, will guard your hearts and your minds in Christ Jesus." (Phil. 4:7)

Prompt

Are you familiar with Palm Sunday? It's traditionally observed as the day Jesus rode into Jerusalem as a triumphant victor... less than a week before he was crucified.

It's truly an unorthodox triumphal parade, with Jesus riding in not as you would expect—on a warrior's horse—but instead on a lowly donkey. But no one cared! People still crowded the street, laid their coats down in His path, and waved palm branches victoriously, like they were celebrating a big win.

They didn't know at the time that they actually WERE celebrating a big win—the biggest win of all time—but that it wouldn't look **ANYTHING** like what they were used to.

Just like Palm Sunday, God loves to bring us peace by showing us wins where we only see losses.

Prod

Read up on Palm Sunday and reflect on what you might have done if you were in the crowd for that parade... or in the same crowd for the crucifixion a few days later.

Praise

 Listen to

"Hosanna Song"

by Paul Zach and Jon Guerra

Pray

Jesus, nothing about you makes sense, and that's part of what I love about you. You look at the conventions we have and you turn them upside-down, and that gives me hope for myself! Thank you for transcending my understanding. Amen.

Proclaim

"And the peace of God, which transcends all understanding, will guard your hearts and your minds in Christ Jesus." (Phil. 4:7)

Prompt

Today is **MY BIRTHDAY!** Around 5:00 pm on this day in 1982, I was born.

I believe God knew *that day* was my day and *that time* was my time. I don't believe that from some self-centered point of view. I believe it because God said this through His prophet Jeremiah: ***"Before I formed you in the womb I knew you, before you were born I set you apart; I appointed you as a prophet to the nations."***

God said that He formed me, knew me, set me apart, and even appointed me!

That blows my mind. I was created, cherished, chosen, and called to walk this earth. I feel so loved and special when I slow down enough to really take that beautiful promise in. But you know what's so cool? God said all those things about YOU, too!

You were created by God, cherished, chosen, and called by Him to walk this earth. You are not an accident or insignificant, and you certainly weren't meant to live on the sidelines of life. God created you for a reason!

So it's from this place we should get up each day—birthday or not—and commit to giving everything we have to furthering the purpose God has created us to live.

Prod

Today's song is the #1 most played song on my Spotify account EVER! I looked it up. This song has permeated my mind and soul for literally days on end... Turn it on full blast today!

Praise

 Listen to

"You Deserve It All"

by Jeremy Riddle

Pray

Jesus, you deserve it ALL! You created me, you gave me life. It's my honor to praise you in all I do, today and every day. Amen.

Proclaim

"And the peace of God, which transcends all understanding, will guard your hearts and your minds in Christ Jesus." (Phil. 4:7)

Prompt

God is eternal. That means, in our limited understanding and our pitiful metaphors, He is both the beginning and the ending... and everything in between.

We're so used to finite thinking that it can be difficult to grasp that God has always been, is now, and always will be. And contemplating that thought can either fill you with tremendous anxiety... or it can fill you with tremendous peace.

Because which of our earthly concerns can faze an eternal God who *cares about us?*

Money? Nah He's got it.

Relationships? NOPE, He's got it.

Future? He holds it all.

Past? He's cleansed every bit of it.

God is in it. No matter what it is.

Now that's some peace that can take you through this day.

Prod

Count off a single second. Now consider that one million of those seconds is about 11.5 days. One *billion* of those is almost 32 *years*. And that's a drop in the bucket to God. Take a few more seconds to reflect on this in your journal pages.

Praise

 Listen to "Vapor" by Gungor

Pray

Jesus, I can't even come close to understanding you and the way you encompass all of eternity. I just know I love you. And that's enough. Amen.

Proclaim

"And the peace of God, which transcends all understanding, will guard your hearts and your minds in Christ Jesus." (Phil. 4:7)

Prompt

God is woven into the fabric of everything, so much that He is the fabric itself. He's the God who was, who is, and who is to come. And yet even though He is so immense, He still invites us into His mystery and welcomes us to join Him in whatever way we can.

It takes peace to embrace God in that mystery, in times of both difficulty and delight. When we are tempted to ask *"Why?"* God guides us instead to ask *"What now?"* so we can serve Him as He served us.

A counselor taught me that. During a session when I was going off wanting to know the WHY behind everything, she said, "You'll never understand WHY, it's pointless to even try. WHY is not the question you should ask. Instead, ask WHAT NOW?"

I've always remembered that and tried to live it out. God always gives us what we need to follow Him. That's why we can follow Him with peace—because we know He's making the way and making it possible. Because He is everything, everywhere.

Prod

When's the last time you asked *"Why?"* How can you turn that into a *"What now?"*

Praise

 Listen to

"Canvas & Clay"

by Pat Barrett

Pray

Jesus, thank you for embracing me with your peace. I can feel you today. You are infinite and holy. Even when I don't understand you, or understand your people, I know YOU care for me and that YOUR promises are trustworthy. Help me today not to get stuck in WHY, but instead ask WHAT NOW? Amen.

Proclaim

"And the peace of God, which transcends all understanding, will guard your hearts and your minds in Christ Jesus." (Phil. 4:7)

Prompt

In Psalm 118, the psalmist writes that God is our strength and our song! But what does that mean? It means that even when we are so weak we can't carry a tune, God lifts us up with His peace and sings over us. He meets us where we are and restores the joy in our hearts.

This reminds me of the few verses of Psalm 140. When David pens this...

"I waited patiently for the LORD; he turned to me and heard my cry. He lifted me out of the slimy pit, out of the mud and mire, he set my feet on a rock and gave me a firm place to stand. HE PUT A NEW SONG IN MY MOUTH...

I've always pictured that new song as being my testimony and that rock my feet are planted on as being my relationship with Jesus. I know He never leaves my side, and that gives me the confidence I need to stand firm on Him, raise my head up with pride, and SING!

God saved me from the pit of Hell and gave me a second chance so I could become a beacon of hope and peace to our world. And He's done the same for you.

So together, let's lift up our voices and sing our new song!

Prod

What's a song that has special meaning to you? How do you experience God in that song?

Praise

 Listen to

"Made to Worship"

by Chris Tomlin

Pray

Jesus, I need you to meet me where I am. Restore me today. Meet me in this song as I listen to it! Amen.

Proclaim

"And the peace of God, which transcends all understanding, will guard your hearts and your minds in Christ Jesus." (Phil. 4:7)

Prompt

In probably the most famous of all the Psalms, David describes God as a *Good Shepherd*. It's one of my favorite descriptions. I love visualizing God leading me, carving the path, never getting tired, and always looking back to check on His flock.

And yes, if God is our Shepherd, that makes us His flock.

To avoid going astray, we should live a life that's fully attentive to His leading. All ears, tuned to His voice, so much so that it's the only voice we hear and follow.

But following our *Good Shepherd* will require us to travel some tough paths. If you are waltzing through life without any trial or any pain, you're probably playing it safe. Sorry!

Since the day I gave my life to Jesus and promised to follow Him wherever He leads, I've found myself in some really challenging situations. Thankfully, I've got a *Good Shepherd* to follow, to trust, and to find my peace in.

Prod

Research the relationship between sheep and their shepherd and reflect on what it means for your relationship with God.

Praise

 Listen to

"Good Shepherd"

by UPPERROOM

Pray

Jesus, I trust you. You're my Shepherd. I'll follow wherever you lead me. You know my name, you know my purpose, you know everything there is to know about me—and you love me. You call me yours! I trust you! Amen.

Proclaim

"And the peace of God, which transcends all understanding, will guard your hearts and your minds in Christ Jesus." (Phil. 4:7)

Prompt

When God speaks, we can believe Him. We can take His promises to heart. We can hold on to them—sometimes as treasure and sometimes for dear life.

As we walk through this world of uncertain futures, uncertain finances, and uncertain fitness, **GOD GIVES US PEACE.** He helps us find firm footing in the resurrected emptiness of Jesus' tomb. In one of God's great ironic jokes, it is that EMPTY tomb that gives us FULLNESS of life.

The peace of God is His antidote to our uncertainty. We can believe Him and take Him at His word; we can rest in the peace of His promises. ***The tomb was empty but His promises are not!***

So as you listen to today's song, let it lift you UP and fill you with peaceful confidence. Because through the power of the resurrection, there AIN'T no grave that can hold you down!

Prod

Do you have a cross that you wear or look at? Today, when you see it, reflect not just on the cross but also on the empty tomb.

Praise

 Listen to

"Ain't No Grave"

by Bethel Music and Molly Skaggs

Pray

Jesus, without the resurrection, you'd just be a failed Messiah. Thank you for the empty tomb! You defeated death! You broke the chains of sin that held me bound and set me free—you walked me out of my own tomb when you walked out of yours! I'm so grateful!! Amen.

Proclaim

"And the peace of God, which transcends all understanding, will guard your hearts and your minds in Christ Jesus." (Phil. 4:7)

Prompt

God is a gardener who deserves to be praised for His creativity, intentionality, and care. He is the one who created flowers and trees, mountains and deserts, leopards and llamas... AND US.

We are beautiful creations, a truth that can lift us up when we feel the absolute opposite, broken and barren.

Today's song, *"The Garden"* by Kari Jobe, is a reminder that God will stop at nothing to lift us out of sorrow, like ivy creeping across a garden wall. There's power in every seed, and every green thing is a reminder that God's peace reigns supreme!

Prod

Go outside and find something green today. As you look at it, remember the seed it came from—and the death and resurrection it represents.

Praise

 Listen to

"The Garden"

by Kari Jobe

Pray

Jesus, thank you for giving me faith that rises up like ivy and for surrounding me with resurrected people. Thank you for your creativity and for creating us all to be uniquely yours. Let me see you in everyone I encounter today. Amen.

Proclaim

"And the peace of God, which transcends all understanding, will guard your hearts and your minds in Christ Jesus." (Phil. 4:7)

Prompt

There's power in our words. Power over others and power over ourselves. Now, I'm not saying you have ultimate power over someone like you're some sort of sorcerer—I only mean that what we say carries a lot of weight, whether we're saying it to another person or if it's the monologue we carry on within our minds.

So, where there are words of despair, let us speak God's hope. Where there are words of fear, let us speak God's truth. And where there are words of anxiety, let us speak God's peace.

Let's use our words. Let's use God's words. **Let's bring the power of peace with the power of our words!**

Prod

Use your words to encourage ten different people today, whether that's in person, by text, or over the phone or email. Start right now by speaking PEACE over yourself as you pray!

Praise

 Listen to

"What A Beautiful Name"

by Hillsong United

Pray

Jesus, help me speak as you would today. Let me use the power of my words to help build your Kingdom and build up those around me today. I want to be a voice of peace in my world! Amen.

Proclaim

"And the peace of God, which transcends all understanding, will guard your hearts and your minds in Christ Jesus." (Phil. 4:7)

Prompt

Will you be going under today? Or will you be resting in the peace that transcends all understanding?

Is God a firm foundation you can trust? Or will He collapse underneath you?

HE WON'T!

No matter what kind of chaos you encounter, you can still have joy.

No matter what kind of mentally distressing nonsense you come across, you can still have peace.

How do I know? I know because God is our firm foundation. He absolutely, positively, truly, wonderfully will not fail beneath you.

Not one bit.

Rest in that peace today!

Prod

Today's song is one of my favorites. It is such an affirming, faith-boosting, peace-giving jam. As you listen to it and pray, ask God to increase your faith and reveal to you where you need to shore up your foundation.

Praise

 Listen to

"Firm Foundation (He Won't)"

by Maverick City Music

Pray

Jesus, sometimes I need help trusting you. I ask you for that help today. Let my heart know you are my firm foundation. I can stand on you because I know **you won't fail me!** Amen.

Proclaim

"And the peace of God, which transcends all understanding, will guard your hearts and your minds in Christ Jesus." (Phil. 4:7)

Prompt

The thing about the sun is that it's always there. We don't always see it—sometimes it's behind the clouds, and sometimes it's, y'know, night. But we don't have to be aware of it for it to shine.

God is the same, shining His light on all of us equally, whether we sense His light or not. Which is why we're called to reflect God's light for those who dwell in darkness, like those living with financial lack or journeying through physical suffering.

WE CAN BE GOD'S LIGHT TO THOSE WHO CANNOT SEE IT. When we do that, we brighten their world and make Him manifest in their lives. We give them peace that God will make all things well. And we increase the peace in our own lives, too!

How will you shine today?

Prod

You know that little flashlight icon on your phone's home screen? Whenever you see it today, think about God as the light of the world and ask Him how you can be that light for someone.

Praise

 Listen to

"Free"

by Good Shepherd Collective

Pray

Jesus, thank you for illuminating this world for me. You shine so brightly that you make everything else seem so dim by comparison. I need that light in my life, and I need to be your light to others today. Thank you for blessing me, God! Amen.

Proclaim

"And the peace of God, which transcends all understanding, will guard your hearts and your minds in Christ Jesus." (Phil. 4:7)

Prompt

Have you ever been called out by someone because you were being **"so heavenly-minded that you're no earthly good"?** It's a real thing! We can often look so far ahead to our existence with God, filled with His light and life, that we can forget to remain grounded in peace on this earth He gave us.

Our lives are gifts from God, so it's up to us to steward them well. Yes, we look forward to our eternal reward, but we can't do that at the expense of the here and now! That's not a peaceful way to live! God deeply desires to pour out His blessings on your home, your city, your state, your nation—and all the people in it.

Be of earthly good! Bring peace to your world!

How?

Serve. Pray. Love. Encourage.

Prod

Turn up today's song and listen to how the artist reminds us that we are HERE (on this earth) to honor God. As you worship and pray, ask God to reveal to you how you can serve, pray, love, and encourage His children today.

Praise

 Listen to

"We're Here For You"

by Jeremy Riddle

Pray

Jesus, you have huge, enormous desires for your people. I want in! Mold my heart to love like you love and serve like you served. Let me bring peace to my world—however that looks. Amen.

Proclaim

"And the peace of God, which transcends all understanding, will guard your hearts and your minds in Christ Jesus." (Phil. 4:7)

Prompt

We're all orphans, adopted into God's Kingdom. So let's act like it! We're His beloved children, so we can trust Him to give us the strength we need to acknowledge our past hurts and failures, as well as the wisdom and resources to seek help where we need it.

Where we've been broken by family, by coworkers, by those in authority, and by the Church, God brings *restoration and peace.*

On the flip side, God also shows us where we need to make amends and seek forgiveness among those we've broken or for any pain we've caused so that we may more fully embody Him in our ever-expanding world.

And in so doing, we can live at peace with others and with ourselves. We're children of the King!

Prod

Do you have amends you need to make? Take the steps to do it today.

Praise

 Listen to

"Jesus Does"

by We the Kingdom

Pray

Jesus, thank you for welcoming me into the family. Thank you for caring for me when I was hurt. Thank you for loving me, even when I hurt others. Help me to be a good sibling to all the other kids in your Kingdom and give me the strength to represent your name well in the world today. I love you! Amen.

Proclaim

"And the peace of God, which transcends all understanding, will guard your hearts and your minds in Christ Jesus." (Phil. 4:7)

Prompt

Today is my Mom's birthday! My Mom is the ultimate servant and caretaker. She's served our family, her parents, and the body of Christ her entire life. She's led hundreds of bible studies, played piano for thousands of church services, and never missed anything in my life.

She passes along the ***goodness of God to others***.

In 1 Kings 19, we find the prophet Elijah fleeing for his life into the wilderness. It was a sudden development that surprised Elijah, but you know who wasn't surprised? God, obviously! Even though Elijah didn't bring anything with him, God cared for Elijah by miraculously providing everything he needed.

When we operate in God's peace, we carry His goodness into the world. We become the ones who care for the Elijahs among us however they may come to our attention. Maybe it's the poor, the sick, or the underfed; the social outcasts, the filthy, or the tattered; the young or old, the orphaned or childless; the grief-stricken and the bereft.

Whoever our Elijahs are, we can care for them. We are called to care, on God's time and with God's goodness and peace.

Prod

Consider who might be an "Elijah" you need to care for today. List them.

Praise

 Listen to

"Goodness of God"

by Cece Winans (my Mom's favorite song!)

Pray

Jesus, thank you for caring for me. You met me in the wilderness and gave me everything I needed—not just to survive but to THRIVE! Thank you for running after me with your love every day. Amen.

Proclaim

"And the peace of God, which transcends all understanding, will guard your hearts and your minds in Christ Jesus." (Phil. 4:7)

Prompt

Too many times in my life, I've felt like an embarrassment to God, like Adam and Eve when they recognize their nakedness and run to hide in shame. But when I was in treatment for my drug addiction during the summer of 2011, I discovered the power of mirror work.

This therapeutic work required me to sit in the middle of a group of people and stare at a mirror for a long time. And then, when I was ready, simply say... "Lance, I forgive you."

This exercise was pivotal in my shame-healing process. While I looked at myself, it felt more like I looked at God inside of me... who was forgiving me.

There's peace in the face of God because He is a God who faces US. God does not turn away, even when we can't face ourselves. We are not an embarrassment to God—we are His children! *He loves us!*

When we forget that love, God will remind us of it. He'll get our attention however He must. But once He reminds us of His love, He'll then turn us into ambassadors of His peace so we can share it with all those we encounter in person, in passing, and online.

We look in God's face and then turn around and represent that face to ourselves and to others. What peace.

Prod

Examine your own face in the mirror and, if you need to, forgive yourself. Whatever it is you need to bring to God, say it. Come clean and ask for forgiveness.

Praise

 Listen to

"Honesty"

by Bethel Music

Pray

Jesus, thanks for being proud of me. You give me peace. Your face is all I want to see in my world—let me see you everywhere I look today, and when I do see you, help me reflect what I see onto those around me today. Amen.

LANCE LANG

Proclaim

"And the peace of God, which transcends all understanding, will guard your hearts and your minds in Christ Jesus." (Phil. 4:7)

Prompt

When I think of peace, I often think of the man we find in Luke 8, a man who was filled with so many demons that he went by the name "Legion." This was a tormented man! But Jesus saw him and freed him, sending his demons into a nearby herd of pigs.

Jesus encountered a man among the dead, saw his need, and asked nothing of him. **All the man had to do was ACCEPT His freedom.**

INSTANT PEACE. In a mere flash, the man went from chaos to contentment.

And then, from this peaceful state, Jesus gave him a simple job: go home and tell everyone what God did for him.

Peace leads to proclamation.

Prod

Today's old school worship song reminds us to SHOUT our victory from the north to the south. I love this reminder. Crank it up and ask God to give you the courage to proclaim your story of freedom today. GO SHOUT IT!

Praise

 Listen to

"Shout to the North"

by Delirious

Pray

Jesus, thank you for saving me when I was among the dead. I cherish my freedom today! I want to proclaim you to everyone I meet today—in whatever way they'll best hear you. Guide me and direct me, Lord! Amen.

Proclaim

"And the peace of God, which transcends all understanding, will guard your hearts and your minds in Christ Jesus." (Phil. 4:7)

Prompt

Yesterday, we talked about the task of proclamation as an outpouring of the peace of Christ in our lives. It's our job to proclaim what Jesus has done for us, just like the man He delivered from the legion of demons.

So what can we proclaim? Here are some ideas:

- The freedom God has brought us.
- The purpose He has given us.
- The majesty He created.
- The delight He takes in us.
- The unearned grace in which He has submerged us.
- The calling He has put on our lives.
- The joy He's planted in our spirits.

We can proclaim God's glory and His desire to deliver everyone the same way He delivered the demon-possessed man. And us.

IT'S YOUR STORY. PROCLAIM IT!

Prod

Pick one of the suggested proclamation prompts and share it with someone today.

Praise

 Listen to "Indescribable" by Chris Tomlin

Pray

Jesus, I proclaim your goodness in my life today. You are truly INDESCRIBABLE! Let me live like it today. Give me courage to proclaim my story to someone who needs to hear it today. Show me who that person is and bring us together through your divine appointments. Amen.

LANCE LANG

Proclaim

"And the peace of God, which transcends all understanding, will guard your hearts and your minds in Christ Jesus." (Phil. 4:7)

Prompt

God is a God of good things. Do you believe it? He really is! He brings good things like joy where we are destitute and peace where we are anxious. And where we need patience and kindness, He gives us opportunities to practice and develop them.

But He doesn't stop there! When our hands are clenched with fear, God eases them open with His generosity and faithfulness, and when we are tempted to berate others or ourselves, He whispers words of gentleness and self-control into our spirits.

God wants us to live entirely from His peace and love. From the Fruits of the Spirit. From good things.

Prod

Identify at least one good thing God has given you in the past month. Thank Him for it.

Praise

 Listen to

"Been So Good"

by Elevation Worship

Pray

Jesus, thank you for the good things you've given me throughout my life—the ones you gave me recently AND the ones you gave me early on. Help me to remember that I AM ONE OF THOSE GOOD THINGS! Amen!

Proclaim

"And the peace of God, which transcends all understanding, will guard your hearts and your minds in Christ Jesus." (Phil. 4:7)

Prompt

We need leaders, but we shouldn't find our peace in them. And I say this as a leader myself! **God is the one who leads.**

Sometimes we get sidetracked and look to other people for answers, like strong leaders to whom we can pledge our allegiance. But Jesus is the One who deserves our allegiance, the One who gives us peace. We should only follow leaders who follow after Him.

So don't go looking for power, whether it be political, spiritual, or organizational. Instead, choose to follow Jesus so closely that He fills your vision and becomes all that you see.

Jesus led with LOVE.

Jesus led with CONFIDENCE.

Jesus led with PATIENCE.

Jesus led with KINDNESS.

Jesus led with PEACE.

Prod

Do you follow a leader who doesn't exemplify Jesus in their behavior? Should you still? Ask God to weigh in on it—and then act on what you hear from Him.

Praise

 Listen to

"All Hail King Jesus"

by Jeremy Riddle

Pray

Jesus, you are my King. You deserve all my praise and all my attention. Thank you for giving your life for mine. You are the best kind of leader I can follow. Let me lead like you today. Amen.

Proclaim

"And the peace of God, which transcends all understanding, will guard your hearts and your minds in Christ Jesus." (Phil. 4:7)

Prompt

Okay, here's a thought that always fills me with peace: God is not a fickle god who grades us on how hard we perform our worship. He's not waiting for us to sweat the right amount, lift our hands the right height, or spend a certain amount of time on our knees before He does anything on our behalf.

No! God is a Good Parent who listens for us, who hears His children when we ask Him questions, no matter how imperfectly we phrase our requests. ***And even when words fail us, God still hears us.***

God is not sitting above us in heaven and waiting for the right incantation to summon Him. What kind of God would He be if that was the case? No, God is with us here and now, longing to act on our behalf. All the time.

That's peace.

Prod

Talk to God today how you would talk to your best friend. Let Him really hear your heart.

Praise

 Listen to

"As You Find Me"

by Hillsong United

Pray

Jesus, thanks for listening to me, no matter how I talk to you. I love your understanding. Here's what's on my heart today: [FOLLOW THE 'PROD' SUGGESTION HERE]. Amen.

Proclaim

"And the peace of God, which transcends all understanding, will guard your hearts and your minds in Christ Jesus." (Phil. 4:7)

Prompt

Who's in your world? Look around and you'll see people who suffer. People who suffer from lack, from unemployment, from sickness, or from grief.

Look around and you'll also see people who rejoice. People who rejoice for bounty, for provision, for health, and for peace.

Look around and you'll see people who do neither. People who are numb to God's world in all its beauty and terror.

Wherever you look, whichever of these kinds of people you encounter, you have the option to be a person of peace, bearing witness to God's grandeur.

I know you will face people today who NEED the PEACE you have. Commit to being a peace-giver today because YOU can bring hope to the suffering. YOU can rejoice alongside the joyful. YOU can shake the numb from their icy state.

God gave you peace. **SHARE IT!**

Prod

Of the three kinds of people above, which kind do you most encounter? How can you be a light to them today?

Praise

 Listen to

"World Needs Jesus"

by River Valley Worship

Pray

Jesus, I rejoice, even though sometimes I suffer or feel numb. Thank you for understanding where I am today because you've been there too. Help me to be a person of peace to everyone who comes across my path today. I love you! Amen.

Proclaim

"And the peace of God, which transcends all understanding, will guard your hearts and your minds in Christ Jesus." (Phil. 4:7)

Prompt

To the outside eye, God's peace looks decadent and irresponsible. Just look at Scripture! He calls herdsmen to prophesy and gardeners to speak truth to the powerful. The Bible is filled with heathens who embody God's peace more faithfully than the holy do.

So should we just be heathens then?

Nah, I don't think that's quite the takeaway!

But we can be peaceful people who embrace these Biblical examples, peaceful people who live as though we're in exile from our homeland of heaven, who see the enemy, the foreign, the stranger, or the alien and run TOWARD them instead of AWAY.

Today's song talks about RUNNING to God. Oftentimes God prompts us to come back to Him, and on the other side of that, He opens up doors for us to help others.

It may be incomprehensible to believe God wants to use you in your current state. But He does. I promise! No matter where you are today, just start heading back to God. Walk to Him. Jog to Him. Run to Him!

Prod

Who are some "holy heathens" that God used in mighty ways? Write about them and what you might take from their stories.

Praise

 Listen to

"Run To The Father"

by Cody Carnes

Pray

Jesus, I know you can speak to me in unexpected ways. I'm listening. Show me yourself through the holy heathens who responded to you in the Bible, and when I see you there, show me who I can run toward in order to bring your peace. Amen.

Proclaim

"And the peace of God, which transcends all understanding, will guard your hearts and your minds in Christ Jesus." (Phil. 4:7)

Prompt

You know what peace does? It looks at our lives as they are and is satisfied with what it sees... while always driving us to be more at peace with both God and ourselves. With God's peace, rather than looking at the world and seeing a barren and limited wasteland, we can see it for what it really is: full of abundant possibilities and promise.

This kind of vision lets us live faithful, peaceful lives—the kinds of lives that speak a resounding rebuke to a culture full of fear and lack. Our lives should NOT look like everyone else's! The fearful, anxiety-ridden world should look at us and say, "I want THAT kind of peace!"

Prod

In what ways have you bought into the "culture of fear and lack"? Ask God to show you His abundance and peace instead.

Praise

 Listen to

"Take Me There"

by Anna Golden

Pray

Jesus, let me recognize your abundance wherever I see it—even when it doesn't look like abundance. I believe in you! Let me be the kind of person who draws attention for how much I resemble you. Let me move and work in the world today as you do. Amen.

Proclaim

"And the peace of God, which transcends all understanding, will guard your hearts and your minds in Christ Jesus." (Phil. 4:7)

Prompt

Sometimes it feels like God hides, but He can always be found. We just have to seek Him. Where? In high places, low places, or even in the ordinariness of our daily lives. We can do this because we know God loves to show Himself to us, especially in unexpected places and with unexpected peace.

The Bible says in Psalm 139:7, *"Where shall I go from your Spirit? Or where shall I flee from your presence?"*

So if there's no place we can go to get away from God, then that means He's always with us, ready for us to seek Him.

God will show Himself among the lowly and the esteemed, among those who work and those who are looking for work, among the outcasts and the insiders, among those whose walk with Him is stronger than ever, and those who experience pain, doubt, and disillusionment at the mere mention of His name.

He can be found anywhere and everywhere. Rest in the peace of that knowledge today.

Prod

What are you doing to look for God in the everyday? Write out some ways you can open your eyes to finding God and His peace in your day-to-day world.

Praise

 Listen to

"Psalm 139"

by Shane & Shane

Pray

Jesus, let me find you today. Show yourself to me in a fresh way. My eyes are wide open and I'm looking for you, but I know you'll still surprise me. I'm looking forward to it! Amen.

Proclaim

"And the peace of God, which transcends all understanding, will guard your hearts and your minds in Christ Jesus." (Phil. 4:7)

Prompt

God wants your cares.

God wants your fear.

What are you holding back from Him?

I get it. Sometimes I only want to give *part* of my fears and cares to God, which doesn't make a whole lot of logical sense, but makes tons of *emotional* sense. These are the things I truly, truly care about, in a perverse way—how can I give them up?

But God wants them. HE WANTS EVERYTHING YOU HAVE, INCLUDING THE BAD STUFF. You can trust him with those burdens—He wants them all. ***Give it ALL to Him.***

Because in return, He gives you His peace.

What a trade!

Prod

Make an inventory of what you're holding back from God. Pick just one thing to commit to giving Him in prayer all week. Then keep working on your list until you're holding nothing back!

Praise

 Listen to

"Give Me Your Peace"

by Gateway Worship

Pray

Jesus, give me your peace! And give me the courage to give you ALL my cares today. I want to give you everything I have—not just the good stuff but also all the rotten stuff and the stuff I can't seem to let go of. I want you to have it all! Amen.

Proclaim

"And the peace of God, which transcends all understanding, will guard your hearts and your minds in Christ Jesus." (Phil. 4:7)

Prompt

There's peace around an open door, isn't there? God loves to open doors! Some of us find the door opens up with a single knock; others have bloodied our knuckles and it still feels like God isn't home. I've experienced both, and though I prefer one over the other, I still know I can rest in God's peace, knowing that He'll open His door in His time.

In the meantime, ***God gives us patience when we need to wait and boldness when we need to step forward in faith.***

And then, He'll open doors. He'll open doors of healing for those who are sick, doors of peace for those who are in turmoil, and doors of joy for those who are numb. God has made us to be people who declare His peace to a world full of closed and locked doors.

Prod

Do you have a door that stays closed? What is God telling you about it?

Praise

 Listen to

"Rest on Us"

by UPPERROOM

Pray

Jesus, I trust you to open the right doors at the right time. You're the one guiding my feet on the path, so you're the one I trust with every step. Give me peace while I wait patiently on you, and give me boldness to act in faith when you open up doors so that I can walk confidently through them. Amen.

Proclaim

"And the peace of God, which transcends all understanding, will guard your hearts and your minds in Christ Jesus." (Phil. 4:7)

Prompt

There's such a remarkable feeling of peace when you know you're known, and no one knows you better than God. He made you! He's the Creator of Heaven, the one who made everything, whether we see it or not. And His creative impulse didn't fizzle out with the stars—He still creates to this day.

You and I are the work of His hands—an ongoing work, ever unfinished. And so we need to remain flexible, submitting to His will while standing firm in His strength and not in our own.

When we do this, when we ask God to search us out and know us, then we get to know Him better too. *We can relax into the peace of a relationship with God.* What a bargain!

Prod

How are you doing with the peaceful work of submitting to God's formation? Spend time on your knees today submitting to His will for your life.

Praise

 Listen to

"Want it All"

by Sean Curran

Pray

Jesus, mold me and make me to look more like you today. I want it! I want it ALL! I want to represent you to the world. I want people to look at me and see you. I want to be a bringer of your peace and love to everyone I meet today. Make it happen, God! Amen.

Proclaim

"And the peace of God, which transcends all understanding, will guard your hearts and your minds in Christ Jesus." (Phil. 4:7)

Prompt

There's peace in knowing your place, and I say that even as a leader. What I mean is this: we *all* sit beneath God. He is Lord over all, high above all our earthly leaders in government, business, ministry... you name it. Whatever the organization, He is above it.

God stoops to conquer and yet meets us wherever we are. He encompasses all space, high and low. There really is none like Him!

This is why we need to lift our leaders up to God—leaders at all levels and in all facets, praying for all in positions of leadership so that everyone in our world can lead quiet and peaceable lives in all godliness and dignity, leading wherever He's called us to lead.

That's the way of peace.

Prod

Listen to today's song, proclaiming God's rightful place in the highest position. Sing your praises to Him and lift up your leaders to the King of all Kings and Leader of all Leaders!

Praise

 Listen to

"Be Lifted High"

by Bethel Music

Pray

Jesus, you showed me how to lead by going to the cross. Let me be sacrificial in my leadership today. Show me how to lead like you, to treat others the way you treat them, and to truly inspire those around me to live a life that honors you. Help me lead by example! We lift your name high today! Amen.

Proclaim

"And the peace of God, which transcends all understanding, will guard your hearts and your minds in Christ Jesus." (Phil. 4:7)

Prompt

The universe declares God's majesty! I love that line from today's song.

You know it doesn't matter what the weather's actually doing outside—according to the calendar, today is officially the first day of autumn, which makes it, just like every other day, a day that God made. Today is another day to live, to breathe in and out. Another day for your heart to pump blood and your synapses to crackle within your brain.

It's another day for your eyes to gorge themselves on the beauty God made, whether that's the grandeur of the night sky or the intricacy of the autumn leaf. God—and only God—could fashion wonders like these!

But as the seasons change, don't forget God's presence. Like the sun: He's always shining, always warming. Even when He's hidden behind clouds or His presence seems dimmed by autumn's chill, He's still there, still radiating His peace.

Prod

Head outside today and find a leaf. Examine it and the intricate way it was created, reflecting on God's miraculous design. What does that level of care mean for you?

Praise

 Listen to

"God of Wonders"

by Chris Tomlin

Pray

Jesus, thank you for your creativity. It's at work in me and for me! I know that your peace is always there, even when I can't see it or feel it, so let me trust that promise and rest in your peace as the seasons change from one to the other. Bless me today. Amen.

Proclaim

"And the peace of God, which transcends all understanding, will guard your hearts and your minds in Christ Jesus." (Phil. 4:7)

Prompt

If you know me, you know I love to quote Jeremiah 29:11. It's full of hope and wonder. But there are lots of other good parts of Jeremiah that speak to the tough times of life, like in chapter 8 where he lifts up his voice in lament and says, "My joy is gone. Grief is upon me. My heart is sick. The harvest is passed. The summer is ended. And I am not saved."

Have you ever felt this way? I know I have. I recently spent over a year feeling depressed and lonely. I couldn't kick it. That's largely why I started writing this devotional book.

When we feel like this—or know someone who does—we can hurt with those who hurt and mourn with those who mourn. And we expectantly await God to fill us again with hope and joy, with peace and comfort.

He came through for me and He'll come through for you. Sadness is only for a time, but God's peace lasts forever!

Prod

Does the arrival of fall fill you with the promise of harvest or the sadness of summer's end? Why do you think you feel that way? Take it before the Lord and ask Him for His peace either way!

Praise

 Listen to

"Lord, I Need You"

by Passion

Pray

Jesus, thank you for hurting with me and mourning with me. I know that my sorrow will only last for a little while and that your peace is forever. Give me peace today. Amen.

Proclaim

"And the peace of God, which transcends all understanding, will guard your hearts and your minds in Christ Jesus." (Phil. 4:7)

Prompt

God is so dependable. He always, always, *always* cares for us, but His care doesn't always FEEL very caring. He brings restoration in His time and in His way, and sometimes that means He brings restoration in ways that break us.

Think of a broken bone. If it isn't set properly, it will HEAL in a malformed way, which isn't good for the bone OR the person it's attached to. Once it heals crooked, it needs to be broken again and re-set so that it can heal more fully and completely.

Sin is our way of trying to HEAL ourselves like an improperly set bone. It doesn't work, and it always leaves us in turmoil instead of peace.

God wants us to HEAL completely, so sometimes our challenge lies in accepting His bone-breaking restoration. It hurts, but we can accept it in peace because we know that, in the end, He makes all things right.

Prod

How do you respond to the idea of having to be "re-broken" in order to mend more fully? I know it can be scary to face these ongoing wounds. But God wants to HEAL you. He can HEAL YOU. Turn up today's song and go to God for the healing you need.

Praise

 Listen to

"Healing Rain"

by Michael W. Smith

Pray

Jesus, I believe you are the HEALER! I ask that you heal me today. I give myself to your guiding hand so that you can do what you need to do to make me new. You make all things right. I trust you... HEAL ME! Amen.

Proclaim

"And the peace of God, which transcends all understanding, will guard your hearts and your minds in Christ Jesus." (Phil. 4:7)

Prompt

God is so patient, loving us at our best and even standing with us in our doubts, our griefs, and our impatient desires.

When we get fed up and cry, ***"How long, O Lord?"*** then He whispers peace in our ears.

Destruction and violence seem to surround us. Shootings, chaos, political division, war in distant countries, toxic air in others, and natural disasters worldwide.

When we look around in despair and cry, "How long, O Lord?" then He whispers peace in our ears.

And even in the midst of our doubts, He can still make us instruments of His hands. Where there is hatred, He can help us to sow love. Where there is darkness, His light can shine through us.

We can do good in His name and hear Him whisper peace through our actions. Peace doesn't have to be loud. Peace can be a whisper.

Prod

Where are you overwhelmed? Write about it in your journal, then cry out to God and ask Him, "How long, O Lord?" Let Him whisper peace in your ears.

Praise

 Listen to

"Open Up"

by The Brilliance

Pray

Jesus, thank you for reassuring me with peace in the midst of my chaos. It's easy to look around at a dying, chaotic world and feel like all is lost, but I know you're at work even when it doesn't seem like it, and that you whisper peace to me. Let me hear you loud and clear today. Amen.

Proclaim

"And the peace of God, which transcends all understanding, will guard your hearts and your minds in Christ Jesus." (Phil. 4:7)

Prompt

We're almost through meditating on God's peace, but we can't let an opportunity go by to reflect for a moment on the fact that we get to talk about God so openly here in these pages. That isn't the case everywhere on this earth.

There is a large segment of Christians worldwide known as the Persecuted Church, Christians who live in places where it's dangerous—*even life-threatening*—to proclaim the name of Jesus. Yet the members of the Persecuted Church are so convinced of God's peace that they embrace it even when doing so could very well lead them to their deaths.

It's good to occasionally remember the Persecuted Church. It should push to pray for those who don't have the freedom we have. It should also fill us with gratitude that we can worship God, sing to God, and praise our God in full freedom today.

Prod

Does it ever hit you, how FREE you really are to worship God? This is a peaceful feeling. Write about it.

Praise

 Listen to

"Find My Peace"

by Naomi Raine

Pray

Jesus, thank you for being so real that you're worth risking it all for. I pray for all those in the Persecuted Church today, those who are putting their very lives on the line just to serve you. Bless them where they are. Guide them, protect them, and bring them peace. I cherish the freedom I have to worship you openly. Amen.

Proclaim

"And the peace of God, which transcends all understanding, will guard your hearts and your minds in Christ Jesus." (Phil. 4:7)

Prompt

Have you ever basked in sunlight? You know, just laid out on a beach or a patio chair while the sun warms you all over?

I love the feeling of peace that washes over me when the sun hits so brightly I can't help but close my eyes.

The overwhelming brightness of the sun is the perfect reminder that where we have faith, the light of God strengthens it. Where we have doubt, the peaceful light of God blesses it.

When we want to run away, His light is there to bring us home.

When we feel alone and useless, His presence brightens our day and fills us with renewed hope.

This is just what God loves to do.

When we bask in God's bright, peaceful light, we can rest assured He will make all things right through His kindness, peace, and love.

Prod

Is there sun out today? Walk outside, sit outside, or better yet, work outside today. And let the sun warm your skin. Reflect on the ways God's light warms your soul.

Praise

 Listen to

"Give Me Jesus"

by UPPERROOM

Pray

Jesus, thank you for shining so brightly in my world and bringing peace to my heart. I am warmed by you and delight in your presence in my life. Let me reflect your warmth to the world today! Amen.

Proclaim

"And the peace of God, which transcends all understanding, will guard your hearts and your minds in Christ Jesus." (Phil. 4:7)

Prompt

In one of God's great contradictions (and He has plenty of those when we consider Him with our human-limited minds), peace can be BOTH a quiet whisper AND a *mighty sound*.

Today's song, *"A Mighty Sound"* by Bethel Music, reminds us of this amazing truth. Angel armies can go to work in our peace! Our songs of praise to God are effective at a massive, earth-shattering level... AND rooted in His ultimate peace.

I don't know how God does it, and I don't even really NEED to know how He does it! I just know He makes His peace exist in the calm of the storm AND in the roar of our praise.

Prod

Crank today's song and let go with a mighty sound of your own! Examine the peace that floods your heart afterward and thank God for it.

Praise

 Listen to

"Mighty Sound"

by Bethel Music

Pray

Jesus, make me an instrument of your peace today. Let me be a mighty sound of your love, joy, and peace that the world around me can't help but hear today. Amen.

Proclaim

"And the peace of God, which transcends all understanding, will guard your hearts and your minds in Christ Jesus." (Phil. 4:7)

Prompt

As we close out our meditation on peace, here's a fun way to practice peace. Turn on today's song, then get a small piece of chocolate—an M&M or a Hershey's Kiss, for example—and pop it in your mouth.

Don't chew! This is key! Instead, as you listen to these bold lyrics about how God is the defender of our peace, let the chocolate rest there on your tongue and dissolve. And while it does that, mentally reflect on what you taste. Really notice it. Focus on the way it melts and dissolves, notice the flavors as they move across your tongue, feel the texture of the candy as it changes form. As you do that, allow your breathing to slow and your mind to be quiet.

Meditate on how God goes before you...

Mediate on how God's mercy is the shade you live in...

Meditate on how God's love has re-shaped your heart...

Stay this way until the candy is gone.

And then thank God for His peace.

Prod

Practice the "chocolate meditation" today.

Praise

 Listen to

"Defender"

by UPPERROOM

Pray

Jesus, you are my defender! Thank you for giving your all for me. Thank you for giving me a peace that passes all understanding. And thank you for helping me to hold on to it no matter what I face. You are the defender of my heart and I give my life to you today. Amen.

Proclaim

"Finally, brothers and sisters, whatever is true, whatever is noble, whatever is right, whatever is pure, whatever is lovely, whatever is admirable—if anything is excellent or praiseworthy—think about such things. Whatever you have learned or received or heard from me, or seen in me—put it into practice. And the God of peace will be with you." (Phil. 4:8-9)

Prompt

Today begins our final quarter-long meditation of the year, and now we're talking about gratitude. I'd like to start with a question:

Are you grateful in the grind?

It's easy to be grateful when you finally reach your goal, but can you be grateful on your way there? During the tough work with no praise? During the grueling practice sessions away from the crowd? During the reps you take that bring no benefit in the moment?

Being grateful in the grind is a gift. And it takes work. Some of the most content people I know have that unique ability to stay steady when things are good or bad, up or down.

You know why? Because they aren't waiting for some big win, big deal, or big moment for permission to finally be happy.

They're just grateful to be in the grind. They've fallen in love with the process because they know that's where real growth takes place.

Prod

What's a part of the grind where you can find gratitude? Each day for the next week, identify something in your life for which you're grateful and write it down.

Praise

 Listen to

"10,000 Reasons"

by Matt Redman

Pray

Jesus, thank you for the grind, and thank you especially for being right here with me. Give me everything I need to grow and to succeed, to make it all the way through with gratitude. There are 10,000 reasons why I'm grateful for you today! Amen.

Proclaim

"Finally, brothers and sisters, whatever is true, whatever is noble, whatever is right, whatever is pure, whatever is lovely, whatever is admirable—if anything is excellent or praiseworthy—think about such things. Whatever you have learned or received or heard from me, or seen in me—put it into practice. And the God of peace will be with you." (Phil. 4:8-9)

Prompt

"Whatever is true."

What does it mean to think about whatever is true?

Our enemy is a liar. That's just who he is. He lies to us constantly. He tells us our lives are over. He tells us we're nothing without whatever he has to offer. He tells us we need that promotion, that like on social media, that next drink, that pair of shoes...

Lies. All of them. The grateful truth is this: all we need is Jesus.

That's what it means to think about whatever is true. Do your thoughts come back to that fundamental truth? When you spiral into whatever has you spiraling, bring it back to Jesus. That's who you need. He is ALL you need.

Rest in gratitude for that truth. Being thankful, Jesus energizes you and clarifies your truth.

Prod

What can you do to remind you of the truth of Jesus in the midst of the devil's lies? Start with today's song. Ask God to renew your mind with the truth of who you are.

Praise

 Listen to

"Fear Is A Liar"

by Zach Williams

Pray

Jesus, thank you for being the Ultimate Truth. Build up my gratitude by reminding me of your truth in unexpected ways today. Amen.

Proclaim

"Finally, brothers and sisters, whatever is true, whatever is noble, whatever is right, whatever is pure, whatever is lovely, whatever is admirable—if anything is excellent or praiseworthy—think about such things. Whatever you have learned or received or heard from me, or seen in me—put it into practice. And the God of peace will be with you." (Phil. 4:8-9)

Prompt

"Whatever is noble."

What does it mean to think about whatever is noble?

Noble things are elevated. Classy. Excellent. Morally upstanding.

When Paul calls us to think on whatever is noble, he's telling us to set our minds on higher things. Not to get dragged down into the world's hollow chase for status but to remember that *true nobility is found in the gratitude of Christ.*

One way to make sure you fill your mind with noble things is by checking what you are letting in.

I spend hours every day with headphones in, filling my mind with words, melodies, and, ultimately, power. The question is, what types of words, melody, and power am I letting in?

Our passage tells us today: they should be NOBLE things.

Prod

Flood your mind with NOBLE things by turning on today's song, meditating on the words, and writing down three noble things you can reflect on throughout the day today.

Praise

Listen to

 "I Believe"

by Phil Wickham

Pray

Jesus, thank you for making me noble! I'm so grateful that you call me toward you in faith. Guide my mind toward the noble today so you can do a work in my heart and spirit. I accept it! Amen.

Proclaim

"Finally, brothers and sisters, whatever is true, whatever is noble, whatever is right, whatever is pure, whatever is lovely, whatever is admirable—if anything is excellent or praiseworthy—think about such things. Whatever you have learned or received or heard from me, or seen in me—put it into practice. And the God of peace will be with you." (Phil. 4:8-9)

Prompt

"Whatever is right."

What does it mean to think about whatever is right?

In my experience, it pays to put a premium on right thinking through the lens of gratitude. Despite the shifting sands of our culture, there is a RIGHT and there is a WRONG, and we are called to gratefully set our minds on what is RIGHT.

When we encounter the many wrongs of the world, we can identify them quickly as wrongs. How? Because we think about whatever is right—we think about Jesus! This is gratitude! By studying Jesus and the way He went through the world, we know what is right and can spot a counterfeit from a mile away.

Aren't you grateful?!

Prod

How will you reflect on what is right today? What will you do when faced with a wrong? Make a plan and write it down!

Praise

 Listen to

"Cornerstone"

by Bethel Music

Pray

Jesus, I'm so grateful that you are the Ultimate Right Thing. May you so fill my vision that anything not of you burns away. I don't want to get led astray by fakes—I just want you! Amen.

Proclaim

"Finally, brothers and sisters, whatever is true, whatever is noble, whatever is right, whatever is pure, whatever is lovely, whatever is admirable—if anything is excellent or praiseworthy—think about such things. Whatever you have learned or received or heard from me, or seen in me—put it into practice. And the God of peace will be with you." (Phil. 4:8-9)

Prompt

"Whatever is pure."

What does it mean to think about whatever is pure?

Purity is an underrated concept in today's culture. Ours is a culture that values experiences, and while I agree that new and varied experiences are a very important aspect of a life well-lived, I also think it's important that we don't dilute those experiences along the way.

In the Christian world, it's easy to hear the word "purity" and think of sexuality, but I prefer to think of it as Undiluted Jesus.

When we think about whatever is pure, we invite all our experiences to be drenched in Jesus.

He must be our everything, nothing added. When we can open ourselves up to the Undiluted Jesus, then we can walk in gratitude. It's the only way to truly experience this world.

Prod

What areas of your life have a lack of Undiluted Jesus? How can you open those up to His power? Write about it.

Praise

 Listen to

"Give Us Clean Hands"

by Chris Tomlin

Pray

Jesus. More, more, MORE. I want MORE of you today. I want MORE grace, MORE mercy, MORE love, MORE beauty, MORE of the raw and undiluted YOU! Fill me to overflowing with you!!! Amen.

Proclaim

"Finally, brothers and sisters, whatever is true, whatever is noble, whatever is right, whatever is pure, whatever is lovely, whatever is admirable—if anything is excellent or praiseworthy—think about such things. Whatever you have learned or received or heard from me, or seen in me—put it into practice. And the God of peace will be with you." (Phil. 4:8-9)

Prompt

"Whatever is lovely."

What does it mean to think about whatever is lovely? And what does "lovely" even mean?

I think of it as being full of love. When something feels lovely to me, that means it's resonated with the part of me that feels love. A garden can be lovely because love blossoms within me. A meal can be lovely because love feeds my soul. A work of art can be lovely because love is an expression of the inexpressible.

Once you start to view the world this way, you'll see God's love everywhere, calling out to you, resonating with you, and connecting with the gratitude in your soul.

Focus on that and you'll be thinking about whatever is lovely.

Prod

Write down five things in your life today that you might find unexpectedly "lovely." Put your focus on them today.

Praise

 Listen to

"Forever Reign"

by Hillsong United

Pray

Jesus, thank you for making such a lovely world. I open up my heart and soul to connect with the lovely things of your creation as I experience your lovely world. Thank you for making ME lovely. Let me see Your love everywhere I look today. Amen.

Proclaim

"Finally, brothers and sisters, whatever is true, whatever is noble, whatever is right, whatever is pure, whatever is lovely, whatever is admirable—if anything is excellent or praiseworthy—think about such things. Whatever you have learned or received or heard from me, or seen in me—put it into practice. And the God of peace will be with you." (Phil. 4:8-9)

Prompt

"Whatever is admirable."

What does it mean to think about whatever is admirable?

Well, what do we admire? I know personally, I admire those people, stories, and ideas around us that call me to be greater than myself. And I don't think I'm the only one. It's almost as if we know we are capable of more, and seeing other people reach higher and climb farther encourages us to do the same thing.

And then, the real miracle happens: *we become admirable!* When those in our world see us living the radically changed lives Jesus has called us to, we become an "admirable thing" for others to think on!

God loves to use others, and God loves to use us. That's admirable. Think about it!

Prod

What or who is calling you to be greater than yourself today? Set an achievable goal and go for it!

Praise

 Listen to

"Great Things"

by Phil Wickham

Pray

Jesus, thank you for putting admirable people and things in my field of vision. I want to be encouraged by them so that I can have the courage to go deeper and fly higher than I ever have before. Give me the strength and will to be admirable to others. Amen.

Proclaim

"Finally, brothers and sisters, whatever is true, whatever is noble, whatever is right, whatever is pure, whatever is lovely, whatever is admirable—if anything is excellent or praiseworthy—think about such things. Whatever you have learned or received or heard from me, or seen in me—put it into practice. And the God of peace will be with you." (Phil. 4:8-9)

Prompt

"If anything is excellent."

What does it mean to think about whatever is excellent?

Chances are, if you mention the word "excellent" to a member of my generation, they're eventually going to say it drawn out and with a Southern California accent, thanks to the movie *Bill and Ted's Excellent Adventure*.

But "excellent" is much more than an overused '80s buzzword. And it's much more than just high levels of achievement.

When someone is excellent, they've gone above and beyond the call of duty. They've brought to the table an attitude that the bare minimum is not enough. They're all in.

This is the attitude of gratitude Jesus brought to us. There is no middle ground with Christ. You have to be all in. You have to go the extra mile. You have to take up your cross and be excellent to one another.

Prod

Identify an area of your life where you are already excellent. How can you take that attitude into *another* area of your life today?

Praise

 Listen to

"All Things New"

by Hillsong United

Pray

Jesus, thank you for demonstrating all-in, flat-out, sacrificial excellence for me. I know you'd never ask me to do something that you haven't already given me the strength to do, so help me be excellent for you today. I want to serve you with EXCELLENCE! Amen.

Proclaim

"Finally, brothers and sisters, whatever is true, whatever is noble, whatever is right, whatever is pure, whatever is lovely, whatever is admirable—if anything is excellent or praiseworthy—think about such things. Whatever you have learned or received or heard from me, or seen in me—put it into practice. And the God of peace will be with you." (Phil. 4:8-9)

Prompt

"If anything is... praiseworthy."

What does it mean to think about whatever is praiseworthy? There are a lot of ways to answer that question, but I think one helpful way is to look at your life and identify any aspects in it that are worth praising.

Are you taking concrete steps to better yourself and your situation? That's praiseworthy. Are you making it through another day with your faith intact? That's praiseworthy. Are you reading this daily devotional, doing the daily "prod," and applying what you learn? That's praiseworthy.

There's no objective, external measure of what makes something—anything—worth praising. If it's good, if it draws you closer to the life God has called you to, or if it honors Jesus in any way, no matter how small, then it's praiseworthy.

And that's worth taking to heart. Praise God!

Prod

How can you act in a praiseworthy manner today? Write out ten ways to be praiseworthy... and then DO them.

Praise

 Listen to

"Son of Suffering"

by Bethel Music

Pray

Jesus, you are so very worthy of praise. Help me put my focus on you, and in so doing, strive to be the praiseworthy person you've created me to be. I want to do my BEST for you today, but I know I can only do that in your strength. Amen.

Proclaim

"Finally, brothers and sisters, whatever is true, whatever is noble, whatever is right, whatever is pure, whatever is lovely, whatever is admirable—if anything is excellent or praiseworthy—think about such things. Whatever you have learned or received or heard from me, or seen in me—put it into practice. And the God of peace will be with you." (Phil. 4:8-9)

Prompt

"Strength for today and bright hope for tomorrow."

These lyrics from the song "Great Is Thy Faithfulness" are a recipe for gratitude. When we stop to identify, rest in, and meditate on the goodness of God in our lives, we can CLAIM the strength we need for the today and ENJOY a bright hope for tomorrow.

Gratitude is a time machine. It provides us with the ability to look back to where we were and be grateful for how God has brought us out... while simultaneously giving us a vision for even better days ahead.

Let's claim that today as we go about our lives. ***Climb into the time machine of gratitude.*** Thank God for what He has brought you through and trust that, if He did it once before, He can and will DO IT AGAIN!

Prod

Where does your gratitude time machine take you in the past? What about the future?

Praise

 Listen to

"Great Is Thy Faithfulness"

by The Worship Initiative

Pray

Jesus, I'm so grateful for being where I am now compared to where I was. You brought me here! What can I do but worship you?! Thank you for this wonderful day you gave me, and give me a vision and a bright hope for tomorrow. Amen.

Proclaim

"Finally, brothers and sisters, whatever is true, whatever is noble, whatever is right, whatever is pure, whatever is lovely, whatever is admirable—if anything is excellent or praiseworthy—think about such things. Whatever you have learned or received or heard from me, or seen in me—put it into practice. And the God of peace will be with you." (Phil. 4:8-9)

Prompt

Over the past decade-plus of my sobriety, I've told my story literally thousands of times.

Would you believe me when I tell you that I think I get more out of it than the people who hear it? It's true!

Each time I share my heart vulnerably and transparently, I walk away incredibly grateful for everything I've been through. It's human nature! The more you share your pain, your struggles, and the hard things you've lived through, the more grateful you find yourself for the life you're living TODAY.

And this is true ***REGARDLESS OF WHETHER YOUR STORY HAS RESOLVED OR NOT.***

When you share your heart with a safe person or safe crowd, you will always walk away more rooted in gratitude than you did before. I'm proof—thousands of times and counting.

Prod

Today's song is one of my favorites. Crank it up and spend time thanking God for your story. Thank Him for everything He has done and allowed to bring you to this place today. Then think about a safe person in your life you can tell your story to... and tell it!

Praise

 Listen to

"Gratitude"

by Brandon Lake

Pray

Jesus, thank you so incredibly much for the gift of my story. Even though it doesn't look perfect and it was tough for me to live out, I know you've been with me every step of the way and that you are glorified through the story of my life. Help me to be grateful for every part of it. Amen.

Proclaim

"Finally, brothers and sisters, whatever is true, whatever is noble, whatever is right, whatever is pure, whatever is lovely, whatever is admirable—if anything is excellent or praiseworthy—think about such things. Whatever you have learned or received or heard from me, or seen in me—put it into practice. And the God of peace will be with you." (Phil. 4:8-9)

Prompt

The end of the most famous Psalm in the Bible says this:

"Surely goodness and mercy shall follow me all the days of my life, and I shall dwell in the house of the LORD forever."

Today's song references this Psalm during the bridge and repeats it over and over again. Some days it gets stuck in my head; when that happens, I always smile with gratitude. Why? Because it acts as both a forecast for my future and remembrance of my past all in one statement, shifting me to a place of grateful expectation.

When we expect GOOD things to come to us, then we naturally end up in a state of gratitude. And that's a great state to live in!

Prod

How can you adjust your state of mind today to be one of grateful expectation?

Praise

 Listen to

"Runnin"

by Elevation Worship and Brandon Lake

Pray

Jesus, you want to give me good things! Goodness and mercy follow me ALL the days of my life! Not just yesterday but today and tomorrow, too! Help me to take that to heart so that I expect something hopeful and good for me today. I believe! Amen.

Proclaim

"Finally, brothers and sisters, whatever is true, whatever is noble, whatever is right, whatever is pure, whatever is lovely, whatever is admirable—if anything is excellent or praiseworthy—think about such things. Whatever you have learned or received or heard from me, or seen in me—put it into practice. And the God of peace will be with you." (Phil. 4:8-9)

Prompt

I took up running a few years ago, and the more I've done it, the more I've learned how much I enjoy it. I don't always love *starting* my run, but I sure do love *finishing* it! I always feel a sense of accomplishment, like I've pushed myself toward what's best for me that day.

Running is as much mental exercise as it is physical. Sure, it takes time to build up your physical body to endure miles and miles of pounding the pavement, but even more difficult is overcoming the mental temptations to quit early, take the easiest route, or just not go out that day.

It helps to run with gratitude for the end. I fully know that, when I finish my race, I'm going to feel amazing! I'll be that much closer to my overall goals, my health will have improved, and who knows what ideas or breakthroughs God might've given me while I'm out there.

The hard areas of our lives become easier when we're preemptively grateful for what lies on the other side of them.

Prod

What sort of gratitude can you take into one of the hard areas of your life today? What can you be grateful for regardless?

Praise

 Listen to

"Testify to Love"

by Avalon

Pray

Jesus, thank you for this breath and the one that follows. Thank you for giving me the strength to do the hard things in my life and see them through. I know the ending is going to be amazing! I'm so grateful for my life today. Amen.

Proclaim

"Finally, brothers and sisters, whatever is true, whatever is noble, whatever is right, whatever is pure, whatever is lovely, whatever is admirable—if anything is excellent or praiseworthy—think about such things. Whatever you have learned or received or heard from me, or seen in me—put it into practice. And the God of peace will be with you." (Phil. 4:8-9)

Prompt

How much would your gratitude grow today if you fully trusted God? How much would it grow if you thought on all the things in this quarter's verse and discovered how foolish it all could look? Would you be willing to look foolish in front of your friends, your family, or your boss?

When's the last time you really trusted God enough to look foolish in someone's eyes?

When you *"think about such things,"* you welcome foolish hope into your life. Because the world isn't always going to seem like it's in line with the foolish thoughts God wants us to meditate on.

But foolish thoughts bring foolish hope. And foolish hope believes for better days.

Foolish hope says nothing is impossible.

Foolish hope believes everything in your past is being worked together for good.

Foolish hope looks **foolish to man but faithful to God** because foolish hope is faith-filled hope.

Prod

Are you willing to look foolish today? Pick one of the attributes in this quarter's scripture and make it your foolish focus for the day.

Praise

 Listen to

"Everything & Nothing Else"

by Chris McClarney

Pray

Jesus, help me trust you enough to let it all out today! Take control of my life. I believe in your foolish hope, and I'm so thankful that I can be foolish for you and know that you'll come through for me. Jesus, help me to be foolish for you today. I'm letting go to give it all to YOU! Amen.

Proclaim

"Finally, brothers and sisters, whatever is true, whatever is noble, whatever is right, whatever is pure, whatever is lovely, whatever is admirable—if anything is excellent or praiseworthy—think about such things. Whatever you have learned or received or heard from me, or seen in me—put it into practice. And the God of peace will be with you." (Phil. 4:8-9)

Prompt

I've come to learn that change rarely takes place until our level of desperation overwhelms our current situation. Whether it's overcoming an addiction, forgiving a spouse, finally starting to exercise or diet the way you need to... all lasting change starts with desperation.

When I am really seeking a breakthrough in an area of my life, sometimes I ask God this question: "Am I desperate enough yet?"

Gratitude springs from desperation, especially when it's fulfilled.

Today and every day, I want to be spiritually desperate for more of God in my life. Enough of me. Enough of selfish desires. Enough of comparisons and ego-tripping. I just want more God and the things of Him.

God, I am desperate for you. And that desperation leads me to be grateful for the changes when they come.

Prod

Do you need a breakthrough today? During your prayer time, ask God to awaken your hope and to open a door!

Praise

 Listen to

"Breakthrough"

by Chris McClarney

Pray

Jesus, I'm desperate for you! Change me, mold me, make me a little more like you today. Lead me down your paths and guide me in my life today so that I can reflect your love and light to everyone I meet. Amen.

Proclaim

"Finally, brothers and sisters, whatever is true, whatever is noble, whatever is right, whatever is pure, whatever is lovely, whatever is admirable—if anything is excellent or praiseworthy—think about such things. Whatever you have learned or received or heard from me, or seen in me—put it into practice. And the God of peace will be with you." (Phil. 4:8-9)

Prompt

Everyone is special in God's eyes. We really are. We are all beautiful, unique creations, purposefully created to do what only each of us can do.

But when it comes to living a life of discipleship and gratitude, you need to hear the other side of this coin: *"YOU ARE NOT SPECIAL!"*

You simply cannot go out and do your own thing and expect it to yield results. *There is a reason why you need Jesus: because your way doesn't work!*

See, there is a solution to all your problems, and that solution has worked for millions and millions of other people, and it leads to a life filled with purpose, passion, and joy! It's a great life, but you won't get to live it if you think you can find your own way to it. You cannot drag your old way of thinking into the life of discipleship; it has to stay behind where you left it so you can follow what God has for you.

And at the end of that path is eternal gratitude.

Prod

What do you need to leave behind? What are you trying to drag into your new life? Make a plan to keep the past in the past today.

Praise

 Listen to

"Not Afraid"

by Red Rocks Worship

Pray

Jesus, thank you for my new life. I'm so grateful. Help me to enjoy this new life and keep my old way of thinking in the past where it belongs. I turn my life, my mind, and my heart over to you completely! Amen.

Proclaim

"Finally, brothers and sisters, whatever is true, whatever is noble, whatever is right, whatever is pure, whatever is lovely, whatever is admirable—if anything is excellent or praiseworthy—think about such things. Whatever you have learned or received or heard from me, or seen in me—put it into practice. And the God of peace will be with you." (Phil. 4:8-9)

Prompt

I made a bold decision early on in my sobriety, one I'm not sure I thought through completely. I certainly didn't have the vision to see what my life would eventually become by making this decision. Yes, it felt like the right thing to do, but more than that, it felt like what I *had* to do. Almost as if I didn't have a choice.

What was the decision? I chose to live my life as openly and vulnerably as possible, giving everyone I could a front-row seat to the emotions and experiences of a rough, raw, recovering drug addict.

What I found, though, was that the more I opened up about the pain of my past, the more others felt like they were given permission to do the exact same thing.

By sharing openly, I became grateful for the impact I could have on others. Imagine how others might feel grateful for your openness.

Prod

Are you living an open and shared life? If not, what's holding you back? What can you do to open up more?

Praise

 Listen to

"Grateful"

by Elevation Worship

Pray

Jesus, thank you for this life of gratitude I get to lead. Give me a way to be open about it with someone today. Help me to recognize the opportunity when it comes and to step into that opportunity with boldness and courage. You're worth it! Amen.

Proclaim

"Finally, brothers and sisters, whatever is true, whatever is noble, whatever is right, whatever is pure, whatever is lovely, whatever is admirable—if anything is excellent or praiseworthy—think about such things. Whatever you have learned or received or heard from me, or seen in me—put it into practice. And the God of peace will be with you." (Phil. 4:8-9)

Prompt

Because of the pain of your past, you might feel like a boiling pot of rage, constantly on the verge of spilling over onto those you love. That's okay. I've felt that way before—after all, anger is a natural human emotion.

But whenever you get tempted to see yourself that way, remember how God sees you: as a bringer of peace and patience, forgiving others just as He has forgiven you.

You simply are not what the pain of your past says about you. That pain doesn't have to define you—God does. He says you're special. Unique. Set apart. Chosen. Accepted. Set free. No longer a slave to darkness but instead a child of the light.

You are not the sum of your mistakes, your poor choices, or the suffering you've endured at the hands of others. No, you're much, much more than that. You've been extended a hand of forgiveness and redemption! You have been made new! You are a victor and a champion!

Prod

Make a list of ten things in your life you're grateful for. These are how you're new!

Praise

 Listen to

"Future / Past"

by John Mark McMillan

Pray

Jesus, I'm so grateful for your forgiveness and grace. Thank you for redeeming my past. Thank you for asking me to be your friend! Thank you for calling me a peace-bringer instead of someone who soaks in anger. Thank you for making me new! Amen.

Proclaim

"Finally, brothers and sisters, whatever is true, whatever is noble, whatever is right, whatever is pure, whatever is lovely, whatever is admirable—if anything is excellent or praiseworthy—think about such things. Whatever you have learned or received or heard from me, or seen in me—put it into practice. And the God of peace will be with you." (Phil. 4:8-9)

Prompt

The longer I've walked with God, the more I've learned that He is a good Father who takes good care of His kids. He has given each of us gifts we can use to expand His kingdom and through which we can worship Him.

But most of all, He's given each of us exactly what we need for *today*.

This is especially useful when you feel short of hope because it frees you up from feeling like you have to manufacture your own hopes for the future. If you have some hopes, then that's great! If not, no worries: God will give them to you sooner rather than later.

But most of all, He'll give you **hope for this day** and this moment in time.

God loves to give us what we need when we need it—even when we don't seem very grateful for it in the process. That's just the way He is!

Prod

What do you need today? How can you demonstrate your gratitude for what God gives you?

Praise

 Listen to

"Hope Has A Name"

by River Valley Worship

Pray

Jesus, I need [NAME ONE OF YOUR NEEDS] today. Please meet my need in your time and in your way, and help me to be grateful when you do. I know you're going to take care of me! I love you so much. Amen.

Proclaim

"Finally, brothers and sisters, whatever is true, whatever is noble, whatever is right, whatever is pure, whatever is lovely, whatever is admirable—if anything is excellent or praiseworthy—think about such things. Whatever you have learned or received or heard from me, or seen in me—put it into practice. And the God of peace will be with you." (Phil. 4:8-9)

Prompt

One of the best ways to demonstrate gratitude in your daily life is to say YES.

If you know anything about me, you know I'm big on saying YES. Before we gave our lives to the Lord, we said YES to a lot of destructive things, but now it's time to say YES to God.

We say YES to surrendering daily.

We say YES to gratitude.

We say YES to our God-given purpose.

YES is a response that acts as a change agent; that's what we're looking for, right? Change? Each time we say YES, we tear down a piece of the walls we so carefully build up around ourselves, the walls we guard so closely to keep everyone at a distance.

As you say YES to helping others or to forgiving someone from your past or to any positive action, the more of that wall comes down. Pretty soon, it's low enough for you to see over. Wow, what a view! It's a whole new world out there.

Prod

What is God asking you to say YES to today? What, if anything, is holding you back?

Praise

 Listen to

"I Say Yes"

by Kim Walker Smith

Pray

Jesus, I can't believe I get to live this life of saying YES. It all started when I said YES to you, so help me keep it going! Give me the courage to say YES to something big today. Amen.

Proclaim

"Finally, brothers and sisters, whatever is true, whatever is noble, whatever is right, whatever is pure, whatever is lovely, whatever is admirable—if anything is excellent or praiseworthy—think about such things. Whatever you have learned or received or heard from me, or seen in me—put it into practice. And the God of peace will be with you." (Phil. 4:8-9)

Prompt

There's an immense gratitude that comes with being the kind of person who says YES, and all that gratitude helps you feel really great.

The more you open yourself up to the idea of saying YES, the more you'll begin to realize how much you enjoy it, because the feelings that accompany triumphing over past fears are exhilarating.

Even people who don't love change would agree that staying in the same routine day after day, saying NO to invitations and NO to offers, is pretty unlikely to lead you to anything new or different.

Try this: say NO out loud three times. How did that feel? By the third time you probably were frowning. Think about it...

Now, say YES out loud three times... go. Say it again. You're smiling aren't you?

Saying YES feels great!

Prod

What God-authored thing can you say YES to today?

Praise

 Listen to
"We Say Yes"
by SEU Worship

Pray

Jesus, you said YES on the cross—you said YES to me and all my pain and shame. I say YES to you! As I navigate this day, help me to recognize what I need to say YES to. I want to follow you! Amen.

Proclaim

"Finally, brothers and sisters, whatever is true, whatever is noble, whatever is right, whatever is pure, whatever is lovely, whatever is admirable—if anything is excellent or praiseworthy—think about such things. Whatever you have learned or received or heard from me, or seen in me—put it into practice. And the God of peace will be with you." (Phil. 4:8-9)

Prompt

Now that you're committed to living a life of gratitude, you'll be surprised by how many new opportunities come your way just through the act of saying YES.

YES has a power to help you find unexpected opportunities, and if you don't say YES, you'll miss out on things you don't even know you're missing out on.

Of course, not every YES leads to something major, wonderful, or unexpected, but that's the point: you never know what lies on the other side of your YES! It could be a new career, a new relationship, a new talent, a new hobby, or just the joy of putting a smile on someone's face.

You aren't responsible for the outcome—you're just responsible for the YES. God's opportunities will knock on your door; your YES opens it, and does so with gratitude.

Prod

Are you missing out on opportunities? What might you say YES to? Write it down.

Praise

 Listen to

"Yes I Will"

Vertical Worship

Pray

Jesus, when you knock, give me the courage to say YES and open the door to whatever opportunity you've sent me. I trust you with my YES today because I know you're trustworthy. Anything you give me is a good gift, so I welcome that good gift into my heart. Amen.

Proclaim

"Finally, brothers and sisters, whatever is true, whatever is noble, whatever is right, whatever is pure, whatever is lovely, whatever is admirable—if anything is excellent or praiseworthy—think about such things. Whatever you have learned or received or heard from me, or seen in me—put it into practice. And the God of peace will be with you." (Phil. 4:8-9)

Prompt

When you live in fear and insecurity, you're avoiding thinking about the very things that Paul tells us to dwell on in this passage.

Do you know the main reason why most people say NO? It's fear. We're scared! We can get crippled by the thought of what new people might ask of us or what new experiences may require of us.

Our walls keep us secluded and our minds trick us into thinking we won't enjoy new practices or that we'll look silly if we decided to try. What will people think? What will they say?

Who cares?! ***Those bricks of insecurity and fear must be demolished.*** We must face them head on! Just remember: with every YES, the bricks of fear and insecurity are falling and a firm foundation of freedom is being built instead! Be grateful!

Prod

Make a list of four fears or insecurities that are holding you back. Ask the Holy Spirit to reveal them to you. Share them with someone you trust and ask them to pray with you to give them back to God.

Praise

 Listen to

"Not Afraid"

by Jesus Culture

Pray

Jesus, you have made me more than a conqueror. Help me overcome my fear and anxiety today. I refuse to walk in fear anymore! Give me the courage to overcome [NAME A FEAR OR INSECURITY] in health and security. I can do anything because you're right there with me! Amen.

Proclaim

"Finally, brothers and sisters, whatever is true, whatever is noble, whatever is right, whatever is pure, whatever is lovely, whatever is admirable—if anything is excellent or praiseworthy—think about such things. Whatever you have learned or received or heard from me, or seen in me—put it into practice. And the God of peace will be with you." (Phil. 4:8-9)

Prompt

Sometimes I look around at the relationships God has blessed me with and I just whisper a giant prayer of thanks. Because when I was drinking and drugging, I had very few true relationships. Legitimate, actual friends were few and far between.

One of the greatest gifts a life of discipleship can give you is the fostering of true, meaningful relationships, and saying YES is the first vulnerable step to get you there.

A **YES** to a Holy Spirit prompting could be the connection point for a lifelong friendship.

A **YES** to a church event could be the setting of your "How I met your mother" story you tell your future children.

You never know who will be on the other side of your **YES.** But you CAN know that you'll be grateful for them.

Prod

How are your relationships? Today during your prayer time, turn up today's song and invite the Holy Spirit to meet with you. Spend time confessing sin and asking for fresh anointing of the Holy Spirit. Then ask God to reveal new relationships that could deepen and strengthen your faith!

Praise

 Listen to

"Here As In Heaven"

by Elevation Worship

Pray

Jesus, you had deep relationships with at least twelve people while you were here; please give me deep relationships as well. I don't need a ton of them—I just need a handful of people I can go super-deep with. Thank you for the people in my life; I'm open to anyone else you want to bring my way. I'm so thankful. Amen.

Proclaim

"Finally, brothers and sisters, whatever is true, whatever is noble, whatever is right, whatever is pure, whatever is lovely, whatever is admirable—if anything is excellent or praiseworthy—think about such things. Whatever you have learned or received or heard from me, or seen in me—put it into practice. And the God of peace will be with you." (Phil. 4:8-9)

Prompt

My hope sprang to life in April of 2011 when I committed to sobriety. During the early days I was taught to build my new life on gratitude. We would practice this each Friday in group therapy sessions by going around the room and listing what we were grateful for.

Each Friday as we did this, the darkness that had engulfed me for years began to fall away. God's hopeful plans for me became more and more of a reality as gratitude began to build in my spirit.

As I grew confident, my addiction grew weaker and weaker, and I began to see a future worth fighting for. One of the greatest gifts of my sobriety has been discovering my purpose in life.

I realized my life MATTERS. And you know what? *Yours does too!*

If you don't believe me, try listening to today's song and not getting fired up for the purpose God has for YOUR life.

Prod

What God-authored purpose are you pursuing? Write it out and keep it in front of you!

Praise

 Listen to

"The Anthem"

by Jesus Culture

Pray

Jesus, WAKE ME UP! Give my calling fuel. Ignite me with your hope! I don't want to wander through this life—I want to live with a purpose! Help me to embody your plans and purpose throughout my day today... and for the rest of my life. Amen.

Proclaim

"Finally, brothers and sisters, whatever is true, whatever is noble, whatever is right, whatever is pure, whatever is lovely, whatever is admirable—if anything is excellent or praiseworthy—think about such things. Whatever you have learned or received or heard from me, or seen in me—put it into practice. And the God of peace will be with you." (Phil. 4:8-9)

Prompt

A random speaker whose name, unfortunately, I don't remember once said something that's stuck with me ever since I heard it:

"I had to realize that if I wanted a life of freedom, I would have to live a life of forgiveness."

This simple statement shook me and changed me. In an instant, I realized what I had allowed to happen and just how far away from God's purpose I had strayed because I chose to stubbornly cling to unforgiveness.

Maybe right now you realize why you've been waking up angry, frustrated, and generally ungrateful. Maybe you, too, are trapped in the land of unforgiveness, just like I've been.

Want to take even more steps toward freedom? Practice **Radical Forgiveness.**

What's that mean? It means you ask God to help you instantly forgive everyone who harms you. Yes, instantly. It might sound daunting, but you'll get there if you start by asking God to help you, today.

Forgiveness is the essence of a life of freedom.

Prod

Ask God to reveal everyone you need to forgive right now. List them!

Praise

 Listen to

"Holding Nothing Back"

by Jesus Culture

Pray

Jesus, help me develop radical forgiveness. When people hurt me. Help me forgive them. When people come to mind who have hurt me, help me forgive them. I know you forgave me, so I ask your help in forgiving [NAME OF PERSON]. I give them entirely to you today, trusting that you will work in their life the same way you worked in mine. You love them, Lord—help me to love them, too. Amen.

Proclaim

"Finally, brothers and sisters, whatever is true, whatever is noble, whatever is right, whatever is pure, whatever is lovely, whatever is admirable—if anything is excellent or praiseworthy—think about such things. Whatever you have learned or received or heard from me, or seen in me—put it into practice. And the God of peace will be with you." (Phil. 4:8-9)

Prompt

When I was in the midst of my addiction, I found what I thought was freedom. At least, it seemed that way to me at the time. The buzz from alcohol or the high from pills seemed like a temporary liberation from my problems, but in the end, it only made them worse.

And then I found freedom in Christ. And that changed everything.

Your life has been changed by that same freedom. And here's another bit of good news—it's not just your life that was changed, it was your ETERNITY. God's freedom is *forever*. It's ETERNAL FREEDOM! It's freedom that's meant to make your life better here and now while ALSO bringing you closer and closer to your heavenly Father throughout eternity.

What more could we thank God for?!

Prod

What has God freed you from? Make a list and thank Him for each one individually.

Praise

 Listen to

"I Thank God"

by Maverick City Music

Pray

Jesus, thank you, thank you, thank you. I'm so grateful for this forever freedom you've given me. Thank you for making me free in this life—help me to live out my freedom today as I look forward to the forever freedom I will share with you on the other side of this life. Amen.

Proclaim

"Finally, brothers and sisters, whatever is true, whatever is noble, whatever is right, whatever is pure, whatever is lovely, whatever is admirable—if anything is excellent or praiseworthy—think about such things. Whatever you have learned or received or heard from me, or seen in me—put it into practice. And the God of peace will be with you." (Phil. 4:8-9)

Prompt

Doesn't it feel good to be forgiven? Doesn't that make your heart leap with gratitude?! Just thinking about it makes me wanna jump out of my chair!

Forgiveness is a transformational power that never EVER leaves a situation the same. Why? Because while forgiveness starts at the cross, it doesn't end there. Jesus paid for our sins and took all our shame upon Him when He was on the cross, but not even the burden of all that weight could hold Him down!

Forgiveness finds its ultimate expression in the empty tomb. That's God's final word about us—that death can't hold us in and sin can't hold us down. Hallelujah we are FREE!

Prod

Carving any pumpkins lately? Or seen any? Next time you look at one, think about how God emptied out the tomb.

Praise

 Listen to

"O Praise The Name"

by Hillsong United

Pray

Jesus, I'm so incredibly grateful for the empty tomb. You rose again! You defeated death and broke every chain that held me down! Help me never to forget what you've done for me and never to take it for granted. Hallelujah! Amen.

Proclaim

"Finally, brothers and sisters, whatever is true, whatever is noble, whatever is right, whatever is pure, whatever is lovely, whatever is admirable—if anything is excellent or praiseworthy—think about such things. Whatever you have learned or received or heard from me, or seen in me—put it into practice. And the God of peace will be with you." (Phil. 4:8-9)

Prompt

I don't know what kind of family environment you came from, but I do know this: when you accepted Christ, you became a part of the best possible family out there. God our Father promises to gather us all into Him, so how can we help but be thankful for our adoption into this Great Big Family?!

And just like every family experiences its ups and downs, so does this one—both large and small. Your community of believers will have times where everyone loves one another and times that are... well, let's just say stressful. But no matter what, our Father helps us be a loving, bonded family, providing for all our needs—emotional, spiritual, financial, and physical.

That's something to be grateful for.

Prod

Write a thank-you note to a member of your Big Adopted Family today. Literally, write an actual note on a card or piece of paper and send it to them in the mail. It'll spread a little gratitude in their direction!

Praise

 Listen to

"Father of Lights"

by Jesus Culture

Pray

Jesus, thank you for this great family to belong to. Thank you for being our mediator when we need it and for smoothing out all our personalities into something truly wonderful and great. We rely on you, and we love you. I'm so grateful. Amen.

Proclaim

"Finally, brothers and sisters, whatever is true, whatever is noble, whatever is right, whatever is pure, whatever is lovely, whatever is admirable—if anything is excellent or praiseworthy—think about such things. Whatever you have learned or received or heard from me, or seen in me—put it into practice. And the God of peace will be with you." (Phil. 4:8-9)

Prompt

This is a time of year when we hear a lot about harvests. And the truth is, a lot of us have a pretty full harvest, all things considered. We generally have enough food to eat, a roof over our head, some honest way of earning money, and a phone that keeps us connected to the outside world.

When we have enough, God calls us to be content but not complacent. In other words, we need to continue pursuing God's peace and purpose for our lives while continuing to call enough "enough."

Because we can fall into the attitude of always wanting more, more, more, which—aside from being unfulfilling—is a fundamentally anti-gratitude way of looking at things.

Be GRATEFUL for what God has given you, DESIRE all He has for you, find COMFORT within His will, and PURSUE the calling He's placed on you. That's the key to a fulfilled life of harvest!

Prod

Check your desires. Write them down. Do they align with God's call on your life?

Praise

 Listen to

"Lord of the Harvest"

by Lindy Cofer

Pray

Jesus, thank you for giving me enough. Let me pursue you and your call for my life first and foremost. I want your harvest in my life, and your harvest is about so much more than just the necessities—it's about people, community, and YOU. It's you I really want! Amen.

Proclaim

"Finally, brothers and sisters, whatever is true, whatever is noble, whatever is right, whatever is pure, whatever is lovely, whatever is admirable—if anything is excellent or praiseworthy—think about such things. Whatever you have learned or received or heard from me, or seen in me—put it into practice. And the God of peace will be with you." (Phil. 4:8-9)

Prompt

Today is Halloween, a time when we generally celebrate kids, which makes it a good time to remember that it's our job as Christians to care for God's kids as well—kids of all ages, from the youngest infant to the wisest elder.

We're all a big family of kids—brothers and sisters—doing our best to get along. We can be grateful to be welcomed into God's family.

So with that in mind, we must remember to treat each other like family: that means we're always hospitable and welcoming to new family members, as well as ready to open the doors of our lives to anyone who knocks in the hopes of getting a treat.

As God's kids, we don't need to compete for His love because He gives it freely and equally—so let's give our love freely and equally, too—to everyone who we encounter.

Prod

Whether you're welcoming kids to your door or just noticing them, use it as a reminder to give the love of Jesus freely to those around you.

Praise

 Listen to
"Kids"
by Brandon Lake

Pray

Jesus, thank you for your love that doesn't ever run dry or run out. You love me as I am, and I'm so grateful and thankful for it! Fill me with your love today so that I can give it away freely—like candy! Amen.

Proclaim

"Finally, brothers and sisters, whatever is true, whatever is noble, whatever is right, whatever is pure, whatever is lovely, whatever is admirable—if anything is excellent or praiseworthy—think about such things. Whatever you have learned or received or heard from me, or seen in me—put it into practice. And the God of peace will be with you." (Phil. 4:8-9)

Prompt

Anger is an unavoidable emotion, and with it often comes regrettable words. I can recall too many instances when words I truly didn't mean slipped out just because I was angry.

Inevitably, we will all make some people angry at some point in our lives. And angry people don't always say the nicest things about the people they're angry at.

Through our relationship with Jesus, when angry words are used against us, we no longer have to wilt in shame or wither in disgrace. He has set us free! He has taken all our shame on Him, so the only words we need to pay attention to are His: the grateful words of life He speaks over us every minute of the day.

But I get it. This is not easy. Words hurt and words can stick. If you have some hurtful words rolling around in your mind from someone, take some time to ask God to replace them with what is true, noble, right, pure, lovely, and admirable!

Prod

Make a list of ten words that describe you as God sees you. Carry it with you today.

Praise

 Listen to

"Greater"

by Elevation Worship

Pray

Jesus, thank you for speaking words of life over me. Thank you that you are GREATER than any of the hurtful words people have used against me. The world tells me I'm miserable and small, but you say I'm blessed and big. The world tells me I can't do anything right, but you say I can rest in you. Forget about the world—I'm listening only to you today. Amen.

Proclaim

"Finally, brothers and sisters, whatever is true, whatever is noble, whatever is right, whatever is pure, whatever is lovely, whatever is admirable—if anything is excellent or praiseworthy—think about such things. Whatever you have learned or received or heard from me, or seen in me—put it into practice. And the God of peace will be with you." (Phil. 4:8-9)

Prompt

Yesterday we talked about the words we hear from others (or ourselves) and how those compare to the words Jesus says about us. If you followed the Prod, you should've written out ten words that Jesus says about you and meditated on them.

So now that you have those words that Jesus speaks about you, in gratitude you can turn that inside out.

Often, Jesus speaks to us so we can then speak the same thing to others, which is how the world can eventually know His truth. Jesus' words aren't always just for us—they're for others as well. We get to speak into others' lives!

Prod

Who in your world needs to hear the words of life spoken to them? Send them a text right now speaking a powerful blessing of encouragement over them. Watch how the gratitude comes back your way.

Praise

 Listen to

"From the Inside Out"

by Hillsong United

Pray

Jesus, give me courage and wisdom to recognize who needs to hear from you today. Give me the words to say to them to encourage them and build them up in you. Let me bring your freedom to others today! Amen.

Proclaim

"Finally, brothers and sisters, whatever is true, whatever is noble, whatever is right, whatever is pure, whatever is lovely, whatever is admirable—if anything is excellent or praiseworthy—think about such things. Whatever you have learned or received or heard from me, or seen in me—put it into practice. And the God of peace will be with you." (Phil. 4:8-9)

Prompt

A wonderful thing about God is that He gives us so much to think about—so many wonderful things that thrill our hearts and cause our souls to rejoice. It's a wealth of richness that guides us to a fulfilling, grateful life.

This makes me think about all the crazy unique things God has allowed me to do since I got sober in April of 2011. From speaking in prisons to baptizing dozens of people in horse troughs, from officiating weddings over Zoom to doing interviews on TV. All kinds of wild stuff I would have never imagined, all blessings given to me by God because I was open to Him.

Part of this life of renewal and recovery is accepting that God wants to bless us in an abundant way!

He may throw some unexpected things in there, but that's His prerogative. Just leave your arms and heart open, leave it up to Him, and be grateful—He is a loving Father who only gives good gifts!

Prod

Take a deep breath and spread your arms wide in a posture of receptivity. Tell God you are ready for what He has next.

Praise

 Listen to

"Doxology"

by Phil Wickham

Pray

Jesus, thank you for giving good gifts, including the best gift of all: yourself. I'm willing to accept whatever you have for me, big or small, scary or peaceful, because I know that you are in control and you have my back at all times. Let me reflect you in the world today. Amen.

Proclaim

"Finally, brothers and sisters, whatever is true, whatever is noble, whatever is right, whatever is pure, whatever is lovely, whatever is admirable—if anything is excellent or praiseworthy—think about such things. Whatever you have learned or received or heard from me, or seen in me—put it into practice. And the God of peace will be with you." (Phil. 4:8-9)

Prompt

Jesus is the light of the world—but what good is light if it doesn't illuminate, if it can't reach its intended targets? A covered light is no light at all!

Fortunately, gratitude turns us into a window. When we're grateful, we become a window to the world that shows Jesus' light.

When we submit to God in gratitude, we become *crystal-clear glass* that reveals Him and only Him.

I don't know about you, but I don't want to block the LIGHT of God! I want it to shine through me SO THAT it reaches those I love, those who are lost, and those who are hurting.

This all begins with our position of thankfulness. When our gratitude is small, then our window becomes dirty and smudged, and God's light gets dimmed. But when our gratitude grows tall, our window is fresh and clean.

Prod

Crank up today's song and spend time in prayer asking God to LET HIS LIGHT IN!

Praise

 Listen to

"Let The Light In"

by Cody Carnes

Pray

Jesus, make me a clear window of your light to the world today. I give you all my bitterness, hate, and anger. Do what only you can do and fill me with gratitude today. I want your light to shine bright through me.

Proclaim

"Finally, brothers and sisters, whatever is true, whatever is noble, whatever is right, whatever is pure, whatever is lovely, whatever is admirable—if anything is excellent or praiseworthy—think about such things. Whatever you have learned or received or heard from me, or seen in me—put it into practice. And the God of peace will be with you." (Phil. 4:8-9)

Prompt

God is the Lord of the least, the last, the lost, the lonely, and the little. That's us! He rescued us and changed us. The world wrote a whole bunch of words about us, words like: *Failure. Fraud. Fake. Feeble. Fiasco.*

But God crosses all those out and replaces them with words like:

First. Found. Friend-filled. Full. Free.

It's a miracle!

These are truths God wants to burn onto our hearts so we can always know them. When we take in these truths, we can walk with thankfulness that God walks alongside us, remaking us as we go.

Remember to think about what is TRUE!

Prod

Look at those five "F" adjectives above that God says about you. Which do you respond most strongly to? Write a reflection on why.

Praise

 Listen to

"The Lost Are Found"

by Hillsong Worship

Pray

Jesus, thank you for calling me what I truly am—what you've made me to be. You rescued me from the worst this world has to offer, you changed my name, and you are changing the narrative about me. You made me victorious and free! Help me walk in this truth today. Amen.

Proclaim

"Finally, brothers and sisters, whatever is true, whatever is noble, whatever is right, whatever is pure, whatever is lovely, whatever is admirable—if anything is excellent or praiseworthy—think about such things. Whatever you have learned or received or heard from me, or seen in me—put it into practice. And the God of peace will be with you." (Phil. 4:8-9)

Prompt

How often do you feel like you need refuge? However you answer that question, whether it's a lot or a little, God offers it. You can call to Him with an expectant heart, in the midst of your troubles, and God will bring rescue and refuge. It's what He loves to do

We can be grateful because God is a deliverer, saving us from the gasping grasp of death, from the conquered clutches of illness, from the frustrated fatigue of poverty, from the attractive appeal of conformity, and from the slain stasis of apathy.

We've been delivered already, and He continues to provide us with refuge whenever we need it. He is a safe place!

Prod

Praise God throughout the day for the ways He's delivered you. He's worthy!

Praise

 Listen to

"You Are Not Alone"

by Will Gaines

Pray

Jesus, thank you for your deliverance. You saved me—and continue to save me. I am a walking, talking miracle, and it's ALL because of you. Hallelujah! Amen.

Proclaim

"Finally, brothers and sisters, whatever is true, whatever is noble, whatever is right, whatever is pure, whatever is lovely, whatever is admirable—if anything is excellent or praiseworthy—think about such things. Whatever you have learned or received or heard from me, or seen in me—put it into practice. And the God of peace will be with you." (Phil. 4:8-9)

Prompt

We talked yesterday about God being our deliverer, and after we fully embrace that truth, it's good practice to keep God's deliverance in front of our eyes routinely. The enemy uses all the distractions of our world to keep our eyes on **EVERYTHING BUT** God's salvation in our lives.

This takes work, and naturally our focus will tend to ebb and flow during our lives of discipleship. In our blessed times of great gratitude and strength, we're called to help those among us who are weak. We need to reach out and remind others of their deliverance in Jesus Christ—but only from a place of humility, to keep ourselves from giving in to the temptations of pride and arrogance.

God gives us a strategy to keep our eyes on Him and our hearts humble. But how much more could our attention stay on God's goodness if we strategically and intentionally identify areas of distraction?

Just call it out today. Name what causes your focus to wane.

Prod

Write down all the areas of distraction in your life TODAY. Use your prayer time to ask God to help you steer clear of those and stay locked in on the ways God delivered you.

Praise

 Listen to

"Overcome"

by Elevation Worship

Pray

Jesus, thank you for your deliverance. Help me not to get pulled in by these distractions... I want to help others who don't feel it as strongly as I do right now, but help me not take pride in how humble I'm being. Let me embody you in someone's life today. Amen.

Proclaim

"Finally, brothers and sisters, whatever is true, whatever is noble, whatever is right, whatever is pure, whatever is lovely, whatever is admirable—if anything is excellent or praiseworthy—think about such things. Whatever you have learned or received or heard from me, or seen in me—put it into practice. And the God of peace will be with you." (Phil. 4:8-9)

Prompt

At the end of the Bible, In Revelation 21, God says He "makes all things new." Friends, that includes us! So we can thank Him for making us new and for being a safe place where we can turn in times of trouble.

At the beginning of the Bible, in Genesis 2, God looks at the dust on the ground and makes a person out of it. So we can thank Him for the very life we live and the air we breathe.

In between the beginning and the ending is the story, over and over, of God taking ordinary things and making them beautiful, of God taking old things and making them new.

We can turn to God with grateful hearts again and again because we see repeatedly how God works miracles and turns the boring into the breathtaking. He's done it before; He'll do it again. He did it with us.

Prod

Read Revelation 21:1-8 and write a brief reflection on it. What surfaces for you the most?

Praise

 Listen to

"Beautiful Things"

by Gungor

Pray

Jesus, thank you for making me new. Thank you for seeing the beauty within me when no one else could—including myself. You are such a wise creator and restorer; I'm so thankful! Amen.

Proclaim

"Finally, brothers and sisters, whatever is true, whatever is noble, whatever is right, whatever is pure, whatever is lovely, whatever is admirable—if anything is excellent or praiseworthy—think about such things. Whatever you have learned or received or heard from me, or seen in me—put it into practice. And the God of peace will be with you." (Phil. 4:8-9)

Prompt

Nothing satisfies like God. Nothing at all.

We tend to learn this lesson the hard way. I remember thinking if I could only work all day and take pills all night, then I would have everything I needed. Boy was I wrong. And just so sick.

But that's what happens to a lot of people. We think we have something that satisfies—***stuff, career, food, substances, family members, relationships***—but it always turns out to be a mirage. Nothing lasts and nothing satisfies.

Which is why we can be all the more grateful when we discover the forever satisfaction we find in the Lord.

His is a satisfaction that outlasts anything this world has to offer, including things that are good! Our relationships with our spouses or significant others, our kids, our creative outlets—all these are God-given gifts... and none of them satisfy like He does. When we turn to ANYTHING OTHER THAN GOD to satisfy us, we'll ultimately be let down.

We can only find satisfaction in God. And that feeling of satisfaction? It feels a lot like gratitude.

Prod

Where is your satisfaction these days? What parts of your life are you holding back from God? Commit to giving Him your all today.

Praise

 Listen to

"Satisfied"

by Chris Tomlin

Pray

Jesus, thank you for being that all-refreshing fountain of satisfaction in my soul. Thank you for the gifts you've given me, but help me not to see them as the end-all of my life—instead, when I look at them, direct my eyes to you, the gift-giver. Amen.

Proclaim

"Finally, brothers and sisters, whatever is true, whatever is noble, whatever is right, whatever is pure, whatever is lovely, whatever is admirable—if anything is excellent or praiseworthy—think about such things. Whatever you have learned or received or heard from me, or seen in me—put it into practice. And the God of peace will be with you." (Phil. 4:8-9)

Prompt

You probably have this quarter's scripture memorized already, but have you ever checked out Lamentations chapter 3? There we read about how God's steadfast love endures forever. **No, literally: forever!**

Think for a moment about every experience you've ever had since you were born. When you start to list them out, it feels a little like <u>forever</u>, doesn't it? After all, it would take a LITERAL LIFETIME to relive all those experiences.

And yet, even as long as they feel, our lives are just the blink of an eye compared to eternity. Our minds are absolutely incapable of grasping the difference between what we understand and what is actually forever.

But that difference? That's the endurance of God's unfailing love. Hallelujah! WE can live lives of gratitude because we know God is vastly, incalculably in love with us!

Prod

Set a timer for five minutes. Close your eyes, take a deep breath, and spend that time focusing on the forever-ness of God's love. It may feel long, but God's love is so much longer!

Praise

 Listen to

"Forever"

by Michael W. Smith

Pray

Jesus, thank you for being the same yesterday, today, and forever. It's so mind-blowing that I don't even need to try to understand it; instead, I just walk with grateful love for all you've done for me and will do for me. Amen.

Proclaim

"Finally, brothers and sisters, whatever is true, whatever is noble, whatever is right, whatever is pure, whatever is lovely, whatever is admirable—if anything is excellent or praiseworthy—think about such things. Whatever you have learned or received or heard from me, or seen in me—put it into practice. And the God of peace will be with you." (Phil. 4:8-9)

Prompt

Been watching any football lately? You better believe I have! After all, we're in the midst of the season, and what would fall be without football? (Boomer Sooner, by the way!)

Culturally, we tend to want to cheer on the clear winners—after all, who doesn't love a champion?—but it's good to remember that God is the God of the scrubs, the benchwarmers, and the outcasts.

Actually, it's GREAT to remember this. Because we have all experienced feelings of being unwanted, left out, or not good enough. That's why God sent Jesus. To rescue the lost and to welcome back the prodigals like me and you.

Today we can live in gratitude because we know that God looked at the B-team and called us starters! We get to suit up, hit the field, and get in the game!

What a privilege He's given us.

Let's leave it all out there on the field!

Prod

The next time you watch some football, check out all the players on the bench. Imagine them coming into the game and earning a decisive victory, and think about how God's given us the ability to do just that.

Praise

 Listen to "Prodigals" by Passion

Pray

Jesus, thank you for making me a starter. Amazing! I was going nowhere and then you called me to go somewhere. You gave me purpose and I'm so grateful. Help me live up to what you see in me today. Amen.

Proclaim

"Finally, brothers and sisters, whatever is true, whatever is noble, whatever is right, whatever is pure, whatever is lovely, whatever is admirable—if anything is excellent or praiseworthy—think about such things. Whatever you have learned or received or heard from me, or seen in me—put it into practice. And the God of peace will be with you." (Phil. 4:8-9)

Prompt

Fall is a time of decay, with leaves falling and starting to rot, fresh pumpkins being carved into jack-o-lanterns and immediately starting to wilt, and the summer heat making way for the chill of winter.

Honestly, it reminds me of resurrection.

How? Because it reminds me of the moment when Jesus had died and all seemed lost. The time in history when darkness seemingly had defeated the light and begun its reign...

And then Jesus snatched it away and rose again! The darkness fled and the shadows scattered! The light of Jesus' resurrection flooded all the corners of the world, and the decay of death was overturned.

As you experience fall, enjoy it—but remember with gratitude that death doesn't have the final say and that resurrection is on its way.

Prod

What signifiers of fall are around you? Fallen leaves or cooler weather? Think how they can remind you of Jesus' resurrection and then live out that resurrection power today.

Praise

 Listen to

"Christ Be Magnified"

by Cody Carnes

Pray

Jesus, thank you for rising from the dead. You defeated all the death and rot in my life and raised me back to life again! I am forever grateful for your love and your sacrifice. It means everything! Amen.

Proclaim

"Finally, brothers and sisters, whatever is true, whatever is noble, whatever is right, whatever is pure, whatever is lovely, whatever is admirable—if anything is excellent or praiseworthy—think about such things. Whatever you have learned or received or heard from me, or seen in me—put it into practice. And the God of peace will be with you." (Phil. 4:8-9)

Prompt

There's a line in a U2 song where Bono sings, "I believe in the Kingdom Come / where all the colors will bleed into one."

It's a nice metaphor and good imagery for God eclipsing the individuality of His creation, but I think the reality is kind of the opposite. It's not that all the colors will bleed into one, but that all the colors will shine out as their true selves! We'll all complement one another and become an almost incomprehensible display of God's glorious design.

We can be grateful that God created us so uniquely while also creating us to complement one another. You are so very special, but you're also meant to be part of a greater community. You fit in both alone AND with others! What a Wise Creator!

Prod

Find something colorful to examine and notice how the different colors work together to create something beautiful. Ponder what that means about your community.

Praise

 Listen to

"I Still Haven't Found What I'm Looking For"

by U2

Pray

Jesus, thank you for making me the way you made me. Thank you for those around me who strengthen me and who I help to strengthen in return. You're such a Wise Designer, and I'm so grateful for all of it. Amen.

Proclaim

"Finally, brothers and sisters, whatever is true, whatever is noble, whatever is right, whatever is pure, whatever is lovely, whatever is admirable—if anything is excellent or praiseworthy—think about such things. Whatever you have learned or received or heard from me, or seen in me—put it into practice. And the God of peace will be with you." (Phil. 4:8-9)

Prompt

As of this writing, my son L.A. has begun to clasp his hands and attempt to pray before each meal. It's really cute!

It reminds me of seeing a young child give thanks for something they're really grateful for, like the perfect Christmas gift! It can be pretty fun seeing how overboard they go, handing out hugs and high-fives while talking on and on about the topic of their gratitude.

It's usually a pretty big contrast to how we adults tend to show our own gratitude. Generally we're pretty reserved, and even when we do go big, it's usually not as big as what you see from the kid I was just talking about.

And that's fine! There's nothing wrong with the WAY you show gratitude. But I think God likes it when we thank Him like we're children, giving thanks with our whole hearts, holding nothing back but expelling everything, living an entire giant life of gratitude.

Prod

Who is a person in your life who deserves your thanks? How can you go slightly overboard thanking them today?

Praise

 Listen to

"Praise"

by Elevation Worship

Pray

Jesus, words aren't enough, so I'm going to thank you with my life today—and every day. Let me become like a child with my gratefulness and really go over the top with my thanks for you. It means so much! Amen.

Proclaim

"Finally, brothers and sisters, whatever is true, whatever is noble, whatever is right, whatever is pure, whatever is lovely, whatever is admirable—if anything is excellent or praiseworthy—think about such things. Whatever you have learned or received or heard from me, or seen in me—put it into practice. And the God of peace will be with you." (Phil. 4:8-9)

Prompt

I'd like to hone in on one particular part of this quarter's theme verse: the part where Paul tells us to "put it into practice."

Ours can be a performance culture. We like to loudly let everyone know which side we're on, but Paul is encouraging us here not just to signify our faith, but to DO it.

It's not enough just to learn or receive or hear or even see Christlike things—we have to put them into practice. **WE MUST DO.** This is the very essence of gratitude.

Doing won't make God love you more—that's impossible—but it WILL open up your heart and change you in ways that make you more like Jesus. And that's what we're here for.

Don't just receive. Give. Do.

Prod

Where in your life do you need to stop being passive and start being active? Name it! Then make a plan to do something today.

Praise

 Listen to

"Follow You Anywhere"

by Passion

Pray

Jesus, thank you for the ability to do. I'm no longer just a hearer or receiver—with your help, grace, and mercy, I'm a DOER, Lord! I receive you and I love you. Help me to honor you in my actions today. Amen.

Proclaim

"Finally, brothers and sisters, whatever is true, whatever is noble, whatever is right, whatever is pure, whatever is lovely, whatever is admirable—if anything is excellent or praiseworthy—think about such things. Whatever you have learned or received or heard from me, or seen in me—put it into practice. And the God of peace will be with you." (Phil. 4:8-9)

Prompt

I have a question for you. Let's say you break the law and get in trouble for it, but when you go in front of the judge, they say, "You know what? I'm gonna give you a break on this one. You're free to go, no problems."

You'd be pretty grateful, right? And so how would you demonstrate that gratitude? Would you go right out and break that same law again?

Probably not!

Instead, gratitude is reflected in repentance—the key to the Christian life. This entire life is one of repentance, where we repent before God, then take that repentance out toward others and demonstrate what kind of just judge God really is.

We live to serve God and others. That's the life of gratitude.

Prod

Think of a time when you received grace you felt you hadn't earned. Write about it. Who needs that same kind of grace from you?

Praise

 Listen to

"Reckless Love"

by Cory Asbury

Pray

Jesus, thank you for saving me! I'm so grateful for your grace that saved me and welcomed me into your family and Kingdom. Help me to repent today and to live a life you'd be proud of. Amen.

Proclaim

"Finally, brothers and sisters, whatever is true, whatever is noble, whatever is right, whatever is pure, whatever is lovely, whatever is admirable—if anything is excellent or praiseworthy—think about such things. Whatever you have learned or received or heard from me, or seen in me—put it into practice. And the God of peace will be with you." (Phil. 4:8-9)

Prompt

Aren't you tired of trying to run your own life? Isn't that level of stress just too much? Why would you try to bring that neverending rat race into your life of discipleship?

Jesus needs to be the King of your world.

When Jesus donned that crown of thorns on the cross, He was sacrificing Himself and enthroning Himself with an entirely different kind of crown—declaring Himself as ruler over all.

The "all" at the end of that last sentence? That includes our lives! All means ALL.

Jesus needs to be the one who wears the crown, and we need to be thankful that He's got it all under control. He is, after all, a Good King. He cares for you! He loves you! He is the one worth being King of your world!

Prod

Are you wearing Jesus' crown and trying to rule all or some of your life? Write out the areas of your life that you need to give back to Him, and then spend time in prayer today doing just that.

Praise

 Listen to

"We Crown You"

by Jeremy Riddle

Pray

Jesus, thank you for going to the cross for my sin. You're a Good King, and I want you to be enthroned over my life. I give you all my stress and anxiety and repent of trying to do this on my own. I'm forever grateful to you. Amen.

Proclaim

"Finally, brothers and sisters, whatever is true, whatever is noble, whatever is right, whatever is pure, whatever is lovely, whatever is admirable—if anything is excellent or praiseworthy—think about such things. Whatever you have learned or received or heard from me, or seen in me—put it into practice. And the God of peace will be with you." (Phil. 4:8-9)

Prompt

Where are your thoughts?

What do you let yourself think about? Where do you guide your mind when it's racing? Do you let it do its own thing, or do you follow the prescription we read in this passage?

I get it—when your mind's going a mile a minute, it can be tough to guide it to a place of gratitude, to think on these things. But the rewards for doing so are immeasurable—including the God of Peace being with you. So wrangle your racing brain and bring it into submission with scripture!

God wouldn't tell you to do it if it couldn't be done, so guide your mind. See what happens.

Prod

Practice! Spend time this morning praying through our scripture for this quarter. Be intentional about bringing to mind a single thought that is TRUE, NOBLE, RIGHT, PURE, LOVELY, and ADMIRABLE. Today's song will help—it's super-peaceful!

Praise

 Listen to

"King Of My Heart"

by Bethel Music

Pray

Jesus, thank you for my mind. It's a trip sometimes, but I still love it—because you gave it to me. When it races today, help me to subdue it and to think on all the things you told me to think about it. Thank you for this gift. Amen.

Proclaim

"Finally, brothers and sisters, whatever is true, whatever is noble, whatever is right, whatever is pure, whatever is lovely, whatever is admirable—if anything is excellent or praiseworthy—think about such things. Whatever you have learned or received or heard from me, or seen in me—put it into practice. And the God of peace will be with you." (Phil. 4:8-9)

Prompt

What is a life worth? It would be practically insane to try to put a dollar value on a human life because human life has inexhaustible value. We are so far beyond value that we enter a new realm of terminology:

We are **PRICELESS.**

And yet—even knowing that we are priceless—there was a price... and Jesus paid it. We were buried in sin, doused in shame, submerged in regret, and Jesus still saw us and said, "I want them."

And then He got us.

How can we do anything but be grateful?!

No matter what anyone has ever called you or how poorly someone made you feel, Jesus calls you **PRICELESS.**

Prod

Get into a quiet place. Crank up today's song. Let the words pour over your soul. God really loves you...

Praise

 Listen to

"God Really Loves Us"

by Crowder

Pray

Jesus, I'm just speechless. You give me worth. You give me dignity. You look at me and see someone worth dying for, and I can barely even grasp that level of love. I can never thank you enough, but I'm sure going to try! Amen.

Proclaim

"Finally, brothers and sisters, whatever is true, whatever is noble, whatever is right, whatever is pure, whatever is lovely, whatever is admirable—if anything is excellent or praiseworthy—think about such things. Whatever you have learned or received or heard from me, or seen in me—put it into practice. And the God of peace will be with you." (Phil. 4:8-9)

Prompt

Here's something to think about: we have an adversary who wants to see us falter and fail.

We know that already, so that's not the thing to think about. Here it is: have you considered that some of the **BEST ARMOR** you can wear against that adversary is gratitude?

What can our adversary do to you when you practice radical gratitude? How can you hurt someone who remains thankful? How can you destroy someone who remains focused? How can you tear down someone who remains grounded in gratitude? You can't! And neither can he.

Gratitude is the ultimate armor. Put it on!

Prod

Think of all the parts of a suit of armor. What are you grateful for? Imagine those individual bits of thankfulness making up your gratitude armor. During your prayer time today, "put on" that armor by offering your thanks to God.

Praise

 Listen to

"Plead The Blood"

by Chris Davenport

Pray

Jesus, thank you for protecting me against my adversary. I'm so grateful I have you on my side. I put on my gratitude armor today and trust that you protect me and keep me safe so that I can walk in this world and impact it for your Kingdom. I'm free! Amen.

Proclaim

"Finally, brothers and sisters, whatever is true, whatever is noble, whatever is right, whatever is pure, whatever is lovely, whatever is admirable—if anything is excellent or praiseworthy—think about such things. Whatever you have learned or received or heard from me, or seen in me—put it into practice. And the God of peace will be with you." (Phil. 4:8-9)

Prompt

Yesterday we talked about gratitude as armor. Today I want to get a little more into that by looking not just at the concept but also at another scripture written by the Apostle Paul, which we find in Ephesians 5. There, he encourages us to "always give thanks to God the Father for everything."

Everything?

Everything.

What about those terrible things that happened to us? What about the rock bottom we hit, the people we mowed over in our quest for the next big thing, the financial, emotional, and spiritual wreckage we've all left in our wake?

Well, if Paul is to be believed... yes. Everything.

Shame has power, but when we give thanks even for the bad stuff, then we remove that shame... which removes the power those things have over us. When we give them to God and call them His, we armor ourselves.

Say goodbye to shame and give thanks for everything. *That means EVERYTHING. It's all His, anyway!*

Prod

What's the hardest thing for you to give thanks for? Write it down and give it to the Lord today.

Praise

 Listen to

"Holy Ground"

by Jeremy Riddle

Pray

Jesus, thank you for everything—even the bad stuff. No matter how bad it was, I know that it brought me to you! Thank you for breaking the power of SHAME over my life so that I can live a live of FREEDOM for you! I can walk unashamed because I walk with gratitude! Amen.

Proclaim

"Finally, brothers and sisters, whatever is true, whatever is noble, whatever is right, whatever is pure, whatever is lovely, whatever is admirable—if anything is excellent or praiseworthy—think about such things. Whatever you have learned or received or heard from me, or seen in me—put it into practice. And the God of peace will be with you." (Phil. 4:8-9)

Prompt

It's the season of Thanksgiving! However you choose to celebrate the holiday, whether that's gathering with family or with friends, whether it's a large gathering or a small one, enjoy it as kind of like a prelude to eternity. In Heaven, we'll all gather together, and when we do, the first thing we'll do is thank God. Then we will eat and watch football. KIDDING! (But that would be cool.)

Today, let's get a jump start on practicing our thankfulness to God.

Thank God for your friends and family, the people in your corner and whose corner you get to be in. Thank God for supply and sustenance, for meeting all your needs according to His riches in glory. And thank God for redemption and restoration, because without Him, well, where would you be?

Everything you have is God's. Enjoy it!

Prod

As we head into the season of Thanksgiving, make a list of things you've been thankful for over the last year. Share it with your loved ones.

Praise

 Listen to

"Be Glad"

by Cody Carnes

Pray

Jesus, thank you for everything you've given me, from the big stuff to the next breath I take. It's all yours! I could never thank you enough. Amen.

Proclaim

"Finally, brothers and sisters, whatever is true, whatever is noble, whatever is right, whatever is pure, whatever is lovely, whatever is admirable—if anything is excellent or praiseworthy—think about such things. Whatever you have learned or received or heard from me, or seen in me—put it into practice. And the God of peace will be with you." (Phil. 4:8-9)

Prompt

As we reflect on Thanksgiving, let's pause and consider how the holiday might hit two different ways.

First, there are those who take great joy in this season because it's never been anything but a (mostly) joyful occasion for them. Maybe that's you? If it is, then I pray along with you that God would be the manifestation of your gratitude, so that when you feel it, you know you're feeling the hand of God.

But then there are those who look at Thanksgiving and see only hurt, pain, and despair, which can make it especially tough to look at this as a holiday of gratitude. If that's you, then I pray God would be your peace and bring healing to all the places where you've been wounded.

Regardless of which of these two Thanksgivings you identify with, you're part of God's Kingdom, which means that in the end, we'll ALL gather together at God's table in blessed thanksgiving. Can you say AMEN to that?!

Prod

Which of the two Thanksgivings described above most accurately reflects your history with the holiday? Today, as the Holy Spirit directs, pray for the people in the other one.

Praise

 Listen to

"Come to the Table"

by Sidewalk Prophets

Pray

Jesus, I'm thankful to be part of your family, and I'm especially thankful that my status in your family doesn't ever change. Let me be a helpful sibling to someone today! Amen.

Proclaim

"Finally, brothers and sisters, whatever is true, whatever is noble, whatever is right, whatever is pure, whatever is lovely, whatever is admirable—if anything is excellent or praiseworthy—think about such things. Whatever you have learned or received or heard from me, or seen in me—put it into practice. And the God of peace will be with you." (Phil. 4:8-9)

Prompt

Yes, Thanksgiving is a special day... but like I said before, it's also a season. Especially those few days leading up to the big day, just before we turn our eyes fully toward Christmas.

We can treat this season as a reminder not just to be thankful but also to cultivate a continual attitude of thanksgiving. Gratitude isn't just for one day on the calendar! We can check our behavior so that when we are inevitably selfish and self-serving, we can instead ask God to place in us an urge to seek His will over our own desires.

When we do that, we are well on our way to living a life of gratitude, walking in an attitude of thanksgiving that radiates out to the rest of the world—all year long.

Prod

What are some concrete ways you can maintain an attitude of thanksgiving? Write them down here, then make a reminder on your phone to help you remember to keep them up.

Praise

 Listen to

"Give Thanks"

by Steffany Gretzinger

Pray

Jesus, thank you for teaching me how to follow you gratefully. Because of what you have done for me, I have a heart full of blessings! Please help this spirit of thanksgiving not just pass away after the holiday, but let it be a lifestyle of gratitude that I live every day. Help me serve you today. Amen.

Proclaim

"Finally, brothers and sisters, whatever is true, whatever is noble, whatever is right, whatever is pure, whatever is lovely, whatever is admirable—if anything is excellent or praiseworthy—think about such things. Whatever you have learned or received or heard from me, or seen in me—put it into practice. And the God of peace will be with you." (Phil. 4:8-9)

Prompt

One thing I can often lose sight of (though we've talked about it a lot throughout the days in this devotional) is that God has promised to be with us no matter what. I always try to remember with gratitude that our mighty and merciful Lord, who is our refuge and our strength, *IS ALWAYS WITH US*. That means He's with us in times of peace AND in times of trouble.

Good or bad, happy or sad, boring or interesting... whatever kind of time we're having—He's there. This truth lets us know we can endure whatever we're in with patience while joyfully giving thanks because we know that all things are held together in Him.

I know it can be tough to give thanks when all seems bleak. It can be tough to find joy when all seems dire. But God is still there. And He is still worthy to be praised.

Prod

In what ways can you thank God despite your situation or circumstances? List five reasons.

Praise

 Listen to

"Better Is One Day"

by Passion

Pray

Jesus, thank you for being you, and thank you for being with me always. I know you're here with me RIGHT NOW. It doesn't matter how my day is going—it's a good day because you're here! Act on me and in me today. Amen.

Proclaim

"Finally, brothers and sisters, whatever is true, whatever is noble, whatever is right, whatever is pure, whatever is lovely, whatever is admirable—if anything is excellent or praiseworthy—think about such things. Whatever you have learned or received or heard from me, or seen in me—put it into practice. And the God of peace will be with you." (Phil. 4:8-9)

Prompt

For the next few days, we're going to look in-depth at one of the four things Paul mentions here that we're supposed to put into practice so that we can increase our gratitude. First up: "Whatever you have learned."

Are you taking a posture of learning into your life? Because learning doesn't end when you're done with school! You don't walk out of that building and into a life of completed education. No! We are called to continue learning throughout our lives, always striving to become better. Growing, gaining, gestating. It's through learning that we develop stronger lives.

Keep learning. Keep loving. Keep striving and keep HOPING. Keep thanking God for the opportunities you have to keep growing.

Prod

What are you learning about lately? Summarize it in a few sentences and share those with someone close to you.

Praise

 Listen to
"Lord, I Need You"
by Passion

Pray

Jesus, thank you for giving me the ability to keep learning about you and about myself. Let me seize that opportunity today. I'm so grateful that I get to continue expanding what I know about your creation: both the world and me. Teach me. I'm learning! Amen.

Proclaim

"Finally, brothers and sisters, whatever is true, whatever is noble, whatever is right, whatever is pure, whatever is lovely, whatever is admirable—if anything is excellent or praiseworthy—think about such things. Whatever you have learned or received or heard from me, or seen in me—put it into practice. And the God of peace will be with you." (Phil. 4:8-9)

Prompt

Before we continue on our in-depth look at the things we need to put into practice, I want to talk today about another facet of learning that I didn't make explicit yesterday.

See, there are basically two types of learning. First, there's the normal kind, the kind where we actively seek out information or knowledge about a topic that interests us or that we just need to know more about. You already know about that one.

And then there's the other kind. The kind where we make a mistake, or we try something and it backfires, or we just outright sin. The kind of learning that folks like to call "the hard way." I have a lot of experience with this one!

I can almost guarantee that right now, in this moment on this day, you are learning something from life! Whether you're actively learning or you just made a mistake.

As you meditate and pray today, ask yourself: what can I learn from what I am experiencing this season? You might be surprised with what God shows you.

Prod

What's a mistake-filled learning experience you've had recently? What did you take away from it? How can you share that with someone else?

Praise

 Listen to

"Abide"

by The Worship Collective

Pray

Jesus, thanks for your grace that teaches me new things even when I mess up big time. Help me be grateful for all opportunities to learn, even when they're from my mistakes. You're the best. Teach me. Amen.

Proclaim

"Finally, brothers and sisters, whatever is true, whatever is noble, whatever is right, whatever is pure, whatever is lovely, whatever is admirable—if anything is excellent or praiseworthy—think about such things. Whatever you have learned or received or heard from me, or seen in me—put it into practice. And the God of peace will be with you." (Phil. 4:8-9)

Prompt

Okay, back to our in-depth look at the four things Paul mentions for us to put into practice so that we can increase our gratitude. Today's is: "Whatever you have... received."

I love this concept of receiving wisdom. Because while learning is an activity, reception feels more passive. You don't have to DO anything to receive; all you need is an open heart and an open hand. That's it! That's the whole job.

And the thing is: sometimes we're receiving these noble things without even realizing it! It's only in retrospect when we can look at where we are based on where we've come from and discover that we've been receiving God's wisdom all along. So let's be grateful for all we've received... and then put that wisdom into practice in our lives.

Prod

Consider your recent past. Is there something noble that you've received—maybe without even knowing it at the time? Share it with someone today.

Praise

 Listen to

"Word of God Speak"

by MercyMe

Pray

Jesus, I'm so grateful for the wisdom you've sent my way throughout my life. Help me receive what you send me today. My heart is open! My will is open! My hands are open! Fill me with your wisdom today so it can overflow into my life. Amen.

Proclaim

"Finally, brothers and sisters, whatever is true, whatever is noble, whatever is right, whatever is pure, whatever is lovely, whatever is admirable—if anything is excellent or praiseworthy—think about such things. Whatever you have learned or received or heard from me, or seen in me—put it into practice. And the God of peace will be with you." (Phil. 4:8-9)

Prompt

Today we're going to continue looking at these four virtues to put into practice. Today's lesson: "Whatever you have... heard."

I like this one. It's like receiving, except where receiving feels more like a gift given, hearing almost sounds like we're listening in, like some sort of spy or party-crasher. Maybe that's just because I want it to feel more mysterious, but I like the idea that God is speaking in ways where we have to sort of tilt our heads and crane our necks to hear.

God rewards active listening. Yes, He'll speak to us in loud, booming voices from time to time, but I also think He wants you to lean forward a little and put your whole self into hearing through a posture of receptive gratitude. It's part of how He teaches us as we walk with Him.

Hear Him. Put it into practice and you'll abound with gratitude at what God teaches you.

Prod

What's a quiet direction you've heard from God recently? Share it with someone.

Praise

 Listen to

"Stir A Passion"

by REVERE

Pray

Jesus, I'm all ears! Speak, because your servant is listening! I'm putting my whole self into hearing you, listening with my whole heart. Stir a passion inside of me. Thank you for teaching me in this special way. Amen.

Proclaim

"Finally, brothers and sisters, whatever is true, whatever is noble, whatever is right, whatever is pure, whatever is lovely, whatever is admirable—if anything is excellent or praiseworthy—think about such things. Whatever you have learned or received or heard from me, or seen in me—put it into practice. And the God of peace will be with you." (Phil. 4:8-9)

Prompt

Okay, last one up as we round out November and head into the final month of the year: "Whatever you have... seen in me."

This one is HUGE, because this is where Paul unambiguously tells leaders—and you and I are leaders, make no mistake—that we are role models. People are looking at us and they are *seeing things in us*. The things they see in us should be worth putting into practice.

What are you seeing in others that YOU could be putting into practice?

What are you showing those who are looking at YOU? When they look at your life, are you showing them something worth emulating? If they did what you did and said what you said, would they be demonstrating grace and gratitude?

You're always an example. Live like one.

Prod

What's something you do that's worth others copying? What's something they might see that they *shouldn't* put into practice? Write them down, then work on amplifying the first and diminishing the second.

Praise

 Listen to

"Rooftops"

by Jesus Culture

Pray

Jesus, thank you for making me someone to watch. It's a big responsibility, but I'm up for it. I believe you are making me into an ever more worthy role model, so when people see me, give me grace so that they see you. Amen.

Proclaim

"Finally, brothers and sisters, whatever is true, whatever is noble, whatever is right, whatever is pure, whatever is lovely, whatever is admirable—if anything is excellent or praiseworthy—think about such things. Whatever you have learned or received or heard from me, or seen in me—put it into practice. And the God of peace will be with you." (Phil. 4:8-9)

Prompt

It's December, which means it's Christmas season, which means we're in for a bit of a wait.

Remember when you were a kid and December felt like the most difficult month? That long wait between putting up the Christmas decorations and finally getting to open your presents on Christmas morning? Remember how it felt like FOREVER?

This time of anticipation is known in the traditional Church as Advent, a time of looking ahead in the midst of the darkest time of the year, hoping and waiting for Jesus to arrive... and for justice to arrive with Him.

But as we look for justice, we need to make sure we look for it AS IT IS, not as we would have it. Because God's justice looks different from our version of it. Sometimes it feels like it will take FOREVER, but it always arrives right on time. And God's justice doesn't punish—it brings restoration and makes everything right under Him.

It can be tough to feel grateful during this long wait... but it's worth it. Jesus is coming, and justice comes with Him.

Prod

What's your concept of God's justice? Write a reflection about it.

Praise

Listen to

"Turn Your Eyes"

by The Belonging Co.

Pray

Jesus, thank you for making all things right in your time. Give me patience to wait for you and grace to trust in your kind of restorative justice. Amen.

Proclaim

"Finally, brothers and sisters, whatever is true, whatever is noble, whatever is right, whatever is pure, whatever is lovely, whatever is admirable—if anything is excellent or praiseworthy—think about such things. Whatever you have learned or received or heard from me, or seen in me—put it into practice. And the God of peace will be with you." (Phil. 4:8-9)

Prompt

Today is my son Lance Adam Lang II's birthday! L.A. has brought so much love, laughter, and FUN back into our lives. I could fill a hundred books with all the joy he's given his mother and me.

But it wasn't always like that. Ally and I struggled with infertility for over five years. It was a dark season of our lives and honestly, near the end, we'd almost lost hope. But then a miracle happened: God gave us a son.

Has there been a moment in your life when it got so dark you could barely see, yet God met you there?

These early days in December remind me a bit of that time. As nights get longer and longer; they can sometimes start to seem unending. But nighttime is the only time when you can see the stars.

In the Christmas story we have some stargazers who make the most of the night. The three wise men had anticipation, just like those who were awaiting the Messiah in the birth of Jesus, and God knew exactly where they would be looking while they waited, so He gave them an unmissable announcement.

God loves to write His name in any place where we'll look for Him, even if no one else will see it. We can be grateful that He meets us wherever we are, including in the darkest night.

Prod

What dark moment did you think of as you started to read today? Talk to God about it while you listen to today's song and pray.

Praise

 Listen to

"What He's Done"

by Passion

Pray

Jesus, thank you for writing your name in the stars and showing up during my darkest nights. Please show me what you have for me today. Amen.

Proclaim

"Finally, brothers and sisters, whatever is true, whatever is noble, whatever is right, whatever is pure, whatever is lovely, whatever is admirable—if anything is excellent or praiseworthy—think about such things. Whatever you have learned or received or heard from me, or seen in me—put it into practice. And the God of peace will be with you." (Phil. 4:8-9)

Prompt

As we've entered the Christmas season and begun to anticipate Jesus' birth, let's not forget something crucial about the Christmas story: Jesus was born so He could grow up, spend time preaching the gospel and making disciples, and then be crucified so He could defeat death and hell and rise from the dead.

Maybe it's not something we think about a lot, but that IS the whole point of the Christmas story. So we can approach this time of year with thankfulness in our hearts! We can enter the Christmas season with thankfulness, as we hear in today's song, for the blood of Jesus that breaks our chains and sets us free!

Prod

What are you thankful for today? Text a trusted friend and tell them.

Praise

 Listen to

"Thank You Jesus for the Blood"

by Charity Gayle

Pray

Jesus, thank you for your blood. Thank you for coming to this earth and being born as a person so we could experience broken chains and true freedom through you. Thank you for restoring our relationships and for making a way where there was no way. I'm so grateful! Amen.

Proclaim

"Finally, brothers and sisters, whatever is true, whatever is noble, whatever is right, whatever is pure, whatever is lovely, whatever is admirable—if anything is excellent or praiseworthy—think about such things. Whatever you have learned or received or heard from me, or seen in me—put it into practice. And the God of peace will be with you." (Phil. 4:8-9)

Prompt

Friend, hear this: God is so, so trustworthy, even though we don't always see it at the time. He won't let us be put to shame, so we can take Him at His word, and most of all, we can rely on His forgetfulness.

Forgetfulness? God is forgetful? Yes! God has a selective memory that keeps no record of our wrongs! Hallelujah!

God loves to work backward and in ways we don't expect. After all, we're celebrating this month the fact that He came to us humbly, in the form of a baby. But even that wasn't a surprise! Through the writings of the Old Testament prophets, He gave us hints of His trajectory, but we can really only see those connected dots in hindsight.

Today you might find yourself in a season that doesn't make sense. It might be hard to trust God that what you are experiencing will ever make sense. Let me be the voice of encouragement to you. THIS SEASON WILL MAKE SENSE ONE DAY. You can *trust Him*.

And more than that: you can be grateful, even though it doesn't make sense. Because someday it will!

Prod

Repeat this until it's in your spirit! "God, I trust you. I know that *THIS SEASON WILL MAKE SENSE ONE DAY.*"

Praise

 Listen to

"Called Me Higher"

by All Sons & Daughters

Pray

Jesus, I love how you work in my life, even though I can't always see it at the moment. Give me a holy trust in you today. Help me to remember that you're there, doing your work in my world, even if it doesn't make sense to me now—or ever. I'm grateful to rest in you. Amen.

Proclaim

"Finally, brothers and sisters, whatever is true, whatever is noble, whatever is right, whatever is pure, whatever is lovely, whatever is admirable—if anything is excellent or praiseworthy—think about such things. Whatever you have learned or received or heard from me, or seen in me—put it into practice. And the God of peace will be with you." (Phil. 4:8-9)

Prompt

Yesterday we talked about how God's plans don't always make sense in the moment. I lived in that place for almost a year after I survived a horrific, fiery car crash in late 2022. From the moment I crawled out of my totaled truck, it felt like I was crawling into the toughest season of my life.

I battled depression, imposter syndrome, anxiety, ruminating thoughts, and insecurity like never before. But with each step I took toward healing, *God was so kind to meet me halfway.* He went with me into my darkness and gave me peace. I sought counseling, experiences, medication, and mentoring to heal the wounds, and while they all helped in their own ways, ultimately, TIME alone with God and intentional TRUST in my faithful (and beautiful) wife were what healed me, both physically and spiritually.

After about a year of living in the confusing season, I began to make my way out of the fog and into my future. I've learned that there will be HOPE on the other side of a WRECK. And that God will turn a horrifically challenging moment into a full season of learning, growing, and developing a greater dependence on Him.

If you're in a WRECK season, don't give up! Keep pursuing God the best way you know how. Depend on HIM! He will never leave you. And one day soon, it will all begin to make more sense.

Prod

Look back over the course of your life. Write down the times you see God's guiding hand in the past. Now consider: what does that mean for trusting Him in the future?

Praise

 Listen to

"Come Out Of That Grave"

by Bethel Music

Pray

Jesus, you've been with me this whole time, whether I realized it or not. Every step of the way you've been walking with me, guiding me where I needed to go and helping me get back on the right paths whenever I got off them. I'm so grateful for your guiding hand. I love you. Amen.

A YEAR OF HOPE IN 5 MINUTES A DAY

Proclaim

"Finally, brothers and sisters, whatever is true, whatever is noble, whatever is right, whatever is pure, whatever is lovely, whatever is admirable—if anything is excellent or praiseworthy—think about such things. Whatever you have learned or received or heard from me, or seen in me—put it into practice. And the God of peace will be with you." (Phil. 4:8-9)

Prompt

Waiting can be hard! This time of year feels kind of like a treadmill—so much to do with so much activity, but it often feels like Christmas is getting no nearer. And as the days get shorter and the nights get longer, we can fall into fatigue and fear, cynicism and despair. Our cries of "How long, Lord?" can turn into sighs of "Whatever."

Maybe for you, it's deeper than just waiting on Christmas. Maybe it's waiting on a spouse, a friend, a financial break, for depression to lift, for anxiety to fall away, for the grief to stop hurting.

Regardless of how we feel and what we are waiting on, **clinging to gratitude** helps!

And may I remind you, you can be grateful because God sees you where you are and calls you blessed, stable, hope-filled, and secure. And oh yeah—there's no waiting for God. Because there is no beginning and there's no ending. He's here right now, with you, right where you are sitting.

Christmas will be here soon enough. But thank God, He is with you *today*.

Prod

In the midst of the chaos, find three things to thank God for today.

Praise

 Listen to

"Bread of Life"

by Citipointe Worship

Pray

Jesus, thank you for giving me patience in the midst of the treadmill. Help me to get on your timeline instead of my own, especially as I look forward to the Christmas holiday. It's good to look ahead, but it's even better to just trust you today. Give me the strength to do that. I believe in you! Amen.

Proclaim

"Finally, brothers and sisters, whatever is true, whatever is noble, whatever is right, whatever is pure, whatever is lovely, whatever is admirable—if anything is excellent or praiseworthy—think about such things. Whatever you have learned or received or heard from me, or seen in me—put it into practice. And the God of peace will be with you." (Phil. 4:8-9)

Prompt

Today as we focus on HOPE, I'd ask you to spend more time than usual sitting with God and experiencing the PROD activity.

One of the key components of this time of year is... **HOPE.** We hope for things! We hope for gifts, for renewed relationships, for the coming of Jesus in the form of a baby.

Sometimes we hope big, but other times it feels like the weight of the world is so heavy that we can have only small hopes. Even then, we can offer them to God in humility, knowing He will multiply them to feed multitudes. And where we do have faith enough to have large hopes, let's offer them to God in gratitude, knowing He gave them to us to share with everyone we meet.

Whether big or small, our hopes are worth giving thanks for. When we hope in gratitude, we can distribute our hopes and brighten the darkness of this time of year, lighting it up with a holy patience and expectation.

Prod

Turn up today's song. Ask God to really open your heart. Write down the small hopes in your heart. List them and then lift them to God today, expecting Him to grow them.

Praise

 Listen to

"Into The Deep"

by Citipointe Worship

Pray

Jesus, I give you all my hopes, big and small, knowing that no hope is ever done in vain. You put these hopes in my heart, God, so I know you want to grow them in whatever way you think is best. Do what you want with my hopes. Amen.

Proclaim

"Finally, brothers and sisters, whatever is true, whatever is noble, whatever is right, whatever is pure, whatever is lovely, whatever is admirable—if anything is excellent or praiseworthy—think about such things. Whatever you have learned or received or heard from me, or seen in me—put it into practice. And the God of peace will be with you." (Phil. 4:8-9)

Prompt

It's no secret that this can be a tough time of year for a lot of people, especially those who have burned a lot of relationships in the past. But even back then, even when we were far, far from living for God, He still spoke to us. He's faithful and unchanging, and He's ALWAYS spoken to us.

Sometimes God speaks directly, but more often than not, He uses messengers. So as we celebrate this season—and maybe even reclaim it—let's make sure OUR hearts are inclined to pounce on God's message, delivered by His messenger, however that message may look to us.

If you're hurting over the loss of relationships, I get it. But sitting, soaking, and souring in that won't help. Trust me!

Create space in your soul today to look for HOPE-FILLED messengers. As God reveals them, give them a chance. Don't judge and don't avoid. Lean in.

Prod

Who might God be sending into your life as a hope-filled messenger? Does someone come to mind?

Praise

 Listen to

"Come See (Glory Hallelujah)"

by We Are Messengers

Pray

Jesus, let me receive your messenger—and your message—today. Remind me of people I've hurt in the past and give me courage to make amends where I need to. You desire all of us to live in harmony; make me a harmonious person today. Amen.

Proclaim

"Finally, brothers and sisters, whatever is true, whatever is noble, whatever is right, whatever is pure, whatever is lovely, whatever is admirable—if anything is excellent or praiseworthy—think about such things. Whatever you have learned or received or heard from me, or seen in me—put it into practice. And the God of peace will be with you." (Phil. 4:8-9)

Prompt

Yesterday we talked about the potential healing that can come from receiving God's messengers in our lives. Today, let's consider a new thought: what if *we're* the messenger for *someone else's* life?

Did you know that John the Baptist proclaimed the message of Jesus... before either of them was even born? Check it out in the gospel of Luke: Mary, pregnant with Jesus, shows up at her cousin Elizabeth's house. Elizabeth was pregnant with John the Baptist, and when Mary arrived, baby John did somersaults. He knew what was up! He knew he was in the presence of God!

We can be messengers like this when we rest in gratitude for what God has done for us. After all, God wants us to be like John the Baptist, too: messengers of His magnificence, couriers of His compassion, proclaimers of His peace... givers of gratitude.

Prod

Read Luke 1:41-44. When have you ever felt like baby John the Baptist felt? Write about it!

Praise

 Listen to

"Go Tell It On The Mountain"

by Maverick City Music

Pray

Jesus, you make me leap with gratitude! Let me carry your message with somersaults today, letting everyone know through my actions about your greatness and grace. Amen.

Proclaim

"Finally, brothers and sisters, whatever is true, whatever is noble, whatever is right, whatever is pure, whatever is lovely, whatever is admirable—if anything is excellent or praiseworthy—think about such things. Whatever you have learned or received or heard from me, or seen in me—put it into practice. And the God of peace will be with you." (Phil. 4:8-9)

Prompt

I'll be honest—I get tired a lot this time of year. It's a busy season for our organization, not to mention all the extra family fun we get to have as the holidays near.

But while this is a time of anticipation as we get closer and closer to the day we celebrate Jesus' birth, it should not be a time of idleness. This is not the time to just coast into the Christmas holiday! God is a co-laboring God. He's called us to His Holy work, laboring alongside Him to build His Kingdom. What a privilege!

So let's not get weary in well-doing, and let's not take our foot off the gas just because a long holiday break might be ahead of us. Instead, let's thankfully ask God to invigorate our faith as we undertake the Kingdom work He's set before us and accept His calling, wherever we might hear it. We get to work alongside God! How much better can it get?! Let's be grateful... and let's get to work!

Prod

Ask God what you can do for His Kingdom today. Do it!

Praise

 Listen to

"On Earth As It Is In Heaven"

by Jesus Culture

Pray

Jesus, invigorate me. Prompt me. Give me strength to live for you all-out today. Don't let me rest just yet—I know you'll give me rest when the time comes, but for now, give me everything I need to make an impact for your kingdom today! Amen.

Proclaim

"Finally, brothers and sisters, whatever is true, whatever is noble, whatever is right, whatever is pure, whatever is lovely, whatever is admirable—if anything is excellent or praiseworthy—think about such things. Whatever you have learned or received or heard from me, or seen in me—put it into practice. And the God of peace will be with you." (Phil. 4:8-9)

Prompt

Christmas is only two weeks away—Jesus is coming soon! And with His arrival into the world comes the promise that God welcomes everyone into the glory of His eternal Kingdom. And when I say everyone, I mean EVERYONE! The blind receive sight, the lame walk, the lepers are cleansed, the deaf hear, the dead are raised to life, and all hear the Gospel of life. What good news!

As we enter these last two weeks before Christmas, let's finish strong and pray this prayer together:

Overflow my gratitude, Lord, until it reaches every shore. Strengthen my resolve to carry you with me into every part of my world so that I can serve you gratefully, without fear. Amen.

When you can pray that prayer and believe God will answer it, you'll be amazed at what God will do in your world.

Prod

Pray the prayer above several times throughout the day today.

Praise

 Listen to

"He Is Worthy"

by Maverick City Music

Pray

Jesus, help me to serve you without fear today. Christmas is so close I can taste it, and I just want to be a light of your gratitude everywhere I go. I need your strength! Amen.

Proclaim

"Finally, brothers and sisters, whatever is true, whatever is noble, whatever is right, whatever is pure, whatever is lovely, whatever is admirable—if anything is excellent or praiseworthy—think about such things. Whatever you have learned or received or heard from me, or seen in me—put it into practice. And the God of peace will be with you." (Phil. 4:8-9)

Prompt

God loves to surprise us in the best ways. Yes, He is steady and stable, the same yesterday, today, and forever, but one way He demonstrates His stability is by showing up in our lives in unexpected ways.

God loves the world—and you and me—so very much, even though it's filled with people who have not yet heard His good news, people who walk in darkness and the shadow of death.

We should know. We were there once. This is a time of longer and longer nights, a daily reminder of the darkness we used to live in. And even though we can experience fear and anxiety in our darkness, we know that in the middle of experiencing those very real feelings, we can also rest in gratitude. God's got us! He'll show up in an unexpected way!

It's just a matter of how we choose to respond. Do we give in to our despair or do we look past it in gratitude for the surprise God has for us on the other side?

We can radiate the light of His love to a darkened world. That's the beauty of the Christmas story—because it's OUR story, too.

Prod

Where are you experiencing fear and anxiety? Can you give those over to God in exchange for more gratitude? Listen to today's song and thank God for shining His light brightly on us!

Praise

 Listen to

"A Light"

by The Brilliance

Pray

Jesus, thank you for being both faithful AND surprising. I know I can count on you! You've given me so much already, and I know you have even bigger plans for me around the corner. Thank you for your love! Amen.

Proclaim

"Finally, brothers and sisters, whatever is true, whatever is noble, whatever is right, whatever is pure, whatever is lovely, whatever is admirable—if anything is excellent or praiseworthy—think about such things. Whatever you have learned or received or heard from me, or seen in me—put it into practice. And the God of peace will be with you." (Phil. 4:8-9)

Prompt

Christmas Day is getting closer and closer. Are you grateful for it? Do you draw upon and embrace God's gratitude as we reach this point halfway between December 1st and Christmas Day?

Though the Christmas dawn will soon arrive, right now we have to endure the darkest, coldest, loneliest parts of the night.

That's why it's such a good thing that God lights up our lives with the flame of His gratitude! This flame burns brightly, renews us in His love, sings loudly and raucously, and dispels all fear, replacing it with warm, glowing thankfulness.

Have troubles today? Be thankful! Have gloom in your life? Be thankful! Have something bringing you down? Be thankful! Christmas will be here soon. Let's enjoy today for the gift it is.

Prod

Take an unlit candle into a dark room. Let the darkness settle on you and then light the candle. Notice how much light it provides and how much the darkness retreats. That's the power of God's gratitude!

Praise

 Listen to

"Set a Fire"

by Jesus Culture

Pray

Jesus, thank you for the flame of your gratitude. Let me experience that power in my life, no matter what's going on. And let me lift my flame of gratitude up to you—and others—today. Amen.

Proclaim

"Finally, brothers and sisters, whatever is true, whatever is noble, whatever is right, whatever is pure, whatever is lovely, whatever is admirable—if anything is excellent or praiseworthy—think about such things. Whatever you have learned or received or heard from me, or seen in me—put it into practice. And the God of peace will be with you." (Phil. 4:8-9)

Prompt

Yesterday we talked about the flame of God's gratitude and how it lights up our lives. And it does that so we can shine brightly! When we're grateful, that gratitude beams out from us, proclaiming our gratitude to others, just as God proclaims it to us. After all, He is our salvation!

So let us **GRATEFULLY** declare God's salvation to a world that is so desperately in need of it. Let's showcase God's love in a way that truly gets the message across—first through the way we act, and then through the words we use to talk about it.

What message are you sending with your life right now? Are you proclaiming God's gratitude with your words? Are you demonstrating God's gratitude with your actions? Be a gratitude messenger today!

Prod

Who do you know who needs a spark from the flame of God's gratitude? Name them here: _____. Now ask the Holy Spirit to guide you in sharing your spark with them today.

Praise

 Listen to

"Shine A Light"

by Elevation Worship

Pray

Jesus, help me burn brightly for you today. I pray for [NAME OF PERSON YOU LISTED ABOVE]. Show them your love, and use me to do it. I believe you want them to walk in gratitude! Amen.

Proclaim

"Finally, brothers and sisters, whatever is true, whatever is noble, whatever is right, whatever is pure, whatever is lovely, whatever is admirable—if anything is excellent or praiseworthy—think about such things. Whatever you have learned or received or heard from me, or seen in me—put it into practice. And the God of peace will be with you." (Phil. 4:8-9)

Prompt

Joy often accompanies the Christmas season, but let's face it—we don't always feel joyful. In fact, this can be maybe the toughest time of the year TO feel joy! The chaos of the season and all the long dark nights can weigh heavy on some of us.

Add to that the fact that joy doesn't always come naturally to everyone. Even though the Bible encourages us to rejoice in the Lord, it isn't always easy—especially in December.

But God loves to give gifts to His kids, and that includes restoring our joy where it is depleted and replenishing our joy where it is needed. Joy is a gift! Hope is a gift! Peace is a gift! Good thing we serve a God who loves to give gifts!

And God gives us these gifts so that, through us, He will liberate the oppressed, heal the hurting, gather in the outcasts, and exchange our shame for praise. What a joyful way to look at Him.

Give thanks!

Prod

Feeling a little low on joy? What areas of your life could use some? Write them down, then ask the Holy Spirit to bring joy to every single one of those areas, even when it might not make sense.

Praise

 Listen to

"Joy to the World"

by The Brilliance

Pray

Jesus, I love you, and I rejoice in you. Thank you for your amazing gifts in my life! I accept your gift of joy. I accept your gift of hope. I accept your gift of love. I receive them TODAY, right now. You're the one for me! Amen.

Proclaim

"Finally, brothers and sisters, whatever is true, whatever is noble, whatever is right, whatever is pure, whatever is lovely, whatever is admirable—if anything is excellent or praiseworthy—think about such things. Whatever you have learned or received or heard from me, or seen in me—put it into practice. And the God of peace will be with you." (Phil. 4:8-9)

Prompt

God's Kingdom is *huge*. Why? Because with the birth of Jesus, He changed the game completely and said, basically, ***"Whoever you are, you're welcome here."*** That includes both the outcasts and the insiders, the tax collectors and the soldiers, the vipers and the virtuous.

And so, if we're going to model the love of God to the world at large, shouldn't we be doing the same thing? Shouldn't we welcome ALL into God's work in this world? Shouldn't we share and share alike, both giving AND receiving love and forgiveness?

Christmas is THE ULTIMATE time that should remind us that everyone deserves to feel accepted by God. Often, you and I are the ones God uses to initiate this time of feeling acceptance, in service of a living, breathing relationship with Jesus.

Prod

Question: How are you doing with seeing ALL God's children at eye level?

Praise

 Listen to

"Never Once"

by Matt Redman

Pray

Jesus, you're so great at just completely upending what I think will happen. Keep me on my toes today! Amen.

Proclaim

"Finally, brothers and sisters, whatever is true, whatever is noble, whatever is right, whatever is pure, whatever is lovely, whatever is admirable—if anything is excellent or praiseworthy—think about such things. Whatever you have learned or received or heard from me, or seen in me—put it into practice. And the God of peace will be with you." (Phil. 4:8-9)

Prompt

If you let yourself think about it this way, the story of the birth of Jesus is really, really funny.

I mean, come on: you're telling me the Savior of the world, the King of all Kings, the blessed Messiah and the only perfect human being ever—THAT GUY is entering the world in a stable, surrounded by a bunch of animals and shepherds?

See? It's hilarious!

But God loves to play the fool, so we can trust Him for comedic courage and be grateful that, when we ask Him, "What would you have us do?" we can hear His answer... and be foolish enough to do it.

Prod

How does it make you feel, thinking about the story of Jesus as comedic? Interrogate those feelings with the help of the Holy Spirit and write down whatever He reveals to you.

Praise

 Listen to

"A Thrill of Hope"

by Building 429

Pray

Jesus, thank you for your hilarious entrance to this world. You can identify with us lowly ones because you started your earthly life that way. Let me be a fool for you today! Amen.

Proclaim

"Finally, brothers and sisters, whatever is true, whatever is noble, whatever is right, whatever is pure, whatever is lovely, whatever is admirable—if anything is excellent or praiseworthy—think about such things. Whatever you have learned or received or heard from me, or seen in me—put it into practice. And the God of peace will be with you." (Phil. 4:8-9)

Prompt

Christmas is getting closer and closer... so close you can almost smell it! It's like God's cooking up His great feast that everyone's welcome to—the aroma has filled the kitchen and the world is about to eat the best, most filling meal they've ever had. Best of all—everyone who wants it has a seat at this table.

Don't you love the smells of the holidays? I know I do, and if you're anything like me, your past few days—and your next few—have been and will be filled with gatherings galore. Parties, dinners, endless rounds of Dirty Santa, and all kinds of family in various places.

Why? What's the point? Don't forget. *This is all because of Jesus.*

So slow down, reset your spirit if you need to, and put your focus on Jesus, as His arrival is coming...

Prod

The next gathering you attend, take a moment to step back, take in the people there, and ask God how you can point people to Jesus during this crazy Christmas season.

Praise

 Listen to

"Breath of Heaven"

by Elevation Worship

Pray

Jesus, thank you that you are really the reason for this season. You are holy. You are wonderful. You are the breath of heaven in my life. Please help me re-center my soul on you today. Amen.

Proclaim

"Finally, brothers and sisters, whatever is true, whatever is noble, whatever is right, whatever is pure, whatever is lovely, whatever is admirable—if anything is excellent or praiseworthy—think about such things. Whatever you have learned or received or heard from me, or seen in me—put it into practice. And the God of peace will be with you." (Phil. 4:8-9)

Prompt

Yesterday we talked about Jesus' birth as an announcement that everyone has a seat at God's table. Today, let's talk about the attitude we can bring to that table.

Because it's a table that's set with grace and gratitude. We can come to it with open hearts and with the mouth-drooling anticipation of a celebratory meal, like people who haven't eaten all day walking in the door to the smell of a home-cooked meal.

We've dined on the bread of despair, we've drunk our fill of tears, and we know those are empty calories that just leave us hungrier. But we also know those past experiences don't have to dull our taste buds on Christmas morning. Instead, we can eat heartily, savoring God's goodness and reveling in His love.

God isn't preparing fast food for us to rush through; He's giving us a meal we will savor for eternity. Come and dine!

Prod

During one of your meals today, slow down and do your best to really taste everything you eat, using it to focus on God's goodness in your life. Give thanks.

Praise

 Listen to

"Draw Me In"

by Paul Zach and Sara Groves

Pray

Jesus, I'm never hungry when I taste your love and grace. Draw me into your fulfilling embrace today. Thank you for filling me up! Amen.

Proclaim

"Finally, brothers and sisters, whatever is true, whatever is noble, whatever is right, whatever is pure, whatever is lovely, whatever is admirable—if anything is excellent or praiseworthy—think about such things. Whatever you have learned or received or heard from me, or seen in me—put it into practice. And the God of peace will be with you." (Phil. 4:8-9)

Prompt

This is how much God loves us: that He sent His Only Son here, to the place where we live, to enter this world as a human baby. You know what that means? It means Jesus understands.

Anything you feel, anything you go through, any trial you encounter—Jesus understands. And because we know He understands, we can begin to grasp a little more deeply God's love for us. Because after Jesus left, He gave US the duty of discipleship. He chose US to carry HIS light to OUR world.

By sending Jesus, God loved us enough to look upon us with favor, with mercy, and with strength. That's why, especially during this time of Christmas, we must work to keep gratitude always before our eyes so we can gain a brighter, clearer picture of God's love for us and then show that picture to our neighbors.

Jesus is how much God loves us.

Prod

Who is someone you love deeply? How far would you go to love them? God goes even further. Write a reflection on that level of love.

Praise

 Listen to

"Because of Your Love"

by Phil Wickham

Pray

Jesus, thank you for loving me enough to come here and rescue me. You understand everything I'm going through because you went through it, too. I'm so grateful! Amen.

Proclaim

"Finally, brothers and sisters, whatever is true, whatever is noble, whatever is right, whatever is pure, whatever is lovely, whatever is admirable—if anything is excellent or praiseworthy—think about such things. Whatever you have learned or received or heard from me, or seen in me—put it into practice. And the God of peace will be with you." (Phil. 4:8-9)

Prompt

It's the first day of winter and Jesus is almost here! The doldrums have arrived, and it's the darkest night of the year—which just means the light is about to dawn... which means we have work to do!

But what does that word "work" mean? We all have our own definitions, though I'd guess that a lot of us have one that boils down, essentially, to "do stuff and look really active and energetic while doing it."

Which isn't really something that leaps to mind on a day like today, when winter has finally shown up and the pulse of our culture is beginning to slow down in anticipation of the Christmas holiday. So let's let God define "work" for us instead of getting trapped in our own limitations. Let's follow His way of work into the holiday, whatever that looks like.

Prod

How would you define "work"? How do you think God wants you to define it? How can you bring those two definitions into agreement with one another? What will you do for God today?!

Praise

 Listen to

"Hosanna"

by Hillsong United

Pray

Jesus, show me how to work the way you want me to. I just want to follow you in everything I do! Amen.

Proclaim

"Finally, brothers and sisters, whatever is true, whatever is noble, whatever is right, whatever is pure, whatever is lovely, whatever is admirable—if anything is excellent or praiseworthy—think about such things. Whatever you have learned or received or heard from me, or seen in me—put it into practice. And the God of peace will be with you." (Phil. 4:8-9)

Prompt

What a gift life is. I mean, we're currently in a season when we both give and receive a lot of gifts, but it's worth pausing a moment and just **thanking God for the gift of our very lives.**

So many of us—maybe even you—almost gave this gift away. I know I was doing just that, squandering my potential and all the additional gifts God gave me in search of my next high. I was on a dark, dark road.

But God spoke to me in an unexpected way and used the love of my friends and family to get my attention so I would stop taking this gift of life for granted and start accepting it for the precious privilege it is.

I said YES to God's gift of life, and I'm so grateful! It makes me so happy to see where I am now—God gave me so much more than I ever thought I could ask, think, or imagine! It's all a gift!

Prod

What's a new way you can say YES to God's gift of your life? Make it happen!

Praise

 Listen to

"Everyday"

by Hillsong Worship

Pray

Jesus, thank you, thank you, thank you for the gift of my life. I accept it, I treasure it, I love it. I'm only here because of your grace, and I'm forever grateful! Amen.

Proclaim

"Finally, brothers and sisters, whatever is true, whatever is noble, whatever is right, whatever is pure, whatever is lovely, whatever is admirable—if anything is excellent or praiseworthy—think about such things. Whatever you have learned or received or heard from me, or seen in me—put it into practice. And the God of peace will be with you." (Phil. 4:8-9)

Prompt

Friends, we are only TWO days away from Christmas! I hope you have all your preparations finished so you can just enjoy the anticipation of the biggest holiday on the Christian calendar.

We've talked about anticipation this month, but one thing I want to talk about today is how much gratitude is wrapped up in anticipation. We usually get excited about something because we know it's going to be something we want! That anticipation is like preemptive gratitude.

When you look forward to something, it's like being thankful in advance.

I love having something to look forward to... It keeps me going and, like I said, it encourages gratitude as my anticipation builds for whatever it is.

So keep that in mind as you await Christmas Day. The festivities, the families, the food... take time today to thank God for what's coming.

It's Hope. It's Joy. **It's Jesus!**

Prod

Make a list of things you are looking forward to experiencing the next seven days.

Praise

 Listen to "Adore" by Chris Tomlin

Pray

Jesus, I'm thankful today for what you're doing in my life tomorrow and the next day and the next. I know you have great plans for Christmas this year. Thank you for every moment I'll experience. Help me to be what you've called me to be to everything I see. Amen.

Proclaim

"Finally, brothers and sisters, whatever is true, whatever is noble, whatever is right, whatever is pure, whatever is lovely, whatever is admirable—if anything is excellent or praiseworthy—think about such things. Whatever you have learned or received or heard from me, or seen in me—put it into practice. And the God of peace will be with you." (Phil. 4:8-9)

Prompt

This is it. Everything's been pointing to this night. All of history is leaning in, waiting, silent with preemptive thankfulness of anticipation.

A Baby is being born tonight.

A Baby who will transform this entire world.

A Baby who will mean the world to you and me.

Jesus is almost here. All is quiet. All is well. All will be redeemed.

The angels bear witness to shepherds. The very stars declare His glory. Creation itself sighs with relief, for the King of All Kings is arriving.

And He loves YOU.

The innocence He will bring to that manger is the same innocence He gives to YOU.

Fresh. Clean. New.

All is silent. He is coming. Just wait.

Prod

Take some time to sit in silence and ponder the majestic irony of the birth of Christ.

Praise

 Listen to

"Silent Night"

by Lauren Daigle

Pray

Jesus, you're almost here! Help me embrace the quiet and the anticipation of waiting for you. Give me patience where I need it today. Thank you for your forgiveness. Amen.

Proclaim

"Finally, brothers and sisters, whatever is true, whatever is noble, whatever is right, whatever is pure, whatever is lovely, whatever is admirable—if anything is excellent or praiseworthy—think about such things. Whatever you have learned or received or heard from me, or seen in me—put it into practice. And the God of peace will be with you." (Phil. 4:8-9)

Prompt

The night is over! The dawn has arrived and Jesus is here! The Light has come! The announcement has been made! The mystery has been revealed and Christ is the solution! It's Christmas!

However you choose to spend this day, take a moment at some point to lift up your eyes to the Newborn King and (metaphorically) gaze upon His Light. Let yourself be so overwhelmed by the love of Jesus that, like the shepherds out in the fields, you nudge your neighbors, point to the sky, and say, "Look!"

Hope is here! Grace is here! Joy is here!

Jesus is here! Rejoice and be grateful!

Prod

Are you giving or receiving gifts today? Anytime you do, silently pause and thank God for the Gift of His Son Jesus.

Praise

 Listen to

"Hark! The Herald Angels Sing"

by Jeremy Riddle

Pray

Jesus, you're here! You're really here! I can do nothing but praise you with gratitude in my heart and your name on my lips. Let me rejoice in your arrival today. Amen.

Proclaim

"Finally, brothers and sisters, whatever is true, whatever is noble, whatever is right, whatever is pure, whatever is lovely, whatever is admirable—if anything is excellent or praiseworthy—think about such things. Whatever you have learned or received or heard from me, or seen in me—put it into practice. And the God of peace will be with you." (Phil. 4:8-9)

Prompt

Yesterday, we celebrated the birth of Jesus. Hallelujah! He is here!

There's something about the relentlessness of the Christmas story, isn't there? So many obstacles tried to get in the way of Christ's birth, but regardless of what happened, Jesus arrived safe, healthy, and adored.

God's always relentless like that. It reminds me of a song by Ben Fuller called "Chasing Rebels," which says, "There's an unrelenting, comin'-for-you Savior who loves chasing rebels down."

Jesus came here LITERALLY for the express purpose of chasing us down. You and me. When you think about the Christmas story, think about that—He's here for YOU. That manger had a baby in it JUST FOR YOU. Jesus chased you down! Now what are you going to do about it?!

Merry Christmas indeed! Hallelujah!

Prod

Weather permitting, run a quarter-mile sprint today, as fast as you can. Now imagine Jesus doing that, running after you with that amount of dedication, for eternity.

Praise

 Listen to
"Chasing Rebels"
by Ben Fuller

Pray

Jesus, thank you for chasing me down. Your relentlessness humbles me and fills me with gratitude. I don't always understand your love, but I'm so grateful for it! I'm so glad to be caught in your love. Amen.

Proclaim

"Finally, brothers and sisters, whatever is true, whatever is noble, whatever is right, whatever is pure, whatever is lovely, whatever is admirable—if anything is excellent or praiseworthy—think about such things. Whatever you have learned or received or heard from me, or seen in me—put it into practice. And the God of peace will be with you." (Phil. 4:8-9)

Prompt

Like we talked about yesterday, God is relentless, which is another way of saying stubborn. He chases us down, no matter what, and He will go to great lengths to speak into someone's life. After all, He even made the skies speak, using a star to guide the wise men to Jesus.

But God doesn't always use supernatural methods to reach people—usually He just uses other people. People like you and me! We are often the "stars" in other people's skies, proclaiming the arrival of a new way of life, of God's boundless riches both to the poor and the oppressed, to those in need and to those in positions of power and safety.

God is dead-set on all of us knowing the wisdom of His mystery. It's a wisdom that He declared with the birth of Jesus: that those who used to be on the outside are now part of the inner circle... And God's inner circle is so big that it includes anyone who wants to join it.

What a stubborn God. Aren't you grateful?

Prod

God used the star to guide the wise men—whose star is God calling you to be today? If you know a specific person, ask God to give you wisdom on reaching them. If you don't, ask God to guide YOU toward guidance.

Praise

 Listen to

"Stars in the Sky"

by Kari Jobe

Pray

Jesus, thank you for your stubborn grace that guided me to you. It never runs out on me! Show me the best ways I can guide people to you today. Amen.

Proclaim

"Finally, brothers and sisters, whatever is true, whatever is noble, whatever is right, whatever is pure, whatever is lovely, whatever is admirable—if anything is excellent or praiseworthy—think about such things. Whatever you have learned or received or heard from me, or seen in me—put it into practice. And the God of peace will be with you." (Phil. 4:8-9)

Prompt

Christmas Day might have come and gone, but the Christmas story is still alive and well. For the last few days of the year, we're going to look at some of the characters in the Christmas story and think about what that story meant for them after it was over. First up: the shepherds.

Think about these guys. They're just out there in the fields, probably asleep with their sheep to protect them from being marauded by wild animals or poachers, and then: boom! Angels! I'd be wide awake for sure!

But it's not just angels—it's angels with a message, a holy vision that compelled the shepherds to travel to a nearby stable and see the baby Jesus. Can you imagine?! Can you feel the way they must have felt? The hype was real! The angels weren't lying! This was truly astonishing. Life-changing!

That encounter with Jesus changed everything for them. **They entered that stable as shepherds, but they left as evangelists.** They would never be the same. How could they be? Encounters with Jesus change us deeply, radically, at the very foundation of ourselves. We aren't shepherds anymore! Aren't you grateful?

Prod

Who needs to know about your encounter with Jesus? As the Holy Spirit guides you, tell someone today. Let your awe at meeting Jesus be real!

Praise

 Listen to

"Love Came Down"

by Bethel Music and Brian Johnson

Pray

Jesus, thank you for being such a life-changing God. Thank you for changing my life and changing my vocation. I used to be a shepherd, but now I'm an evangelist. I'm so grateful! Amen.

Proclaim

"Finally, brothers and sisters, whatever is true, whatever is noble, whatever is right, whatever is pure, whatever is lovely, whatever is admirable—if anything is excellent or praiseworthy—think about such things. Whatever you have learned or received or heard from me, or seen in me—put it into practice. And the God of peace will be with you." (Phil. 4:8-9)

Prompt

Today we're continuing our look at some of the characters in the Christmas story, this time thinking through the story of the Wise Men.

Our modern Nativity sets always show the Wise Men there at the stable with Jesus, but if you read the story in the Bible clearly, you'll discover that the Wise Men and the shepherds don't actually show up together (or even in the same gospel—the Wise Men are in Matthew and the shepherds are in Luke!).

Church tradition has long held that the Wise Men didn't show up right away—in some traditions, they don't get celebrated as part of the Christmas story until early January on a day called Epiphany.

I love that our two main witnesses to the Christmas story are some lowly shepherds who showed up right away and some highbrow Wise Men who didn't show up for a while. Jesus is for everyone: rich or poor, early or late.

It doesn't matter WHEN you come to know Jesus, just that you DO. It doesn't matter what you have (or don't have)—only that you give everything you have to Jesus. The circumstances don't matter! Just come!

Prod

Epiphany is generally celebrated every year on January 6th. Make a reminder on your calendar for that date and, when it arrives, write a reflection on Jesus welcoming the late-coming Wise Men.

Praise

 Listen to

"Lord of Lords"

by Hillsong Worship and Brooke Ligertwood

Pray

Jesus, unlike us humans, you're never early or late, but always on time. You were on time for me and I'm so grateful! Show me who I need to be "on time" for in my world today. Help me to be like you. Amen.

Proclaim

"Finally, brothers and sisters, whatever is true, whatever is noble, whatever is right, whatever is pure, whatever is lovely, whatever is admirable—if anything is excellent or praiseworthy—think about such things. Whatever you have learned or received or heard from me, or seen in me—put it into practice. And the God of peace will be with you." (Phil. 4:8-9)

Prompt

Okay, we're on our third and final day of thinking about our extra characters in the Christmas story, and today I want to think about some people who don't really get mentioned much.

Why do we know Joseph and Mary had to go to the stable to have their baby? Because we know the inn was full of other guests!

So my question is: did those other guests know what was happening in the stable right next to their rooms? Were they aware of the incredible, marvelous, history-changing miracle happening mere feet away from them? Or were they completely oblivious?

I think it was the second one. Why? Because I think if they'd come to witness it, we'd have heard about it in scripture. What an enormous missed opportunity!

But what about us? How many miracles happen around us that we aren't aware of? What life-changing instances are going on right next door? If our eyes aren't open and our ears aren't listening, we might miss something.

Don't miss out on what Jesus is doing! Don't crowd Him out of your life and into a stable—welcome Him!

Prod

Take notice of the everyday miracles around you, like the miracle of creation or the miracle of the people in your orbit. Thank God for them, and then list them out.

Praise

 Listen to "Be the Centre" by Jami Smith

Pray

Jesus, I never ever want to miss you and your miracles. Don't let me be like those other guests who had no idea you were being born right in the next room! I want to experience you! Help me see you! Help me listen for you! Amen.

LANCE LANG

Proclaim

"Finally, brothers and sisters, whatever is true, whatever is noble, whatever is right, whatever is pure, whatever is lovely, whatever is admirable—if anything is excellent or praiseworthy—think about such things. Whatever you have learned or received or heard from me, or seen in me—put it into practice. And the God of peace will be with you." (Phil. 4:8-9)

Prompt

And now we come to the close of another year. Regardless of how this year has been for you—whether it's been triumph after triumph or difficulty after difficulty (or some combination of the two)—you're here at the end of it, and that's something worth celebrating. GOD BROUGHT YOU THROUGH!

Today's song is all about starting fresh and new, drawing on the picture of moving to a new apartment and beginning life anew. It's a quiet reminder that God is always on our side and that wherever He calls us and whatever He calls us to, He will bless and bring us through.

So let's close out this annual cycle and start the new one by praying this prayer together:

Lord over all, as we end this year and begin a new one, we ask that you be our focus. Let us rest in your grace, your justice, and your righteousness. Work in our hearts in the new year, that we will grow closer to you because you bring us through. We can find our feet in you.

Amen? Amen! Go now in the light, love, peace, and joy of God!

Prod

Did you finish this year strong? What can you do to set yourself up for success in the new year? Make a plan and write it down right here.

Praise

 Listen to

"Finding Your Feet Again"

by Denison Witmer

Pray

Jesus, thank you for walking with me throughout this year. Give me hope and promise for next year. It's going to be great, because you're with me! I believe it! Amen.

About Lance

Lance Lang has devoted his life to inspiring hope in those affected by addiction through sharing his own decades-long journey from addiction to freedom and brokenness to wholeness.

In October of 2012, Lance and his wife Allyson Lang founded Hope is Alive Ministries, a program providing next-level mentoring homes for recovering addicts and alcoholics, as well as support groups providing help and hope for loved ones impacted by substance abuse.

Since then, Hope is Alive has grown from one home and five residents to 25 homes across 6 states with over 200 residents and an 80% success rate, as well as over 50 support groups attended by over 700 loved ones every month.

The impact of Hope is Alive is being felt in thousands of homes and will be evident for generations to come.

Lance has written multiple books, with his previous book reflecting on the lessons learned during his decade of sobriety, *10 Years Sober: Taking Steps Toward Freedom*. In addition Lance is a dynamic speaker, who has told his story thousands of times across the country.

Connect with Lance

@LanceLang

LanceLang.com

More Books

Hope Is Alive
One Addict's Story of Hope
Lance Lang

This book is the story of how Lance Lang's hope departed, how it was restored, and how he's kept it alive. He wrote it for drug addicts, alcoholics, gamblers, sex addicts, hurt people, prideful people, and angry people. He wrote it for the fear-ridden, the guilty, the insecure, the obsessed, the perpetually disappointed, and anyone else caught in the tornado of destruction that is addiction.

10 Years Sober
Taking Steps Toward Freedom
Lance Lang

More than just a memoir, *10 Years Sober* is Lance Lang at his most vulnerable, reflecting on ten miraculous years as a husband, a father, and a leader. It chronicles not just the establishment and rapid growth of Hope is Alive Ministries, but also the ups and downs that come with following Jesus wherever He leads you. Lance learned lessons both glorious and painful during this decade—he shares them all in this book.

Hope Changes Everything
Claim Your Pain, Rescue Your Dreams
Lance Lang

Dreams are universal. The hopes we all have for our future, the plans we all sketch out in our minds. And then, somewhere along the way, those dreams slip out of our grasp. Whether through some kind of pain or worry, some guilt or mistake, or just the dull routine of life getting in the way, we lose hope and start to slide into normality. But it doesn't have be this way! Those dreams can fuel your world once more. You just have to discover the transformative power of hope.

Finding Hope
A Field Guide for Families Affected by Addiction
Lance Lang

Worry. Fear. Pain. You think something might be wrong with your loved one— your son or daughter, your husband or wife, your mom or dad—but you can't be sure. Can it just be a phase they're going through, or can it be something worse? Can it even be addiction? *Finding Hope* was written with you in mind. Starting from diagnosing whether your loved one has a problem with addiction and taking you all the way through treatment and beyond, Lance Lang has created this field manual to help both you and your loved one get the help you both need.

available at

For over a decade, Hope is Alive (HIA) has focused on their mission, to "radically change the lives of drug addicts, alcoholics and those who love them." HIA fulfills this purpose through a variety of means, including:

Dozens of long-term, highly intentional, **Mentoring Homes**, unlike any other in the country. Men and women leave the HIA program equipped emotionally, professionally, spiritually, and financially, with their families restored and a toolkit of life skills that enable them to live healthy and fulfilled lives.

A breathtaking **Residential Treatment Center** that houses men during their first 45 days of sobriety, providing a customized rhythm that focuses on building their relationship with Jesus, healing core wounds, and preparing them to thrive when they transition to an HIA Mentoring Home.

Finding Hope and **Hope After Loss** support groups, which serve the families and loved ones of addicts through over 50 nationwide, community-based support groups. These free groups are held bi-weekly and facilitate a powerful, life-changing curriculum developed by HIA staff.

HIA Online, the same life-changing, innovative HIA curriculum that residents receive but delivered online, tailored for those who, for whatever reason, cannot participate in the HIA residential programs.

Corporate Support, an outreach program that provides 24/7 assistance to companies facing anything that might come across the HR desk, utilizing HIA Online as a means of recovery from substance abuse, along with education and prevention initiatives drawn from HIA-developed curriculum and guest speakers.

University and School Support, an outreach program focusing on prevention and awareness education, while building relationships with students and faculty to provide a safe place to process anything related to substance abuse. These programs offer initiatives similar to the Corporate Support program but geared more specifically toward students, faculty, and staff.

Made in USA - North Chelmsford, MA
38625_9780990311850
12.02.2023 0518